Adieu Bellapais

(Farewell, Beautiful Country)

and Collected Short Stories

By Jirair (Jerry) Shekerdemian

Adieu Bellapais
copyright © Jerry Shekerdemian 2019

First Edition
This is a work of autobiographical fiction. I have tried to recreate events, locales and conversations from my memories of them. In order to maintain their anonymity in some instances I have changed the names of individuals and places, I may have changed some identifying characteristics and details such as physical properties, occupations and places of residence.

All rights reserved. No part of this publication may be reproduced, stored in, or introduced into a retrieval system, or transmitted in any form, or by any means (electronic, mechanical, photocopying, recording, or otherwise) without the prior written permission of the author, except in the case of brief quotations or sample images embedded in critical articles or reviews.

ISBN-13: 978-1-945587-43-6

Jerry Shekerdemian
Adieu Bellapais
1. Memoir; 2. Immigration; 3. Armenia; 4. Canada

Book design: Dancing Moon Press
Cover design: Dancing Moon Press
Cover Art: Jerry Shekerdemian

Manufactured in the United States of America
Dancing Moon Press
dancingmoonpress.com
Bend, Oregon USA

Contents

Foreword	1
Bellapais Abbey	2
Voices from a Buried Past	4
Cyprus Memories	21
My Introduction to Shakespeare	22
Valley of the Nightingale	25
My Grandmother's Culinary Traditions and Healing Rituals	28
Black Dog Apparition	36
My Grandmother's Patchwork Blankets	39
Of Kaleidoscopes and a Table of Memories	40
The Key	43
Vanishing Trades of Cyprus:	
The Mattress Maker	45
Requiem for a Brave Workhorse	48
Donkeys for the Italian Campaign	51
Donkeys: Postscript	57
Turning Points	58
My Regrets	
Two Windows Facing	59
Shakespeare to the Rescue	65
Coiled Message	72
My Brother K	82
Mediterranean Crossing	85
Mistaken Identity	86
Lebanese Transactions	88
Civil Disorder Comes to Beirut	93
Escape From Beirut	98
Port Saïd	104
Alexandria	106
Northward to Greece	113

Photos 117

Immigration 121
Coming Into The Unknown
The Importance of Where You Come From 122
London Drizzle 133
Vancouver-Bound 138
Immigrant Story 141
Immigration and Employment Office Interview 145

Canada 149
A Fistful of Diamonds 150
A Trigger Of Memory 154
Lured by Sirens at Deep Cove 155
A Letter To Burl Ives 158
Real Canadian? One Man's Question of Identity 162
Union Meeting 166
Christmas Bonus 170
Hail Vancouver 180
The Big Rock Mountain Ship Registry of Vancouver Island 184
Squamish Highway 191
Long Beach Holiday 201
How We Raised a Robin Chick 206
My Daughter's Wedding 209

Tales of Travel and Work 213
Sidetracked to Salvador 214
An Affair at an Arctic Hotel 217
Stranded in Panama 224
Bizarre Philippine Encounters 233
California Fireworks 238
Fast Taxi to Caracas Airport 242

Additional Writings 247
Khatchatur Abovian (1808-1848) 248
The Secret Mission of Tissaron Stonaris 251
The Foreboding 256

Woe Is Me-ow!(Big Red, the Alley Cat Meets Milady, the Aristo-Kit)
261

About the Author **267**

To Tom & Anne

With Best Wishes

from Jerry Shekerdemian

@ Tapestry

Foreword

Bellapais Abbey

The ruins of Bellapais Abbey dominate the village of the same name, high up in the Kyrenia mountain range, on the northern coast of Cyprus.

Travelers planning a visit to the Island can see, in guidebooks and postcards, cypress trees, very appropriately growing among the ruins. Though the spelling of its name differs from that of the Island, yet it confirms the source and origin of the slender evergreen.

The name of the Abbey, however, has often been presented in different spellings, ascribing to it different meanings. Laurence Durrel, English author, who lived in Cyprus in the early 1950s, bought a house in the village of Bellapais and had it remodeled over a period of many months. In a book titled "Bitter Lemons," he describes, in beautiful prose, his experiences in the then-British Colony of Cyprus, as well as his observations as a teacher in a Greek school, and later as Public Information Officer during the era of the Cyprus revolt, in the mid-1950s, when dissidents among the Greek population waged a campaign for "Union with Greece," (which, later, escalated into guerrilla warfare and terrorism). In that book, referring to the Abbey and the Village, Durrell has used the spelling "Bella-paix." This spelling is said to be based on "Abbé de la Paix," (Abbey of Peace), the name believed to have been given the Abbey by French Crusader monks who built it in the Fourteenth Century.

To me, however, the name of the Abbey will always remain the way the local people have called the Village for centuries—Bellapais, a unified word, meaning beautiful country. The name has an Italian ring, I believe, and was probably used by the Venetians when the Island belonged to them in the Fifteenth and Sixteenth Centuries. (Remember Othello, the Moor of Venice? He was Governor of Cyprus, was he not? Shakespeare's story takes place in Cyprus.)

I plan to write a story some day; or, perhaps a series of stories... well...maybe a book, and title it "Adieu Bella Pais: Goodbye, the Beautiful Country." In it I will describe how I never intended to emigrate, when, as a consequence of the Cyprus revolt, I left the Island to seek employment in nearby Beirut and found myself adrift in the tide of revolution that swept all countries of the region in that era of its history. Aspects of that history will probably serve as background to my personal experience. (I realise, of course, that the project may be an impossible dream for an amateur, and that the idea may never even leave that realm.) I will mention, as well, that Bellapais, and the whole of northern Cyprus, is now occupied by Turkey who, upon a pretext, invaded the Island in 1974, inundating the occupied zone with Turkish troops and hordes of tribes from Eastern Anatolia. I will conclude my story with a description of my arrival in a land that many have rightly called "God's Country" — British Columbia.

This book brings the entire journey to fruition.

Voices from a Buried Past

Civil war in the early 1960's between Greeks and Turks in Cyprus disrupted the lives of all inhabitants making refugees in the tens of thousands of people on both sides in their own land. Many who had no traditional or ancestral roots tying them to the soil, or who, through displacement, were robbed of such attachment, and could still afford the passage, pulled up stakes and migrated: Most, who had kept their British citizenship after independence, to England; many to Australia and perhaps an equal number to the Americas.

Among those who relocated in Britain was Araxie Damatyan, a woman in her early sixties who with her aging husband had accompanied their son's family and settled in a garden town not far from London, where their son and daughter-in-law found work.

Araxie's husband, by then close to eighty, had trouble learning English and, accustomed as he was in Cyprus to spend his evenings and leisure hours at the community men's club, succumbed to the isolation and loneliness and died. Araxie's grief was compounded by the unleashing of memories of a long-lost past: memories that had been repressed, buried and locked up, unresolved, but that her husband's death had revived.

"You can't live with those memories," she had been chided for the past forty years; words which her son now repeated. "You have your grandchildren to think of," he counselled.

It was true. Her two grandchildren, both girls, now on the threshold of their teens, reminded her of her own youth and her memories were sweet and pleasant. It was the manner in which life's evanescent spring had been snatched from her that she could not reconcile. But she had learned to repress her emotions and was resigned to her fate. And though melancholy marked her deep-set eyes, she would occasionally take her granddaughters' hands and dance around the living room. "I'll teach you a Caucasian dance," she would say to one girl while the other practiced her piano. "I used to be such a good dancer when I was you." She was slim and even at her present age her movements were still very graceful.

Often Araxie would engage the girls in conversation. She had noticed that since immigrating to this new country they had been gradually weaning themselves from their mother-tongue of Armenian and finding it much easier to express themselves in English. Her efforts at teaching them the old language and her insistence on answering their English with Armenian were being eroded and tolerated only reluctantly. It pained her to see the gradual loss of a past that might have been, yet in her own life she had witnessed the uselessness of clinging to bygones. The past, she had learned, had a cruel way of betraying its devotee. It was wiser to embrace the present, she thought, and endeavoured to improve her own English in halting conversation with the girls. A passable fluency in English would be handy in communicating with friendly neighbours commenting on the weather, or in better understanding the sermon at church, and responding in kind to the warm greeting of the members. In the absence of an Armenian church, or even a fair-sized community in town, Araxie's family had wisely joined a Methodist church in their neighbourhood and become active members.

Araxie's son and daughter-in-law had attended English and American schools, respectively, in Cyprus, and not only spoke the language fluently but felt quite at home in an English or Western church. Moreover, they enjoyed the friendly fellowship of a congregation where their children had many schoolmates and where they were made to feel welcome. As a regular weekly activity they preferred it to the ritualistic atmosphere of the National Orthodox Church where the preservation of tradition and cultural identity of a people deprived of its homeland seemed to have taken precedence over the nurturing of the soul.

At times, when the lure and yearning of tradition overwhelmed them, they would dress up and travel to London, on Christmas or Easter, and attend Mass at the Armenian Cathedral in Kensington—a Gulbenkian endowment, built in classic Armenian architectural style. After Mass they would exchange greetings with old-country acquaintances, then return home, exhilarated by the ceremonious liturgy and the uplifting performance of the choir, their bodies and apparel steeped head to toe in the scent of the permeating incense.

༓ ༓ ༓

Araxie sat alone in the living-room dozing before the babbling television set. It was a quiet Sunday afternoon in early Spring. Her son had taken the girls to a community function at their school. Her daughter-in-law was preparing Armenian dishes for dinner. The aroma of a variety of spices, mixed with the bouquet of freshly chopped herbs, gently caressed in a mild envelope of garlic, emanated from the kitchen. They had made it a family tradition for the Sundays. Araxie's knitting fell limply onto her lap and in the tranquility of the moment she mused, half asleep, on the turn her life had taken of late. There was much to be thankful for...Keep your feet firmly grounded on the present and face the future with hope and trust. Bury the unanswered questions of the past...Bury the past...Bury the past...

It had now been many years since the death of her husband. She had long become accustomed to life in England and wondered why she, along with all her acquaintances back home had dreaded the English weather. This was home now and the weather was preferable to six months a year of intense heat they used to endure.

She loved England, Araxie told herself, and her thoughts became dominated by flowers...her daughter-in-law grew such lovely flowers in their front yard...The whole town was like a big garden ...Flowers in all the splendor of their colours spun before her eyes as she reeled in a dreamy consciousness, as though trapped in the eddy of a whirlwind.

She was vaguely aware of the doorbell ringing and, in a state of stupor, sensed that her daughter-in-law was attending to it. Words spoken at the door reached her ear only as muddled voices. Her floral reverie became interrupted. The spinning flowers were suddenly no longer there...

Swept on a plume of the twister, transported in time and space, Araxie was abruptly carried back fifty years into the very past and the lost world she had resolved to bury. Her senses still in the misty realm of shadows, but with images more vivid than in a dream, she found herself re-living a time of her life that had brought an end to her best and happiest years; a time she had never been able to banish from her mind but the loss of which she could not bear to remember; a world she dreaded to visit, for fear it might hold captive her sanity, yet wished she had never left. Like a curtain between acts in a play, an impenetrable barrier had come down between the early chapters of her life and all that had followed since.

≀≀≀

A young girl of seventeen, Araxie was in the process of boarding a ship at Batum, port city of Georgia, on the Black Sea. Warmly dressed in an astrakhan fur coat and matching headgear, she elbowed her way toward the railings through the crowd of frenzied passengers cramming the deck. She scanned the swarming multitudes of quayside, below, looking for her family who had come along to see her off. Wiping her tears, she caught sight of the group, guided by the colourful toques her little sisters and young cousins Grigori were wearing. Her parents, waving handkerchiefs, were yelling a last-minute message, but in the deafening din of the noisy crowd no words were audible.

There was a babel of languages being shouted back and forth, ship to shore and shore to ship: oft-repeated messages and instructions and farewell endearments, in Russian, Armenian, Georgian, Turkish and Greek, some in several dialects and all mingled with dockers' and seamen's jargon.

Araxie could not make out the message her mother, Olga, was yelling, though she could tell the words were uttered in Russian. She knew that, although her mother had learned to speak Armenian and spoke it fairly fluently at home, yet in situations like this she usually lapsed into her native Russian. But they frequently switched languages at home. It was nothing unusual. Araxie herself was perfectly bilingual, having been educated at a private Russian girls' school—from whose graduating class she had just been snatched, half-term, to be sent abroad. Araxie's father, Anton, now relayed the message in Armenian—still to no avail. It was young Grigori who finally transmitted the message. "We too will soon be coming to join you!"

The assurance had, over the past several weeks, been repeated many times during discussions at home, in Baku, where Araxie's father was a petroleum engineer in the Caspian oil refineries of Azerbaijan. It was little comfort for a young woman whose life, in all its aspects, had been so hastily, so rudely interrupted. And yet, she was not altogether incognizant of the reasons that had given rise to her parents' decision to consign her to the custody of relatives in Constantinople.

Constantinople! That, as Araxie reflected on her parents' discussions, had seemed the most worrisome thought regarding her departure.

"How can you send my daughter to Turkey?" her mother had argued. "Have you forgotten what happened to your people there, under cover of war?"

"It will be a temporary arrangement," her father pointed out. "Besides, Constantinople is Turkey's cosmopolitan showcase before the world. No harm will come to her there," he reassured them. Then, hesitating, as though reluctant to reveal the balance of his thoughts, "A more dangerous situation is developing right here in the Caucasus," he said. "We will all have to leave one day, and the sooner the better."

"What about your position in the refineries?" Olga asked. "You are a valuable employee of theirs. They should be able to protect us."

"The oil companies themselves may not survive," Anton said, lighting his pipe. "I haven't talked about it in order not to worry you," he said, his fingertips smoothing out the furrows of his brow. "you see...the situation is this: The war—the Great War, as it is being called—ended two years ago. It is now Autumn, 1920. Our three small states of the Caucasus, Armenia, Georgia and Azerbaijan, have been in limbo ever since. They declared independence, yes, but not because they are self-sustaining or able to defend themselves against any major attack. Their status and borders have not been ratified. The American mandate they were hoping for has been rejected by Congress. They are a vacuum waiting to be stormed. Armenia, moreover, is groaning under an overpopulation of starving refugees—helpless survivors of the massacres and death marches, seeking asylum in an equally helpless, newly-proclaimed republic.

"Turkey, though defeated in the war, has been allowed to rearm as a bulwark against communist Russia, and is poised to strike.

"Russia, on the other hand, may still be preoccupied with the Bolshevik revolution, but cannot allow Turkish domination of the area.

"There is going to be a war," Araxie's father said, concluding his assessment of the prevailing situation. "Most probably a double invasion...We don't want to live under either regime...What is more, many of the workers in these three republics are communists sympathizers. They will go on the rampage. A talented girl, like our Araxie should not be trapped in that chaotic upheaval. She must not be deprived of the opportunity to further her inclination in music and dance, perhaps in Paris. We'll send her to my cousin's now and we'll follow as soon as we are packed, in a week at the most."

≀ ≀ ≀

On the voyage Araxie saw her father's fears justified when she learned that the passengers were, almost all, in flight from the deteriorating conditions in the region. Many, dressed in expensive furs, were Russians who had managed to escape the brutalities of the revolution that victimized the rich. The discovery set her mind at rest about the wisdom of her departure and eased her anxiety somewhat.

In Constantinople Araxie was met by her father's relatives and taken to their modest apartment. They were a young couple with a small child, kind and hospitable, and from the start Araxie felt quite at home in their house. Their child, a little boy of four, took a fancy to her, called her "tantie" and ceaselessly flooded her with a deluge of questions, which provided a pleasant diversion for Araxie. She was fascinated by the sights and sounds of the ancient city and only wished for her family to arrive soon for her joy to be complete.

A week had passed when a telegram arrived from her father. "We have begun packing," it said "as soon as we have disposed of some possessions we'll be setting off and we'll see you soon."

Two days later the news spread in Constantinople. The Russian army had overrun the Caucasus and Turkey had invaded Armenia.

Communications were cut off and Araxie sank into sudden despair.

Had her family managed to get out? Were they, perhaps, on their way? "We should find out in a few days," her relatives suggested, in an effort to quell her panic.

The waiting proved futile.

A frantic effort to make contact through the Church, other religious bodies and embassies, produced no response. The invaders on either side were deaf to all appeals.

Araxie's relatives kept her busy doing things and seeing places and tried all they could to comfort her and keep alive her hopes. Though she was appreciative of their efforts she felt she had become an uncalled-for emotional as well as financial burden on them. "Nonsense!" they said. She was family! Besides, they too were concerned about their own relatives, her family.

It was the uncertainty and the lack of news that aggravated Araxie's anxiety. She dreaded the thought that her family may have been killed in the fighting and began asking why she should have been spared.

While she worried about what had become of her family Araxie was overtaken by concern about what was to become of her.

She had been in Constantinople for several weeks when she began noticing furtive goings-on in her relatives' household, as well as a change in their conduct. At first it was the appearance of suitcases and a large trunk, delivered by hired hands, which were hurriedly hidden out of sight. Araxie felt awkward for having seen them and sensed that her hosts would rather she hadn't. Then, she would occasionally, inadvertently surprise them, interrupting stealthy, whispering conversations they would be engaged in. It was not until their son innocently revealed their plan that the mystery was solved. "We are going to America," he blurted out as he and Araxie walked to the neighbourhood grocer's one day.

Her relatives admitted it when Araxie confronted them. They had applied for immigration, they said, and had been waiting for their "quota" for some time. They had expected her parents to have arrived by then, but told her not to worry. She could stay with good friends of theirs until some news of her family could be obtained.

Araxie's personal troubles multiplied as her apprehension and longing for her family grew. What was she to do? Stay with so-called friends when her relatives departed, as they had advised? She would be reduced to an object of their pity! She would have no means of repaying their kindness. How "kindly" would they treat her, a bewildered, dependent stranger? And how long would she be able to tolerate the predicament?

The thought of becoming a nun crossed her mind. But being forced into the service of God out of necessity rather than dedication seemed wrong.

She felt tormented as her mind foundered in the mussy confusion of options she envisioned:

She could apply to the Church and become a ward of the Community. The thought of it was so demeaning she began hating herself.

Perhaps she could claim to be an orphan (for all she knew her parents' fate she might well be one), and enter one of the orphanages run by European or American Missions in neighbouring Greece or Syria. Surely they could take one more victim, though they were said to be filled to capacity with surviving children of Armenians.

Dispossessed of all property, the children's parents, along with the rest of their nation (more than a million of them, Araxie was told), had been driven from their historic homeland in the Eastern and Southern provinces of what had become Turkey, and killed or marched off to their death in the hot sands of the Syrian desert. Araxie felt an affinity and sympathized with them, though her own people, Armenians of the Russian sector in the Caucasus, had not experienced the brutalities that befell their brethren in Turkey.

A twinge in her heart for the sufferings of her kindred made her troubles seem, briefly, insignificant, and, in a flicker of hope, Araxie began entertaining thoughts of self-reliance. Could she not earn her own keep, she asked herself. But then, she wondered what she could do. Not only had she no training for a profession, but, wrested from school when her final year had hardly begun, she had not even graduated. She could think of no occupation a respectable woman without proper education might engage in. Her mother had been a schoolteacher, but Araxie doubted whether she herself was qualified to follow in her mother's footsteps. What difference would it make though, she thought, if necessity forced her into a humbler choice. Survival was the objective, she told herself. Besides, it would be only a temporary interlude. She was convinced and wished to God that news of her family's welfare and whereabouts would be forthcoming before long. The confusion of war and the paralysis of communications could not last forever!

Though she tried to keep her hopes and spirits high, it was mostly at night that a sense of abandonment overwhelmed her. She shuddered at the thought of being left alone in the world and, haunted by thoughts of the worst possibilities, she often cried herself to sleep. Yet she prayed, kneeling by her bedside, every night before retiring, as she had since childhood.

If she couldn't be a schoolteacher, Araxie thought, she could perhaps be a private tutor to some rich family's pampered child. She rated it higher than being a nanny and certainly higher than a housemaid. She was inspired with some hope in that possibility when she learned that a large population of wealthy Russian emigres had been on the increase in Constantinople since the Bolshevik revolution.

When, with the help of her relatives, Dikran and Anahid, she embarked on her enquiries, Araxie began to get a glimpse of the confusion and uncertainty that seemed to reign in Turkey two years into the aftermath of the Great War that ended in 1918. While leaders of the participants—victors and vanquished—met in Europe negotiating peace settlements, the situation in Turkey, which had lost the war, was becoming more and more unsettled. The victorious Allies—Britain, France and Italy—had begun to view each other with suspicion as to which of them might be making secret agreements to gain more advantageous concessions from Turkey. The Greek army, with the approval of Britain and France, had been allowed, a year after the war had ended, to march, unopposed, into western coastal Turkey, which since ancient times had been a land of Greek settlements. It had taken control of the great port city of Smyrna whose population consisted of vast numbers of Greeks and a large minority of Armenians as well as Turks. There was talk that the Army was on the move toward Constantinople, bent on recapturing the grand old capital of the glorious Byzantine Empire, which had fallen to the Turks in the fifteenth century.

The city was bustling with foreigners. Russian aristocrats, bejeweled and fur-clad women, accompanied by their husbands, former officers of the assassinated Tsar, in uniform, road in carriages up and down the waterfront. An Allied occupation force under command of a British general had taken control and, on her outings to town with her relatives, Araxie could see soldiers of different complexions in a variety of military garb. Besides European Allied servicemen there were French troops from Africa and Indo-China, British units from India, and even forces from Japan which had become an ally later in the war. Local residents also watched parades of soldiers in kilts marching to the music of bagpipes.

A rumour that Constantinople might be ceded to Greece and that Britain would keep permanent control over the straits was said to be causing a stir among the populace. Turks grumbled and resented the notion, and though there was excitement among part of the Greek residents, as well as most Armenians of the city viewed that possibility with some concern.

"It is a delicate situation, my child," lamented the Patriarch of the Armenians of Turkey, with whom Araxie was granted an audience. She had wished to pay her respects and seek help and counsel in confronting the problems that bewildered her. "Unless Britain or France occupies the city in full administrative and military force," the Patriarch explained, "we minorities cannot feel secure."

Although in her home in the Caucasus Araxie had, in recent years, lived through a historic period of political upheaval and military traffic, she had been young and had not felt personally touched by events as she did now, listening to the venerable priest with keen interest. If world affairs had something to do with the sudden severance of communications with her family, could she not, she thought, perhaps find a clue to their fate by probing all avenues of information and learning what exactly was going on.

There was as yet no embassy in Turkey of the Bolshevik revolutionary regime, but the Patriarch promised to put Araxie in touch with the Russian Orthodox bishop of Constantinople. If there was any news at all trickling across the sealed and war-bound border, the Church, with her ear tuned to all sources, would be the first to be informed. He advised her, however, to be patient. "No one can tell how long it will be before these ungodly assassins open their borders and join the civilized world," he said. "On the other hand," he continued, after a pause immersed in deep thought, "if your family was caught across the border, ending up on the Turkish side..." He did not wish, it seemed, to expound on the possible consequences. Besides, the scant information he had on the obliteration of the fledgling state of independent Armenia did not inspire much hope. "You must be brave, my child," he said, in a tone of consolation, "and trust in the Lord."

The old churchman seemed distracted, his thoughts detached from his immediate surroundings. Absently stroking his scraggly beard, his deep-sunken eyes focused far away as though on a scene beyond his reach or control, his soul burdened with the cries of his flock, trapped, like sheep in the slaughterhouse, he spoke wearily, as though to an equal, or perhaps to himself, forgetful that his audience was a young woman of tender age and vulnerable emotions. Araxie could sense the heaviness that seemed to hang over the old shepherd's heart for the fate of his flock.

"A rebel Turkish army," he told her, "has, in defiance of the current government with whom the victors are, at this moment, in peace negotiations, taken control of the interior and eastern provinces. It has already wiped out, apparently by secret agreement with the Russians, what had been proclaimed, and we had hoped would continue to be, an independent Armenia after centuries of subjugation. The rebels' commander, an officer by the name of Mustafa Kemal, disillusioned by defeat and unhappy with proposed conditions of settlement, has vowed to purge the country of all Christian elements, Greeks and Armenians, regardless of the fact that this is our native land and has been our historic home since thousands of years before the Turks set foot in the region.

"Even as we speak, he is on the rampage in the southern province of Cilicia, the orphaned kingdom of the Armenians, putting to the sword and driving out, yet again, the few straggling survivors who, urged and encouraged by assurances of the victorious Allies, had come back from their burial grounds in the fiery sands of Syria and Mesopotamia. Though hopelessly decimated in numbers, their bodies, wasted and reduced to skeletons, they had returned, with gratitude in their hearts toward their new-found saviours and Christian protectors. They had returned with renewed hope to resettle their ravaged land and rebuild from the ashes their pillaged and plundered homes."

The initial anxiety that had brought Araxie to seek counsel from the leader of the Church and steward of his nation seemed reduced in importance, if not vanished from her mind. She listened with rapt attention to the Patriarch's soliloquy and her heart ached for the tribulations suffered by the western branch of her people.

"How can I help, Your Grace?' she asked, when the old priest had fallen silent for a moment, her voice, hardly audible, trembling with emotion, tears running down her cheeks.

The old man appeared not to have heard her. "Cilicia, O, Cilicia," he signed. "Mountain fortress of a proud race of peace-loving warriors. Friend of the Crusaders. Their gateway to Jerusalem. A little Europe in Asia Minor. Cilicia was supposed to have become a French protectorate at the conclusion of the war. But she was abandoned and betrayed. The Allies, realizing that the rebel, Kemal, might emerge the dominant ruler of the country, vied for his favour by providing him, each in assumed secrecy from the other, with much-needed arms for his irregular, insurgent army. Then, reneging on their mandate over the conquered territories, they stole away and vanished in the night. Their new-found hero now had a free hand to carry through his campaign of extermination and genocide which his predecessors had left unfinished when they lost the war."

Tears welled up in the old Patriarch's eyes and he seemed to sink deeper into a pensive mood. His lips moved, as though uttering a silent prayer, and his body swayed gently to and fro, almost imperceptibly, in the manner of a remorseful penitent or helpless, exhausted mourner.

Araxie sat patiently through the long ensuing silence, dabbing her eyes and nursing her own emotions.

"Woe is me! O, woe is me!" the Patriarch's subdued, rueful muttering broke the gloomy suspense. "History will never forgive me," he lamented. "I deserve the eternal reproach of my people. How can I exonerate myself? How can I wash the stain of my own people's blood from my hands? O, woe is me! God forgive me, for

I am, in great measure responsible...I was chief among leaders of our nation in encouraging our young men to join the Ottoman army when there was a call for conscription. We were anxious to dispel any doubts of our loyalty to the Government. They gathered them all and killed them."

Araxie could not restrain a sudden, audibly convulsive sob. The Patriarch continued undisturbed, as though confined in his own, private confessional, oblivious to the presence of anyone in the room.

"Then, in one lightening swoop, in the middle of the night, they hauled in every single one of our intellectual leaders, thinkers, writers, teachers, poets, artist, all...My People were reduced into a defenseless and headless body of women, children and old men. Though, unopposed and unresisted, they started a ruthless search for arms, beating, raping, imprisoning and torturing their helpless prey to the content of their barbarous nature. And still we admonished our people not to resist, in order not to provide the murderous horde with an alibi for sweeping, wholesale bloodshed. The memory of the Mamidian massacres of the 1890's, when 300,000 of our people were slaughtered, was still fresh in our mind. But that era was past, we tried to convince ourselves. This was now a new regime. These were the "Young Turks," the "Committee of Union and Progress." Hadn't they deposed the "Bloody, Red Sultan"? Proclaimed "Equality" and "Fraternity" under a new "Constitution" in 1908? We wanted so desperately to embrace those empty slogans as their commitment in gaining entry into a civilized new century. We were even ready to discount the more recent massacre of 30,000 that occurred under their rule in 1909, and that they had done nothing to punish the culprits. With misgiving in the depths of our soul, we wanted to deny the blatant fact that the Turk's nature had not changed, that, though cloaked in endearing, romantic words borrowed from a civilized world, he was the same bloodthirsty barbarian at heart. Fools that we were! Criminal that we were. We deemed it better to sacrifice the few than give cause for the murder of the entire nation. But that is exactly what we have invited upon our heads.

"Eternal glory to the many towns and villages where our people saw through the diabolic intent of the deportations, ignored our admonitions, resisted with the scant arms they had clung to and fought bravely to the death. They have given future generations reason to hold their heads up with pride, though it may never absolve our shame and want of courage that would have forbidden their act of valour.

"Glory to the brave! Praise to God, and may He forgive our misguided wisdom and the fatal decisions taken in our moment of desperation. May He look kindly upon his people who have borne the suffering of the Cross for the sake of His Son, and save them from being consigned to extinction."

The disconsolate churchman appeared to have wound up his confession. His countenance had let up. A pervasive calm filled the decorous drawing-room, engulfing the two occupants in its comforting tide. They sat in silence, basking in the cathartic peace that, like a receding after-glow, permeated briefly their all-too-transient, deceptive world.

The Patriarch reached for a small bell that lay on the table beside him and gave it short tinkle.

"I have burdened your young soul with the woes of our long-suffering people, my child," he said, turning to Araxie. "But it is incumbent upon you, the surviving youth—such as have survived—to be armed with knowledge of your history—the glory of it, as well as the agony—and carry the torch of your culture to future generations. Our mission is more imperative, the task more arduous and the challenge more formidable now, with our nation deprived of homeland, survivors scattered and struggling to keep alive in foreign lands, drifting, like grains of sand, their identity at risk of being washed away in the torrent into oblivion."

The sexton entered and, with a boy, brought over a tray of tea and platter generously piled with a variety of home-baked pastries. He poured tea for them and, again with a respectful boy, departed.

Araxie was grateful for the hospitality. She had listened to the Patriarch's monologue with emotion, and though she appreciated the knowledge she had gained and was glad for her visit, she welcomed a refreshment break at this time.

The Patriarch's tone had become more conversational now, though it still seemed tinged with pain.

"Massacres are nothing new where the Turk has trod," he said.

"over the centuries Turkish raiders and Mongol tyrants terrorized our native people into subjugation with indiscriminate periodic massacres, killing women and children. But nomadic parasites that they were, they recognized that their livelihood depended on looting and plundering our productive peasants, our wealthy merchants and our skilled craftsmen. And so, they knew better than to destroy the whole nation. But these modern-day vultures, these twentieth-century "Young Turks," these "civilized," misguided "patriots," they are cutting their own life-line, severing the hand that feeds them. They? How can they be such idiots?"

Araxie knew the questions were not meant for her to answer. She realized that, weighed down as he was with the plight of his people, the Patriarch could not help becoming agitated now and again.

They sat in silence, savouring the refreshing tea and the delectable pastries that Constantinople was famous for and the Patriarch's housekeeper took pride in preparing.

The Patriarch turned toward Araxie.

"Do not be disheartened, my child," he said, seeing the anguish in her face, becoming suddenly aware of his immediate business at hand.

"We have survived countless onslaughts in our long history and have outlived many of our mighty contemporaries. It will be more difficult now, deprived of our homeland. But, this too we shall survive. God will never allow us to be wiped out, my child, though He may seem to have abandoned us and will often allow us to be martyred for His name." The Patriarch's mood became suddenly pensive again. "Perhaps He is trying to teach us a lesson," he said. "A lesson we still have not learned: to love one another.

"We made a covenant with God when we proclaimed His Son's creed our official state religion in the year 301. It introduced a flood of light into our nation. It inspired the creation of our alphabet, resulting in the beautiful translation of the Holy Bible, as well as a torrent of great literature. The fifth century was the Golden Age of our culture.

"Our culture will sustain us. Our Church and our faith will sustain us. And we will survive.

"We must survive, my child. It is vital and imperative that we live through this holocaust, in order that we may bear witness. For, if this evil that has been committed in the dark is not exposed to the light of international inquiry; if it is not brought to trial and a judgement passed, but is ignored and forgotten; if the perpetrators go free, gloating over their butchery, and are admitted into the family of the world's nations without condemnation, and make no restitution or reparations; if this blatant inhumanity of man toward his fellow-man is not soon redressed, then woe unto the civilized world, for the stain and stench of blood in the dawning of this new era of progress bode ill for the future of the twentieth century. For, in this crowded world of intermingled races on a group of people — whether nature or settler — inspired by bigotry or dreams of racial purity, may find reason to end mutual tolerance and, encouraged by the international reluctance to punish this first holocaust of the century, decide to exterminate, one the other.

"This "War to End All Wars" has been a sham. This century, then, is bound to become the century of genocides.

(*Voices from a Buried Past* is the onset of a novel.)

Cyprus Memories

My Introduction to Shakespeare

When I was about six years of age, living in the asbestos mining village of Amiantos, my birthplace in the snowy mountains of Cyprus, I once attended a concert presented by the children of the Small Armenian community in their one-room schoolhouse.

While I may have forgotten many of the faces and recitations that crammed the event, a play, staged by the older pupils, has clung to the recesses of my memory to this day. A popular farce in Armenian amateur theatre—though its title, Varda la Bomba, may suggest a translation from another language—it was destined to play an important initiating role in my randomly self-programmed education when my formal schooling was cut short.

The theme of the play is an overbooked hotel room at a festival town. A peasant hawker rents the last available room and goes to bed early in order to be well rested for the morning when he intends to display and market his sackful of squashes that he has dragged along. While he is asleep the hotel keeper re-rents the room to an actor with the understanding that his sleep cycle will not coincide with that of the peasant and on the assumption that the peasant may not even become aware of another's occupation of the room. The actor, however, seeing the peasant sunken in deep sleep, and taking advantage of the idle hours of waiting, decides to rehearse for his upcoming performance.

The peasant is awakened by noises in the middle of the night and is startled to see a stranger holding a dagger to his throat, demanding the handkerchief.

"I didn't take your handkerchief!" pleads the peasant, trembling.

The actor, shaken into the real world, apologizes profusely. "Don't worry," he says. "Go back to sleep. I won't bother you again. I am Othello, you see!"

"So what, if you're in the 'otel? Says the peasant. "I am in the 'otel, too!"

Sometime later the peasant is again awakened to find the actor holding a dagger, this time to his own heart, and, in a despondent mood, contemplating whether "to be or not to be."

"Don't do it!" cries the peasant. "Nothing can be worth taking your own life for!"

The actor, apologizing again, says this time he was Hamlet.

"Ah!" the peasant exclaims. "You like it too?"

"I like what?"

"Omelet! My favourite dish!"

˃˃˃

The War years saw me moving from village to city, chasing a school from hill-town to coastal town. Then, in my mid-teens, I found myself reluctantly dropping out of the American Academy. It was to be the end of my formal schooling.

Had I been able to continue to graduation I would have acquired business or office skills that would have qualified me for the job market. As it was, my main asset in seeking employment was only a passable fluency in English. I was determined to improve on it and since there were no facilities for continuing education, I would have to rely entirely on my own personal effort. I had a vague idea of where and how I ought to start.

The prospect of employment was not the only incentive in my determination to further my language skills. The pages of our English readers were interspersed with quotations from works of literature. The beauty and the magic of language as well as the depth of thought expressed in those gems had captivated me. I had even come across short passages from Hamlet and Othello, names that had fascinated me since childhood—not only for the humour they evoked through their connection with the play that I remembered, but also because I imagined myself an actor performing the roles.

My decision, then, came naturally: I would embark upon furtherance of my grasp of English by reading the books where such beauty and charm, contained in words, were to be found. I knew where I would start.

I went to the school librarian and asked if she could tell me where I might read about Hamlet and Othello.

She smiled. "You're looking for Shakespeare's plays," she said.

"Shakespeare? If I had heard the name before it had made no connection in my mind. The librarian gave me two small books, the kind prepared for schools, with the text paraphrased in small print between the lines.

The language of the plays, though elucidated by the explanations, was not at all unfamiliar. Regular Bible classes at the Academy, augmented by church and Christian Endeavour on Sundays, had well acquainted me with the tongue spoken in the era of King James. I had little trouble understanding the dialogue and was, moveover, dazzled by the beauty of the poetry, charmed by the brilliant twists of language, amazed at the grasp of human behavior in comic or tragic situations, enraptured by the wit and wisdom and awed by the depth of thought that filled every page.

Upon quitting school I immediately bought myself the complete works of Shakespeare. A fair-sized volume, with clear print, it was a treasure-trove. I sat leafing through the whole book, caressing each page with a sense of elation mixed with awe and reverence. It was to be my school, my teacher, my friend and companion for many years. Although it was not paraphrased, as the school-texts I started with had been, I delved into the volume and soon caught on to Shakespeare's wit and poetry, savouring the magic of each beauty-laden passage. I was occasionally lucky to have one or other of the Bard's works playing at the local cinema. (We had no live theatre. I read Hamlet and saw Olivier's rendition four times.)

And then I discovered the sonnets. An unfamiliar word or idiom often called for interpretation. I enlisted the help of the Oxford Dictionary and was thrilled to learn that 'treading the measures,' an expression that had impeded my enjoyment of a sonnet, meant dancing. I would sit with a ruler and a red pencil and, between Shakespeare and my Oxford, study and underline passage after ecstatic passage.

My mother, who also delighted in the beauty and wisdom of a passage when I translated it for her, cautioned me, nevertheless—devout Christian that she was—not to allow Shakespeare to become my idol. She was not far wrong. Shakespeare had become my religion, my idol and my obsession.

Valley of the Nightingale

Many summers of my childhood were spent at a village in the lower hills of Cyprus—that history-laden little island in the sunny Mediterranean.

Often, in the cool of a late afternoon as the sun went behind the mountains, my two older brothers and I, along with our grandmother, walked to a viewpoint overlooking the valley, at a wide bend of the road that wound up the mountain range bypassing the old village. It was a hike of several miles from our rented house in the new town which spread randomly into the orchards and up the hillside with rustic bungalows built mainly for summer tenants escaping the heat of the city in the plains. We sat there on a bench and rested in silence as we gazed at the peaceful landscape, our senses feasting on the balmy gifts of nature, lulled by the sounds that awakened with the speedily spreading shadows enveloping the valley and darkening the glen, intoxicated by the savoury scents that drifted in whiffs up the sun-warmed mountainside.

The ancient hamlet stretched below upon a narrow strip of land between two streams. Its weathered mud-brick houses, huddled tightly together as though pushing each other for perching space, lined the single cobbled street that zigzagged the length of the village, their red-tiled roofs blackened with age.

Although the hill on the far side appeared rocky and barren, (conforming to the name of the village—Kakopetria—a place of bad rocks), except for a sparse patch of grape vines or a straggling almond or carob tree here and there, orchards of apple, plum, peach and apricot trees as well as numerous small vegetable farms provided a lush green carpet on the floor of the valley, while the creek on the closer side flowed beneath a thick dark canopy of oak trees.

The streams merged under an arched stone bridge marking the cobbled entrance to the old hamlet as well as the approach to the new village. The main highway swung past and wound its way through the new town and up the mountain range. The village flour mill, perched on a promontory above the bridge, gushed out its churning waters through a gaping vent below, with a roar whose whoosh, permeating the glen, had become an identifying aspect of the village and greeted all visitors, caressing their faces with the cool mist that arose from the turbulence.

The refreshing smell of wild mint that grew in abundance by the water, blending with the aroma of the sage brush on the slopes, floated past now and then, carried on a gentle upward breeze and, aided by the whispering murmur of water and leaf, caressed our senses into a restful reverie.

A delicate smell of dry grass also lingered in the air. The threshing floor was in a clearing among a group of old, gnarled and twisted olive trees down by the roadside. We had passed by it on our way up. The winnowers and the oxen had gone home, and the heavy threshing board lay idle on the flattened golden straw. A pair of turtledoves and a woodpigeon swooped down on the yellow grass to feed on the abundant barley. We had also heard, on our way up, the clacking of a partridge calling her brood at the close of day.

Darkness was now setting in and lights came on in houses and coffee gardens in the village below. But the moon, on its way up behind the opposite mountain, spread a milky wash, lightening the sky and revealing the ridges in silhouette.

The crickets started chirping now. They seemed to be everywhere in the surrounding shrubbery. Their short, staccato, rhythmic rasps provided a muted chorus to the shrill, ringing solo of another, perhaps of a different variety. This one piped from the thicket beyond the curve of the road, yet it echoed unchallenged in its territory, its long, measured trills further enhancing the tranquil dreaminess of the magic hour.

The raspy chirping and high-pitched trill of the crickets were no competition nor were they a hindrance or challenge, but rather, accompanied by the soft, distant murmur of flowing water, provided a fitting background to the haunting yet ecstatic and melodious outburst that rang forth from the gloom of the creek below. All other sounds seemed to fade as the mysterious lament of the Nightingale echoed through the valley in what appeared to be a meaningful hymn chanted by a shy genius, doomed, in hiding, to pour out the depths of its soul, steeped in the forgotten glory of a mythical paradise, tinged with a sadness at its loss.

My Grandmother's Culinary Traditions and Healing Rituals

My grandmother, Gulizar, my mother's mother, lived alternately with us and with my aunt's family. Of all my grandparents she was the sole survivor of the Genocide and the only one I knew. She had brought with her to Cyprus, my birthplace, not a few Old Country traditions and little else from her Armenian homeland in Ottoman Turkey.

Though resourceful in the kitchen, Grandma (our Medzmama, as we called her) was not an exceptionally gifted cook, but was good at preparing certain food items, some as general staples, most to see for much of the family's diet through the winter months.

We spent the summers of my younger days at a village, by the name of Kakopetria, in the middle hills of Cyprus, where the sun was more tolerable than in the city on the plains. Grandma made use of those sojourns to prepare bulgur and other provisions whose success called for continuous, dependable sunshine.

Bulgur has perhaps always been the major staple of the western Armenian and neighbouring countries' cuisines. Foreign travelers and expatriate residents who have been introduced to it have conveniently, though mistakenly, called it "cracked wheat." The term is not entirely incorrect, of course. Bulgur is wheat, and it is cracked. But what makes wheat bulgur is that it is par-boiled before it is cracked.

Grandma, working together with my mother, would boil the wheat in a large copper pot over wood fire, outdoors. When it had attained a measure of boiling time or intensity—a measure determined by Grandmother's long-tested, infallible instinct—it would be drained and spread to dry, over clean sheets, on the sunny patio of the rented cottage. When fully dry, it would be ready to mill, usually with a pair of borrowed, portable millstones. My two elder brothers and I would take turns, down on our knees, turning the heavy stone, testing our strengths, exercising our muscles.

The final step in the production of bulgur would be the sifting of the milled grain to obtain coarse, medium and fine grades of product. And Grandmother would spend a whole day patiently carrying out the tedious and tiring chore, shaking and tossing the sifter, as though the job came to her instinctively, while the expression on her face betrayed that her thoughts were far away, meditating on past woes and lost kin.

Other food items that Grandmother dried or processed in the village sun were apricots and tomatoes. The latter would be bought from the farm market and selected for full ripeness. The two women would then get busy cutting up and crushing them by hand. (Once or twice, I remember, when the quantity had justified it, I stomped the tomatoes in our large cauldron.) They would then strain the juice into a pot, salt it, cover it with fine netting to keep the flies out, and place it in the sun to reduce and thicken into tomato paste. Often the juice would be spread into several shallower pans to speed up the thickening process. And Grandma would be in her element during the whole activity, from beginning to end, supervising the purchases for quality, inspecting utensils and equipment for cleanliness, checking the final products for doneness, until she was satisfied with the results.

Apricots, selected for drying, would be ripe but firm. When slit, they should open freely into the form of a bivalve, without sticking to the stone. Done with a sharp, small paring knife, this was an operation for the adults. We children hung around, cracked the stones and ate the seeds, which tasted no different from regular almonds. We also gobbled up any of the fruit that happened to be too ripe or considered rejects. A piercing "tummy-ache" would eventually put an end to our feasting.

A different variety of apricot had bitter kernels. Grandma said they had medicinal properties and encouraged us to eat a few while we were at it. She saved a handful of the shelled seeds and placed them in a bag where she kept an assortment of medicaments ready for the time of need. There were dried flowers and leaves, aromatic herbs, grass roots, flax seeds, cherry pits and stems in her well-tended hoard. She knew the curative qualities of each little bundle. Hollyhock flowers had to be strictly of the pure white variety, naturally matured and shriveled on the plant and spontaneously fallen off. Sweetened with honey, they made an important tea for colds, chest congestions and sore throats. Grandma's collection of natural cures also contained remedies for headaches, fevers and stomach aches, as well as expectorants, diuretics, calmatives and digestives. Mint, perhaps the most common remedy for milder ailments, such as headaches, upset stomach, indigestion and abdominal pains, was always available in ample quantities, in the kitchen, as a condiment in many foods.

Grapes, varieties of which abounded on the farther slopes of the valley, provided much excitement for us boys one summer. Villagers, often women, trudging through town as they returned from the vineyards with their donkeys laden with the fruit, would sometimes pass by our cottage on their way to market. My mother had bought a fair-sized basketful of the black variety from one such woman the day before. And now, rinsed and checked over by Grandmother, the grapes—delectable, of intoxicating sweetness, vine-ripened, vineyard-fresh—were heaped in the cauldron, to be rendered into juice, by the traditional method of stomping. My brothers and I, with washed feet, took turns in the ritual. But they were soon bored with the monotony of it, and, to my delight, preferred to go and play, or explore the surroundings with friends. As for me, I enjoyed the activity as a game, a dance, a performance, or...exhibition. In fairness, though, because I was younger and smaller than they, I may have been a better fit in the cauldron.

Treading the fruit was, of course, only part of the fun that the excitement about grapes entailed. The prospect of the end product—soojooko—made us wait with mouthwatering anticipation. As the next step in preparation, the juice, finely strained into a large pot, combined with cornstarch and cooked over wood fire, was first made into pudding, a delicious dessert in its own right, which we all sampled before the final procedure began. Soojooko is probably a Cyprus specialty, but imitated in neighbouring countries: a series of walnut meats, strung on a length of cotton string, dipped in grape pudding, hung up to cool and set; then dipped again, and again, over and over, until the accumulation has grown to more than an inch thick, the walnuts are well hidden and only recognizable by the evenly spaced lumps, richly covered with layer upon layer of chewable, delicious, nutritious confection, preservable through the winter months, dealt out, to the joy of the children, as a dessert, or treat, on New Year's and Christmas festivities.

An occasional activity, to which my Grandmother lent her expertise during her stays with us, was the processing of sheep's tail to obtain cooking fat. Sheep, in Cyprus and in countries of the region, are endowed with fatty tails of considerable bulk. Often a good-sized tail, well rendered, would provide an average family with its yearly supply of essential cooking fat. Olive oil, as well as other vegetable oils, such as sesame seed, peanut and cotton-seed oils, and, on a smaller scale, dairy butter, were always available commercially, while margarine and other imported shortenings began showing up in stores following WWII. But traditions die hard when eager perpetuators live on, and accustomed palates prefer the familiar.

I remember, once, in 1940 or '41, when a blubbery tail of enormous size was delivered home from the butcher's. Grandma got busy cutting it up and dicing it into small cubes. These were melted, or rendered, in a large copper pot, on a charcoal burner. The pool of melting oil was ladled into jars, as it welled up, and left to cool and gel into soft, buttery consistency. Unlike lard—favoured, in Cyprus, mainly by the Greek majority of the population—tail fat can be spooned and spread, much like soft butter or margarine. Spread on toast, sweetened with honey or a sprinkling of sugar, it served, in our home, during WWII, as an occasional substitute for butter. Contrary to the generally held reputation of mutton, tail fat, processed, is neutral, or at least more tolerable, in taste and odour.

The shriveled, crispy residue of the rendering process was by no means wasted. Grandma incorporated it into biscuit dough of her own creation, rolled and formed it into loops, brushed them with egg, lined them on large trays borrowed from the local bakery, and sent them to be baked into crackers. They served, throughout the winter months, as afternoon snacks, or dunkers with tea at breakfast.

A visit, or "expedition," to the "hammam" (Turkish bathhouse) occasioned the provisioning of an appropriate "picnic basket."

Water has always been a scarce commodity in Cyprus. Few houses, in the days of my childhood, had a storage tank to collect the sparing ration; fewer still a bathing facility. A portable galvanized metal tub, however, was a common utensil in every home. Going to the hammam, therefore, was a festive occasion; literally so at Easter and Christmastide.

My introduction to the hammam (my first and only glimpse of it) may have coincided with one or the other event, but was truly in culmination, as well as celebration of my recovery from a disquieting illness. I have long forgotten the nature of the ailment, but the very remembrance of my Grandmother's loving treatment, the application of her traditional remedies and the performance of her healing rituals, still gives me comfort whenever I feel out of sorts, to this day. Whatever cures my frequent indispositions called for, Grandma was ready with the full range of her remedies. Many times, she applied cups on my back, rubbed my chest with Vick's VapoRub, made me inhale steaming eucalyptus leaves, drink a variety of herbal teas, and, more memorably, anointed my head with olive oil and vinegar. When all was found lacking, she yielded, as a last resort, to divine intervention, through a supplicatory observance.

Though I am affectionately reminded of my grandmother on many a trigger occasion (such as, dressing my salad—with my favourite: olive oil and vinegar), the image, which often is also called forth, of the mystic ritual of blessing she performed when all remedies seemed to have failed, still fills me with the most serene sense of well-being and warmth. I remember lying in a feverish, trancelike state of oblivion, yet basking in my grandmother's, as well as my mother's solicitous ministrations. I could hear their muted voices, sounding as from a distant void, as they weighed the merits and timeliness of the blessing ceremony.

Then all fell silent, and I drifted away, as though under a hypnotic spell, into a state of perceived boundlessness, oblivious of my body, as though I existed, not as physical matter, but as an ever-expanding ethereal entity. I was remotely aware, nevertheless, of the soft "whisp-whisp" of my grandmother's slippers, as she paced back and forth the distance from my head to my feet. And I felt warmed and comforted by the assurance of her loving presence.

In her hand she held a large kitchen knife, with a thick slab of bread pierced at the end, (symbolizing, I learned later, the pierced body of Christ) with which she made the sign of the Cross, many times, at different spots throughout the length of my body.

If she uttered an incantation during the ritual, I could not hear it, though a whiff of a whisper seemed to escape her lips occasionally.

My grandmother's mother tongue (she spoke no other) cannot be said to have been her native language. It was a patois of Turkish, the language of the invaders, forced upon the native population since the Middle Ages, intermixed with Armenianized expressions and Christian terms. Her invocation was possibly a prayer in Classical Armenian, which she would have learnt by rote, even as a child. She used to draw, with the tip of her cane, and relate, with some pride and more pain, how she had learnt the first letter of the Alphabet on her first and only day at school. Her great uncle, patriarch of the family, dragged her out of school the next day. Education for girls, in the prevailing culture of the land and of the times, was an alarming concept. Even though missionaries, European and American, had established schools, for boys and for girls, throughout the country, in the second half of the nineteenth century, and mainly Armenians, including girls, took advantage of them.

There is an irony in that my grandmother's brother had been a well-educated man, versed in several languages, author of a translation into Turkish of the Armenian Prayer Book, and had served as superintendent of schools, as well as French teacher in the Gessaria (Caesarea, Kaiseri) district. Inducted, subsequently, into the priesthood, he had become a popular pastor of the surrounding communities. Targeted as an intellectual by the Ottoman Government, he was arrested and, along with all Armenian intellectuals, was among the first victims of the Genocide of wartime 1915.

I regained my health in good time and normalcy returned to the household. I needed now to wash away the sick-room scents and residue of all the liniments, salves and embrocation rubbed into my skin, head to toe. The two women in whose tender loving care I had been restored to good health thought I needed the cleansing magic of the hammam. Bathing in a portable tub, at home, with no basic facilities and comforts, was an arduous and risky undertaking, primarily in consideration of a convalescing child.

The hammam was open for business in two shifts: daytime for women, evenings for men. My father was away attending to his chain of stores in the asbestos mines on the central mountain range, and came home only at intervals. I was to accompany my grandmother to the hammam. I could overhear fragments of a stealthy conversation between my mother and grandmother regarding the admissibility of a six-year-old boy among a crowd of females during their allotted time in the bathhouse. The consensus was that I should be presented to the manageress on the appointed day, and let her decide.

The manageress was, propitiously, an Old Country compatriot and acquaintance of my grandmother's. She scrutinized me, viewing me asquint, while they exchanged civilities. "He's harmless," she pronounced, with a meaningful flicker of a smile and a twinkle in her eyes.

It was, perhaps, the lengthy confinement in the steamy, poorly lit, cavernous chamber, and the torturous "massage" at the hands of the professional "scrubber" that induced hunger or stimulated the appetite that had given rise to the need of a respite and the tradition of a "picnic" following the cleansing "infliction."

Whenever she stayed with us, Medzmama would rise at daybreak every morning and busy herself with preparations for our breakfast, before the Church bell summoned us to school. She would start the day with a splash of cold water on her face, cross herself, facing the sunrise, and, standing in awed reverence, with her palms held upward at her sides, she would utter, in whispers, a standard prayer—in Classical Armenian, the language of the Church, which she neither understood nor enunciated correctly. The mystery of the ancient, incomprehensible language, it seemed, lent her devotions a magisterial voice and a sense of the veritable presence and protection of the Divine, further deepening the blissfulness that sustained her simple, ever-hoping, ever-trusting generation. She was careful not to wake us up with any noise or clatter, but we could hear the shuffle of her slippers as she stirred about in the kitchen. Soon the house would be filled with the balmy aroma of cinnamon boiling in the tea water (sometimes a clove would be added) and we would know it was time to rise and dress up for breakfast and a hot cup of ambrosial, aromatic tea, before joining the neighbours' children on our way to school.

Black Dog Apparition

I was paralyzed with fear when, returning home from kindergarten one day, I climbed our stairway and found a massive black dog sprawled at the door of our apartment. I stood frozen in my tracks and called "mama." The animal made whimpering sounds and looked at me with sad and plaintive eyes, knitting its brow. It did not move but rather clung to the floor as if it were glued down. In a fervent display of non-aggression and friendliness it wiped the floor with frantic waggings of its tail.

I was not totally unfamiliar with dogs. In my younger childhood, several years earlier, we did have a pet — a white, docile, woolly terrier. It was run over by a Model-T when cars were a rare sight in the town where we lived. Then there was a stray pup — a white mongrel that my brother found abandoned in the street and brought home. We were not allowed pets inside the house, so we kept it on the roof-top patio of our concrete building. We three brothers cared for it, fed it and washed it. It proved to be a wonderful companion. By the summer it had grown too big and too lively to be kept on the roof. We took it with us to the village on our summer holidays and traded it for a bag of apples with a villager who needed a guard dog for his orchards.

I was, thus, not totally unfamiliar with dogs. I was shocked, nevertheless, at the sight of this strange, dirty and fearsome animal blocking our doorway. It left just enough room to sneak past its snout. But I was too scared to try. I stood back, petrified, and all I could do was yell for my mother.

She opened the door and was herself startled at the apparition. Whose dog was it? No one we knew in the neighbourhood had a dog like this. A poodle or terrier, perhaps, kept indoors, but nothing so big and scary, and dirty. Indeed, judging by its appearance, this dog for a long time had not had an owner who cared for it. Its shaggy fur had grown long and unkempt and was matted at the ends. It had obviously not had a wash for a very long time. The odd stray dog in the neighbourhood would occasionally be scrounging in a garbage can or chasing after a noisy car thundering by—when cars had no mufflers. But this was no ordinary stray dog, for, dirty as it was, there was an indefinable reflection of good breeding in its demeanor, strange though it may have been. All our efforts at driving it away—with words, for we dared not go too close—were met with even more frantic waggings of its tail and pleading whimperings. It would not bark or growl.

My mother, always a religious person, now became superstitious and wondered whether this were an omen of some kind. A visitation, perhaps, from the spirit world? Why else would it choose to climb several flights of stairs and park itself at our door? It reminded my mother of her uncle who used to be the head priest of the parish in Kaiseri, Turkey. We had a picture of him—black robed and black bearded—on the front page of a prayer book he had translated from the ancient Armenian into modern language his people could understand. Father Aristakes Timourian, an intellectual and a poet who, along with all intellectuals of his ethnicity, had been arrested and hanged or tortured to death, some 25 years earlier, in 1915. My mother saw in the dog a physical resemblance to her uncle and became convinced that the phenomenon of the animal's appearance at our door was an effort on the part of her uncle's spirit to communicate with the living. She became well-disposed toward the animal and brought it food and water. The dog took a few licks of the water but ignored the food, never standing on its four legs.

My father, who had his business in a mining town, came home later that day for the weekend. We were not sure how he would handle the situation, but his presence was reassuring. He had been commander of a militia unit in the defense of his hometown in Turkey. Surely, he could make a dog obey his orders. But he too seemed perplexed at the predicament. Verbal commands produced only further whimperings from the dog and more obstinate determination to hold its ground. He tried pushing the dog with his foot cautiously, anticipating a bite. But the dog lay even flatter and clung to its spot on the floor like a doormat.

There was only one solution. My father had fashioned a sturdy walking stick from the slender branch of an oak tree, which we kept in the clothes closet. Ignoring my mother's pleas for restraint, he took the stick, went carefully behind the animal and started beating it on the rump. The dog took the beating literally lying down. It turned its head backward to face my father, its brow knitted and an expression of entreaty in its eyes. It did not squeal, bark or growl. But for a faintly audible whimper it made not a sound or even an aggressive gesture and kept wiping the floor faster and faster with its tail.

Frustrated and defeated by the dog's willful determination, my father himself began thinking that there might be a tacit meaning in the animal's appearance beyond its physical manifestation.

The situation had to be turned over to the city authorities. There was a police station at the end of our street. My father went to talk to them. He returned, accompanied by an officer. The two men had hardly scaled half the first flight of stairs when the dog pricked its ears at the sound of the policeman's heavy footsteps, jumped to its feet, shot out of its corner like a bullet, threw itself into the stairwell at lightening speed, bolted past the policeman and my father and disappeared into the street never to be seen again.

My Grandmother's Patchwork Blankets

My grandmother has been dead for more than sixty years. But an occasional unexpected sight or smell will suddenly usher vivid memories of her, pleasantly imbuing the moment with feelings of comfort and peacefulness, warming my heart, caressing my soul. Such was my sensation when I heard the owner of a cinnamon rolls bakery confess to a customer that he boiled the spice in order to entice potential clientele, evoking images of my grandmother, as I remembered her method of making cinnamon tea.

One object that provided true warmth and comfort, not only at first sight but for many years to come, was a bedspread which immediately caught my attention, some forty years ago, at Army and Navy Department Stores. It was an imported item, made somewhere in Southeast Asia, of inexpensive material and of no sturdy weave. But its pattern of squares, in a variety of colours, summoned memories of the patchwork blankets that I had seen my grandmother make.

She would collect scraps of worsted fabric, of different colours and patterns, left over or salvaged from suits and costumes, and cut them up into four-inch-square pieces. When she had enough of them accumulated, she would join them together by a method of hooking—with two short, hooked needles—into a good-sized bedcover. I still vividly remember the colours of the squares—browns, blues, greens and reds; striped navy-blues and light-browns, all knitted together with sturdy yellow cotton string, in a herringbone type pattern.

Of Kaleidoscopes and a Table of Memories

I had been feeling miserable and remorseful over a promise I had made a beloved and respected friend but had failed to keep. In exploring the theme of turning points in our lives, I had mentioned, in writing class, that during the first summer after dropping out of school, I had attempted to earn pocket money by making and selling kaleidoscopes, which skill I had learned from a magazine in the school library. When asked by members of the group what exactly was a kaleidoscope, I had taken on the challenge and promised the teacher that I would make one and bring it to class. Now the teacher had passed away and I had managed to get my hands on only one item of the required parts for the project. I existed for days in a dejected spirit, ruing my tendency for procrastination, which weighed down on me as an incorrigible trait of character.

I sat, past midnight, absently gazing at the TV screen, and, oblivious to the shifting pictures, was transported, in a state of reverie, back to the land of my former domicile—the far-away Island of Cyprus—and the summer of my last school year of 1947. I could see, in my mind's eye, the table, set in the hallway at the top of the stairs, which had served as my workbench. It had been a labour-intensive but creatively satisfying process, fabricating from scratch those "magical" instruments. The most laborious part of the project had been the tube, or cylindrical outer casing, which I fashioned from sheets of pliable cardboard wrapped around a wooden rod. Truly magical was the effect of the kaleidoscope on all who took a peek into the device. They were amazed and captivated by its display, at the slightest rotary motion, of an endless variety of surprise patterns and colour combinations. It provided hours of spellbound viewing to members of my family and all who bought them.

The table I worked on had been among our family's periodically dwindling possessions through the many houses we moved to since my early childhood. Covered with an oilcloth of floral pattern, it served the household in a variety of functions. It was a kitchen and dining table; a study desk during our school years for my two elder brothers and me; a workbench where my mother styled and sewed her own dresses and all our shirts and shorts for many years, and it also served as her ironing board. Above all, I remember my grandmother kneading, rolling and shaping traditional pastries on that ample surface. A single shallow drawer ran across the full length and width of the table. It held an assortment of items, such as our schoolbooks and supplies; the big family Bible; a songbook which contained all my parents' favourite Armenian songs; and of course all the equipment I needed for the production of my kaleidoscopes.

My grandmother, who was illiterate and normally passed her quiet hours knitting, crocheting, or working on a patchwork blanket, perhaps more than anyone, enjoyed the thrill of gazing into the kaleidoscope. She could not enunciate the word, but whenever she had her chores taken care of and had a moment to spare, she would ask for the "karidoop," sit on her divan and spend an interval rapt in a breath-taking world of beautiful, ever-changing, polychromic designs.

Remembrance of one thing triggered another, and soon a kaleidoscopic array of images, locales and episodes, and a parade of colours reminiscent of cathedral windows, began milling about in my hypnotic consciousness. Each image and each sensation assumed an almost tangible reality, as in a trance. Then, as though caught in the upward swirl of a whirlwind, the elements of the milling throng spiraled and spiraled into invisible space, losing their specific identities, and evolved into a nameless, dizzying sensation. Epochs merged. The distant past seemed to intermingle with the present. And I was alone in a rudderless boat, tossing about on the violent billows of a stormy, fog-bound ocean. And I heard a voice in the wind. And I became aware that it was my own voice, pleading for Peace and Tranquility. And I knew that in my altered state the words had assumed individual personalities and were the names of angels. And I heard another voice in the wind, and it sounded like a familiar directive I seemed to remember: "If you build it, they will come," repeated the refrain several times before I became aware of the connotation. Two beautiful angels appeared briefly through the fog, as it lifted, and all was calm and quiet again.

I woke up with a smile. I had attained atonement. Now all I had to do was make the best kaleidoscope I was able to, in memory of my teacher.

The Key

In the village where we spent our childhood summers, in Cyprus, my brother and I would devise activities and exploits to allay our boredom.

One ingenious project, I remember, gave us a great sense of accomplishment. It was the construction and use of a contraption, whose success, my elder brother and I, aged twelve and eleven, respectively, celebrated with a big bang.

We put our invention to reverberating sound use on the hill behind our rented cottage. Then, having run out of supplies, we returned home, elated with the results, albeit with some trepidation. Our inflated ego received a sound thrashing from the scolding that our mother gave us.

I don't remember whose idea it was, my brother's or mine, but when it came to fabricating things, I, though younger, was the handyman. It was, in fact, a simple gadget, made up of three simple parts: a key, a nail, and a length of twine. But who had originally taught us to make it? Was it George, perhaps, who, when we first met him in our new neighbourhood in the city, had his finger wrapped in bloody bandage with a three-inch nail sticking through it? We found out later it was only a bent nail that fitted around his finger.

I spent several stealthy hours, cautiously working on our creation. The parts fitted well, and it worked. Of course, finding the right parts was half the battle. The nail and the twine were the easy parts. The hard part was the key. No ordinary key would do. The problem was to find the right type of key. It had to have a hollow barrel, which was a rarity even in those days. And the nail had to be a sliding fit into the barrel of the key—not too sloppy and not too tight.

We had a variety of old nails in a tin can, where we also kept small tools. But where to find a key? And then, presto! There it was, staring at us! And the nail was a perfect fit! Now all I had to do was file the end of the nail round, connect the heads of the nail and the key with the twine to form a sling when inserted, and we were in business! We put our apparatus, along with a box of matches and a penknife, in our pockets, and sneaked out up the hill behind our house.

And now the fun began. We had to put our "toy" to the test. With the penknife we shaved off the heads of several matches and carefully dropped the "powder" into the barrel of the key. At an appropriate place beside a rock, with the nail inserted in place, I swung the sling several times, back and forth, then vigorously slammed the head of the nail onto the rock. A deafening bang followed. It worked! It gave me a scare but it was exciting! I could tell, by the hurried pace in which my heart was trying to palpitate out of my chest.

I repeated the process several times, while my brother, holding a broomstick against his shoulder, aimed at an imaginary game bird: a partridge or woodpigeon. It was hunting season. A real hunter and his dog suddenly appeared from behind a shrub further up the mountain, and stared at us for a brief moment of scornful disregard.

On our return home we were met by our mother.

"Boys!" she said, "I heard hunters on the hill behind the house. I'd like to keep our door locked, but I can't find the key! Also, we seem to have run out of matches. I can't light the stove to cook our dinner."

Then she noticed! My bare legs were peppered with blisters from the spatter of the "gunpowder," and evidence hanging out of my pocket betrayed our "firearm." She went into hysterics. "You could have blinded yourselves!" she screamed. "Where did you learn to play with dangerous toys like this? Who taught you?" And then, shaking her head, "It must have been that George!" she said.

Vanishing Trades of Cyprus: The Mattress Maker

If you were planning to furnish your bedroom in Cyprus, the procedure today would perhaps be no different from what it is in Canada, or in any other developed country, for that matter. You visit a furniture store or two; view all required items—including box spring and mattress—displayed on the floor; make your selection; agree on a price (this phase of the transaction may, perhaps, still hold true to tradition in Cyprus. Haggling, or bargaining, is a trait, or art, that may not have vanished with the trades); then pay for your purchase, by cash or credit card, and have the goods delivered, and even installed, if you so wish.

There was a time, however, barely fifty or sixty years ago, when a young girl, engaged to be married and planning her wedding—assuming that she had already been given a dwelling house as customary part of her dowry—would first shop for a reputable cabinet maker. (Her parents, needless to say, would accompany her and play an active role in the quest.) She would then pick out her favourite styles from the artisan's catalogue: dresser, wardrobe, chest of drawers, headboard (very likely carved with images of a pair of doves symbolizing purity and mutual fidelity), all to be handcrafted from raw material. She might choose local woods, such as walnut, cherry or oak, or opt for mahogany or other imported material.

The basics taken care of, it would be time now, before any furniture were delivered into the bedroom, to prepare the most important item that symbolized the true reason, the natural motivating urge, the incentive that led to the marriage rite in the first place: the mattress.

The mattress, with its accessories, was perhaps the single piece of furnishing that had to be made on the premises of the user's home. A competent craftsman would be engaged and called in for an estimate and discussion, not only of the price but also of the amount of material (cotton filling and fabric covering) required, and selection, from samples, of colour, pattern and quality of fabric preferred.

The room where the work was to be carried out—preferably in a cooler part of the house—would be swept clean and sponged free of dust. The craftsman would now get busy procuring material—appropriate quantities of cotton and fabric, as well as needles of all sizes and thread—and having receptacle bags sewn for each item to be made.

When all requirements had been delivered to the premises, the "yorganji," this master craftsman, mattress maker par excellence, skilled practitioner of a most rare and vanishing art highly deserving of respect, yet viewed among the lowlier professions, would arrive on a bicycle, carrying the major item of his scanty tools of trade on his shoulder. The senior mistress of the household would welcome him with a demitasse of Tuurkish coffee and show him to his "workroom," wishing him facility in his arduous job and God's participation in his dexterity.

The room would be bare, except for a small flat cushion, or "kilim," on the clean floor and a jug of water or lemonade, and glass, in a cool corner. The "oosta" or "mastro," would empty the bale of natural, dense cotton onto a corner of the floor, and envision enough space in the opposite corner for the modified product to pile up on. He would now embrace the gadget—the implement to which he ascribed the greater part of his expertise—and lovingly inspect its few parts for wear or damage. This was the main tool of his trade, a strange contraption that looked somewhat like a cross between an archer's bow and a prehistoric musical instrument, the frame made of rigid wood of substantial thickness, strung with a single chord made of twisted and dried cow's gut. It was about five or six feet in length, the farther end curved to a point, the closer end square, and equipped with a tensioning device. The top of the frame was fitted with a padded loop through which the operator would insert his left forearm, grab the frame, and with his elbow hold the instrument firmly to his side.

The "master craftsman" would next produce, from his saddlebag, a round mallet made of heavy hardwood. It had a beveled bead machined at the head end, so that, when struck against the chord of the bow in a downward motion, would flick it smoothly but powerfully enough to produce the necessary vibration (along with a dull twang). He would test the tension of the chord, make adjustments if needed, settle in a low, squatting position on the "kilim," and be ready to begin. But being physically ready would not guarantee success. He must, without fail, commit his performance to the direction of a Higher Operator, whispering a few words in Arabic, quoted from the Quran, if he were Turkish; or, if he were Greek, he would cross himself and utter the names of Christ and the Holy Virgin.

And now he must begin without further ado, for he would have several days' work ahead. He would strike a blow on the chord with the mallet, holding the bow above the pile of cotton barely stroking the surface, whereupon fluffs of cotton would be captured in the vibration of the chord, and, reduced to downy plumes, would take to the air, then slowly float down, landing on the floor in a cloud-soft accumulation away from the original pile. And "Yorganji" would be caught up in the rhythm of the process: Trumm-ta-ta-tumm, trumm-ta-ta-tumm. And he would no longer be a mere "yorganji," but an artist, a musician, a dancer. And the twang of the chord was now music to his ears. And the rhythm was a drumbeat he could dance to as he worked. Trumm-ta-ta-tumm, trumm-ta-ta-tumm. And he would bounce to the rhythm as he squatted on his heels.

The monotonous twang that reverberated through the house would cease at last. It would now be time to stuff the bags, sew them up and work the bloated blobs into cozy and inviting components of a bed. The craftsman now, in his quiet solitude, had the opportunity to reveal the most creative aspects of his skills. At the end of another day's work he would present the lady of the house with exquisitely stitched and sculpted quilt and mattress.

"May you use them long and in good health," he would wish the household, as he departed with his payment and their eternal gratitude.

Requiem for a Brave Workhorse

Who can know the agony of an animal in the throes of death? Does it need a voice or a language to convey the pain? A defiant dash up and down the hard-paved slopes of a narrow street, clouds of steam billowing from her nostrils, her head turning and directing her gaze at a human, a young man out on the street in the dizzying heat of the midday sun, cowering against the walls of the street, alarmed and shocked at the unfolding spectacle, trying to keep out of her way as she passes him by in her faltering gallop, her eyes wide with fear and panic, but also flashing with anger and accusation, and yet not without a certain tenderness and pleading—not for mercy, but as though apologizing for the accident. It was not her fault!

A magnificent workhorse, big and strong, well-fed and well-groomed, she hauled water—a heavy ton of it—to customers in the industrial section of old Nicosia, that ancient, walled capital of the Mediterranean Island of Cyprus. Running water was a luxury there in the late 1940's, and well-water was delivered to commercial establishments in owner-driven, horse-drawn tanks.

She came down the slope of the narrow street, slapping the pavement confidently with her large heavy hooves, her reddish-brown curves glistening in the midday sun. The driver pulled her to a halt beside a row of short steel posts barring the entrance to an industrial yard between two towers of a building. Her muscles tensed as she resisted the downhill momentum of her heavy load, but with determined and practiced effort she came to a full, abrupt stop, as she had done many times before. The driver dismounted and walked through the untidy yard, strewn with sheets and bars and scraps of steel, into the shops lining the two sides of the yard, to see about his clients' requirements. The water in the tank was set in a back and forth rocking motion, applying an on-and-off pull via the harness, taxing the horse's resistance. Still she resisted. She stiffened her front legs and tensed her shoulder muscles and did not give an inch of ground. The hammering motion of the water, now pressing, now relieving, would have been no problem on level or softer ground. She snorted angrily and dug her hooves in. But the ground was hard, and the force of the hammering water, meeting her resistance to move forward, was converted into a sideways motion, and her front legs began moving gradually apart on the slippery pavement, until they had opened so wide she could no longer lift herself. The weight bore down mainly on her shoulders. She made a frantic effort with her hind legs, and her hind legs slipped apart. And though she had lost her ability to stand upright, she still held her ground and kept the cart where her master had stopped her, but came helplessly down on one of the steel posts at the entrance of the yard, puncturing her soft underbelly. Violently struggling to rise, battling the contraptions that kept her trapped, she scraped and kicked the pavement with all four hooves. She snorted angrily, steam spouting from her snout. Horses, it seems, do not scream when met with physical injury or violent death, though there was panic in her eyes.

There were few people out in the hot midday sun; but her predicament was noticed, and her master eventually appeared on the scene. Alarmed at what he saw, he quickly placed a couple of wood blocks under the wheels of the cart, cursing his neglect that had caused the irreparable disaster. Carefully trying to avoid the wild kicks of the struggling animal, he undid and cut loose the restricting harness.

Freed from restraint, the animal managed, after further struggle, to pull herself into an upright, standing position. There was hardly any blood spilt, but the damage was done. A small coil of her intestines hung from an opening in her belly.

She looked left and right for a brief moment to find her bearings, lost in a strange world. Where was she? The narrow street dipped into the main road, then rose again on the opposite side. She ran down and up the street, then turned back. Her bouncing motion shook and exposed more and more of her intestines until they trailed behind her for yards, dragging between her hind legs. Still she ran back and forth, frequently tripping over her own guts, falling on her rump, looking around with an expression of dazed panic, then rising and aimlessly running again.

But now her expression was one of wonderment at the strange universe that surrounded her. She was now no longer a workhorse delivering water in an unfamiliar and cruel world. She was a newborn baby foal romping about on weak and unsteady legs in her village field. She was tired. She sat down and could not rise again. There was a scratchy sensation inside her. She felt hungry. She must go and find her mother in the stable. It was getting cold and dark. She could not see. She could sense her mother's presence. It was peaceful in the stable. She was asleep.

Donkeys for the Italian Campaign

Toward the latter years of World War II, when invasion of Italy by the Allies had begun, pack animals were requested by the military to transport supplies over that country's rugged mountains. Horses and mules may have been considered, but less testy (and, perhaps, less expensive) manageable beasts were apparently preferred, for reliable portage over difficult terrain.

Donkeys, it seems, emerged as the favoured choice. But donkeys, though known to be more docile than horses and mules (despite a reputation of occasional inexplicable obstinacy), are, in general, smaller, and, perhaps, not as strong.

The British Army knew better! On the Island of Cyprus, which was then a British colony, not far from Italy, there is a breed of donkey, known for centuries by the Ottoman Turks as the 'Cyprus Donkey.' Not all donkeys in Cyprus, however, conform to the attributes of that particular breed. This famed donkey is a hardy animal, tall, big, and strong as a horse. Its spine is bony, straight and solid as an iron beam; its legs long yet sturdy and powerful. Perhaps not as graceful or dashing in appearance as a horse; patient by nature, pensive and philosophical in countenance and demeanour, the donkey is capable of carrying disproportionate loads, and at times, even take undeserved abuse with great tolerance. This almost saintly aspect of its character may well have prompted the use of its alternate appellation as a derogatory epithet by arrogant humans, calling all who do not meet their pretentious expectations an ass.

A team of three men, assigned by agents of the Army for the purchase of the requested animals, included my father. He acted as treasurer and supervisor of the transactions. The other two were the driver of the little Renault which had been provided for the project (the Company acting as agents of the Army were also dealers of several makes of cars); and a horse trader, whose expertise apparently included the humbler genus of the species. This last man was a rough and hefty fellow and proved an effective, if not an intimidating bargainer. He was Turkish, as also was the driver. The driver, a smaller and kindlier man, was an old acquaintance of my father's. He had been in my father's employ when my father owned a thriving chain of stores in a mining town on the upper hills of the island, before the War.

With three in the team, there would be room for one more passenger in the four-seater Renault.

"I'd like you to come along on this trip," my father urged me. "We'll be going where you went to school for the last two years."

The plan was to head toward Lefkara, a town in the central mountain range of Cyprus, and make the rounds of a group of villages in the vicinity. The region reputedly bred the brawniest and most stalwart of the famed Cyprus donkey. Lefkara was also where the American Academy, the school I had attended for the past two years, had relocated during the earlier years of the War to escape the anticipated invasion, or air raids, by the Italians or Germans. Other schools from the cities had also relocated to villages and smaller towns presumed to be safer. They had all moved back to their hometowns now, when it had become obvious that the war was not coming to the Eastern Mediterranean, as threatened. The fierce resistance of the Cretans, it was said, had held it back.

I was nearly fourteen, on summer holidays, bored, and in doubt whether I would be going back to school at all. The Academy had returned to its coastal hometown of Larnaca; our family to the capital, Nicosia. There was no justification in chasing a private, missionary school beyond our means. It was my summer of uncertainty as well as boredom. The friends and acquaintances I had made in those two years at school, as I entered adolescence, were gone with the school. Friends of my earlier, childhood years now regarded me with envious awe for the scant English I had learned. I had begun a new life and it had come to an abortive end. I welcomed my father's offer for the diversion it would provide, as well as for the nostalgic memories it would evoke.

We started late and arrived at Lower Lefkara at nightfall. Unlike the more populous and prosperous, mainly Greek upper town, this annex of a village, several miles detached, was a small Turkish hamlet, made up mainly of sheepherders, woodcutters, and growers of carobs, olives and figs. A narrow dirt path branched off from the gravel road and in the deepening darkness appeared to be meandering among a randomly laid-out group of humble dwellings. There seemed to be no streetlight or any electricity in the village. Dimly lit windows at some dwellings denoted the presence of kerosene lamps. Our horse trader had been given, by an acquaintance, the name of a resident of the village, a shepherd, with whom, we were told, we could lodge for the night. The little Renault rambled down the scarcely discernible path and pulled up at the first house where a faint light was visible through cracks in the shutters, our arrival heralded by the barking of every dog in the village. There was some question whether this was the address we were looking for, but the occupant, a simple shepherd of middle age, insisted on putting us up and would not let us go any further. Hospitality, almost a religious rite, is an age-old tradition in the villages of Cyprus, and the peasant, whether Greek or Turkish, will not refuse food or lodging to a stranded stranger.

The shepherd made tea, served in clear glasses, and bade us make ourselves comfortable in his humble front room, furnished with homemade divans and rustic chairs laid with kilims and woolly sheepskins. He disappeared through a doorway hung with a heavy canvas curtain for a door. We could hear muted whisperings beyond. Our spokesman, the horse trader, called after him not to go into elaborate trouble to feed us. The shepherd shyly stuck his head through the doorway and, with an almost apologetic smile, said it would be no trouble, but to, please, be comfortable. It shouldn't take long.

A table was set in the middle of the room, and soon generous portions of fried chicken, freshly killed, served with piping hot bulgur pilaf, accompanied by a large bowl of yogurt, were laid out for four.

We were awakened at the crack of dawn by a contest of crowing roosters, each vying to excel the other in its throaty welcome of the rising sun. Soon a more distant sound, the calmer and soothing call of the muezzin, at times barely audible, began softly intermingling with the crowing of the roosters. Our Turkish friends stroked their faces with cupped palms, invoking, in whispered Arabic the blessings of breaking day. My father held his cupped palms at his sides, calling in whispers, no doubt upon the same Source, in classical Armenian.

Our plan was to have an early start, circle the mountain, skirting past the larger town of Lefkara, canvass a number of villages on the other side, and return home the same evening, having, hopefully, filled our quota of a dozen donkeys. Breakfast consisted of tea, fried eggs, and slabs of fried halloumi cheese—unique to Cyprus, halloumi, unlike other cheeses, does not melt when fried, but, rather, forms a crisp crust, with a chewy inside. The shepherd would not hear of any payment for his hospitality; it was his providential good fortune, and he was grateful to have been granted the opportunity. He was unyielding in his refusal, but some money was furtively left in the room, without offending the man. We thanked him heartily, invoking Allah's blessing on his household, and bade him convey our thanks also to his wife, the hanim, whom we never heard nor set eyes upon.

My father had not taken me along on this trip with the purpose of introducing me to the donkey trade. He may well have been genuinely concerned about my state of despondency and dejection that summer, and perhaps thought, rightly, that I needed the diversion. I was to discover, as the day wore on, what was perhaps the true reason why my father needed me on the trip.

Skirting the upper reaches of the bigger town of Lefkara, our Renault climbed the winding dirt road up and around the white limestone mountain, to the first village on the planned circuit. (The geology of the region consists of white limestone. Hence the name of the dominant town, Lefkara. [The Greek word for white—lefkos—has crept into international technical—mainly medical—language in the formation of compound words, such as leukemia.] Often quarried in large chunks, the stone was carved into utensils, such as washtubs. It was also the main building material in the region. Most houses were made with it, and, in single level, humbler homes, which were the majority of the village dwellings, it also served, in its crushed form, as roofing material: piled on top of bamboo webbing over the rafters, it was packed down to a thickness of about a foot and rolled to a solid, cement-like finish. Every roof of that type had its own heavy limestone roller, ready for a booster pack-down after the first rains, or whenever the roof leaked, which was quite frequently.)

We drove into the first village square early when the mountain air was still cool and life in the valley was just beginning to stir. The village coffeehouse (which originally may have been a warehouse) had its big gates open and several men—a few in baggy breeches—were seated sipping their demitasse of 'Turkish' coffee. It seemed a good place to advertise our intent, make preliminary inquiries and send for the mukhtar (mayor) of the village.

The purpose of our visit and the official nature of our business was communicated to the mukhtar in the best halting Greek that all three of our "team," combined—two Turks and one Armenian—could command. His approval and assistance were obtained, and soon sullen-faced animals began arriving, led by their equally glum owners. Though tempted by the prospect of cash, the owners seemed reluctant to part with their beasts of burden, for they well knew that their already-hard-working wives would not, readily, be willing to assume the duties of the departed quadruped.

Our horse trader was now in his element. He stood aside and, viewing the presented animals from a distance of a few paces, passed each one through a detailed and thorough visual inspection. He watched for a limp in its gait and, on closer examination, checked for general grooming and for signs of abuse or injury. He said he could tell by the brightness of the animal's eyes if it was a healthy and willing worker or bore a grudge against its owner. The hooves were inspected next for condition and whether they were well shod. To verify its age, he pried the animal's lips apart, much to its displeasure and discomfort, and checked the colour of its teeth. Then, as a final examination, which, he claimed, further indicated the age as well as the general health of the animal, he lifted its tail, standing aside to avoid the animal's kick of protest, and took a quick glance in the region of its posterior anatomy, ordinarily modestly hidden by the tail.

When all inspection had been completed it was time to haggle over the demanded price. My father would often step in to offer a compromise, and the deal would be closed with a handshake. My father then carved a mark on the hair of the animal's smooth rump with a small round-tipped pair of scissors he carried in his pocket, branding it for identification when it would be delivered at the seaport for shipment. Full payment for the purchase would be made at that time. It was necessary now to make a partial installment for good faith. The animal's owner then wrote his name in a book my father carried, acknowledging the amounts paid and owing as well as the delivery date. My father then asked me to stand close beside him during the transaction and produced a thick bundle of banknotes from an inner secret pocket. I felt a sense of responsibility and realized then that in my father's view I was not just an idle bystander; that with my presence in the "team" he knew he was not outnumbered and gained an added sense of security guarding the cash he carried.

We completed our quota of a dozen donkeys by the fourth village and by mid-afternoon set out on our return home. Our peppy little Renault had withstood the rigours of the rough ride on the winding loop that traversed the chain of villages, but, a mile or two short of rejoining the main road and entering the town of Lefkara, the driver pulled to the side and shut off the engine. A peek under the hood confirmed his suspicion. The fan belt had snapped! Talking rather to himself than to the rest of us, he proposed several impossibilities, then settled on the only alternative available: coast down in neutral, with the engine turned off. We were already on a slightly downward grade and the feat could be accomplished with occasional rests to cool the brakes—and the engine, if necessary.

As we rounded the mountain and re-entered the main road, several miles uphill from where we had exited, the sprawling town of Lefkara came into view on the left, spread over the gentle incline beyond a barren gravelly expanse of limestone. The steep mountain rising to the right, Ay. Sotira (St. Saviour), was named after the old Byzantine chapel perched on the summit. It served as an observation post for the Royal Air Force, with a solitary soldier stationed there at all daylight hours, his binoculars aimed at the skies and distant waters of the Mediterranean to the south.

My father and I were just in time to catch the bus home. The driver and the horse trader remained behind to have the Renault repaired.

Donkeys: Postscript

When my friend, Roy Beith, a member of our Lifewriting class, mentioned that he had served in Italy during the War, I thought I'd ask him whether he remembered seeing any donkeys during his term in the campaign.

"Oh, yes!" he beamed. "We had a bunch of them, and they were a lot of fun!"

He said the men had never seen donkeys before, and treated them like circus animals. They dressed them up with colourful bows and head wraps, and, in fact, named them the "MacNaughton Circus" after their Commanding Officer.

"They were fun," he said, "except when they started braying, especially at night. And then the Germans would aim their fire toward the noise."

Turning Points

I dropped out of school at the age of seventeen with no training in any marketable skill. I did have some talents, and, though undeveloped, I made an effort that first summer to exploit my abilities for monetary gain. From magazines at the school library I had learned to make various toys, one of which was a kaleidoscope. With the help and encouragement of family members I gathered the raw material I needed and set to work on the dining table. Everything had to be made from scratch. It was time-consuming, but I managed to make about five dozen of them through the summer. Now I had to market them, but that calls for a totally different set of skills and aptitudes. I received no encouraging response from two stores I approached. I felt dejected, and decided I needed a wage-paying job. I started hunting for one. In the meantime, a friend of mine who was beginning in business as a freelance salesman said he would try and sell my kaleidoscopes. And he did. He took his cut and gave me my share—a little more, a little less—and I was glad to get rid of them.

I discovered, while looking for a job, that my knowledge of English, such as it was, was my best marketable asset. I found a job at a photographer's establishment. The pay was poor, and so, after about a year I moved on. The technical branch of an airline company that had recently started hired me. After fumbling through various duties I finally landed in the maintenance, or service department: specifically, in the hydraulic overhaul shop. This gave me the opportunity to learn new skills and, at the same time, put my innate talents and manual dexterity to profitable use.

After some experience and the help of a correspondence course I passed an exam with the British Air Registration Board and became a full-fledged Licenced Aircraft Engineer, Category "A."

I had reached a turning point in my life. There would be many more—some upward, some downward, others sideways.

My Regrets
Two Windows Facing

When my eldest brother, Kay, returned from the Navy, in the summer of 1946, we moved from the coastal town of Larnaca to Nicosia, capital city of Cyprus, where he would be looking for employment. My elder brother, Van, had already moved there, working in the office of Cyprus Mail, the Island's leading English language newspaper, and had been boarding with family acquaintances.

My father had hurriedly rented the upper level of an old house, in a predominantly Turkish neighbourhood, from an Armenian friend of his who had leased the whole dwelling from the Turkish owner and lived on the ground floor with his elderly house-bound wife.

Our quarters upstairs consisted of a large bedroom, with two windows that looked into the street at the front; a smaller bedroom with a window to the backyard—where the outhouse was located at the far end, and a cistern midway, against the wall of the yard, to store the weekly quota of piped-in water. A windowless, gloomy little room in between the bedrooms served as a kitchen. (We carried water upstairs by the bucket and filled a "remodeled" 4-gallon "petrol" tin, adapted with a faucet, hanging over the "sink.") A single, bare electric bulb hung from the ceiling in each room. The landing at the top of the stairs, as well, had a window to the backyard and was roomy enough to accommodate a fairly large all-purpose table. A lamp also hung there.

In the larger bedroom (our "fraternal dormitory" where we three brothers slept) my bed was located in a corner with a window at my foot-end. My window looked out into the front street and also faced a side of a two-storey building complex. On the ground level of that building, in the rear alley that ran the length of the block, perpendicular to our street, and which I could also see from my window, there were two or three "shops" with roll-down doors, but

I rarely saw any activity there. A sign hanging on a wire across the alley marked the oncoming zone "Out of Bounds" for British soldiers. (Cyprus was, at the time, a British colony). The area indicated was a labyrinth of narrow, poorly-lit streets and old, run-down dwellings, built of mud-brick (mud mixed with straw and sun-dried). The area was considered unsafe and dangerous for soldiers unfamiliar with the language or culture to stray into. (In keeping with the age and condition of the tenements, rumours were occasionally repeated of how more than one lucky occupant, while trying to repair a crack in the plaster of an inside wall, had been surprised and flabbergasted out of his wits by a sudden avalanche of Victorian and Georgian silver shillings pouring out of an abandoned cache, left behind and long-forgotten.)

On the street level of the building complex facing our side, there were two Turkish business enterprises. One was open at all hours of the day, but, judging by the wild disturbance frequently arising from its site, it seemed busiest in the late hours of the night. It was a taxi office. I once peeked out through the louvers of my window (it must have been past 2:00 a.m.) and saw two or three Gurkha soldiers, in uniform, complete with their special hats, their heavy, webbed belts in hand, inflicting weighty blows upon the roof and windshield of the taxicab, shouting in a language no one understood. They were obviously drunk and were incensed at being denied service. Military police soon arrived and took them away.

The last business enterprise, at the end of our street, was a strictly night-time affair. It was a tavern of sorts, and it was noisy. But the noise rarely persisted past midnight, due, perhaps, to city residential restrictions. And its most offensive aspect did not emanate from the clientele. It was, rather, the voice of a female singer. She was an import from Istanbul, as advertised in a poster pinned on the door. She had a hoarse, somewhat raspy voice, and sang doleful Turkish songs of unrequited, unattainable, or lost love. I sometimes peeked through the louvers of my window, when I heard her speaking voice, and saw her standing on the narrow sidewalk having a smoke and shooting off vulgar and obscene retorts at harassing male patrons, in her "refined" Istanbul Turkish.

Musical accompaniment was provided by a solitary accordion.

It would occasionally break solo, into universally popular tunes or perhaps some Gypsy melody, but never any dance music. The place was not a cabaret, and, I'm sure, the singer was the only female present. I was surprised, however, when I heard the accordion play, quite frequently, the tune of a popular Armenian revolutionary, patriotic song that praises the exploits of an Armenian guerrilla band rushing, on a moonless night, to the rescue of Armenian villages from marauding Turkish soldiers in the old Armenian homeland under Ottoman rule. (I learned later that the accordionist was an ethnic Armenian, well known in the community.)

At the end of our street, next to the "tavern," was a pharmacy whose door faced a wide city square into which our street also opened. The pharmacy was a clean, brightly-lit dispensary, open until midnight. Its owner-druggist, a mild-mannered, highly respected Turk of middle age who always wore a spotless white frock, bore the title of doctor and was said to have been educated in Paris.

The city square dated back to antiquity, marked by a grey granite Roman column of impressive size. Surrounded by an iron fence, it served as a "round-about" for vehicular traffic.

In spite of the street-level stir and bustle that I witnessed every night, the upper level, second floor of the building complex remained a mystery. It had windows on the two sides of the building that were visible to me—one window almost squarely faced mine—but they were always dark and always shuttered. There just was no sign of any life on that floor. I had begun to imagine that, perhaps, the space had not been fully finished and was being used as a warehouse by some business whose entrance faced the city square. I had, further, convinced myself that the mystery was not for me to solve, accepted it for whatever it was and had stopped being concerned about it.

Summer nights in Cyprus can be oppressively hot and often humid. It had been one of those sleepless, sweltering nights when, at long last, I sensed a cool breeze stirring at the break of day. I immediately hopped to my knees on my bed and pushed my shutters open to let that balmy air in before the sun warmed up to scorching heat again.

To my jolting surprise, the shutters of the window across the street started moving and burst open at precisely the same instant as I opened mine. Framed in the window, adding amazement to surprise, stood the figure of a young girl of breath-taking beauty. My heart leapt as we both gasped, gaping at the "miraculous" appearance of each-other, both of an age conducive to mutual attraction: I was seventeen; she, possibly fifteen, but certainly not a day older than sixteen. She may have slept in the night, but was not in night clothes. She wore a light dress, somewhat crumpled, with pink and green floral pattern. Her hair, light in colour, trimmed short and tousled, gave her an aura of self-assertion, defiant of tradition. She could have made a classic model for a French Impressionist painter, I thought, as I had seen in pictures at the school library.

Despite my captivation with her beauty and the novelty of her miraculous appearance on the scene, two alarming thoughts immediately invaded my mind: What is a Greek girl doing in a Turkish secret house? I asked myself. (Communities of different ethnic or racial background forming the mass of a country's common population seem to develop an "instinct" for identifying each-other.) I had no doubt in my mind that the girl in the window was Greek; however, whether Greek or Turkish, I was, moreover, convinced that she had been abducted and was being held captive. I had heard of the predicament of poor village girls coming to the city to seek employment and save money for their Greek traditional dowry of a house. They were often said to fall victim to exploiters for "work" in a "pension." I felt like asking her—in a voice audible across the street—whether she was Christian. (Christian, in Cyprus parlance, means Greek). But to be discovered communicating would endanger her life, and might even result in "consequences" for myself as well as my family.

We froze, gaping, staring at each other in silence. The shadow of a smile flickered on her lips, her face blossomed like a rose, her eyes sparkled with anticipatory excitement. It was an evanescent glow. It soon faded into a look of caution and suspicion. She glanced left and right and down into the street, then slowly pulled the shutters closed and disappeared.

A tremendous sense of responsibility suddenly weighed down on my consciousness. What could I do to avert the fate that awaited her? Go to the Police! Not any officer on the street! They're all Turks in this neighbourhood! They wouldn't be too worried about involving you in the investigation! Nor would Greek officers, for that matter! There must be a Colonial superintendent of police who can be trusted! In the end, I concluded that I, as the source of information, could not remain a secret. The girl herself might reveal the fact that she had seen me and had herself been seen; in which case I would be exposed, but her captors would be in a panic to hide her and hope that I had not informed police.

My observations the following night seemed to confirm my suspicion. I was at my window in the small hours after midnight, peeping through the louvers of my closed shutters. There was light in her room. Her shutters were closed, but the louvers were not turned down and afforded a revealing though limited scene. There was a man in the room, a giant of a man, with a big head and a barrel-chested massive torso, wearing an orange-brown double-breasted suit and light blue tie, sitting like a statue in the back of the room, though his legs were not visible. His lips were not moving. They could be having language difficulties. She wouldn't understand Turkish; his Greek would be very poor. But he was blond, and perhaps could impress the girl as being English, and therefore more trustworthy and less intimidating. But intimidation, I was sure, was the purpose of his presence; intimidation and watchfulness. He sat, without a word or any movement, patiently, like an Easter Island monolith.

Who was the boy who had seen her last night? Would he come again to-night? I was not going to give him the satisfaction. I could see the girl cowering on the floor. She looked very small, squirming like a worm, crushed. I couldn't hear whether she was moaning or crying, realising that she was captive, a prisoner with no chance of escape.

I cried myself to sleep, in anger that I could do nothing to save her.

The next night the second floor of the building was as it had been before: dark, windows shut, uninhabited. A man's mournful voice was heard on the street just before daybreak, calling "Maria!" Twice he called, two days in a row, "Maria! Maria!" Was it her father, perhaps? Maria is a common Greek name.

I have lived for seventy years with the torture of a forfeited dream that I could have been the gallant knight who rescued the abducted damsel and made her my princess, but am now doomed, rather, to die with the remorse of my failure and my life's major regret rankling in my heart.

Shakespeare to the Rescue

"You are welcome, Sir, to Cyprus." (Othello)

In the early 1950's the majority Greek population of Cyprus, a British colony in the eastern Mediterranean, began agitating for "Enosis" (Union with Greece). The sentiment was not new. Ever since the Ottoman Empire had leased the island to Britain in 1878, the Greek natives had hoped that Britain, a true friend of Greece during her struggle for liberation from the Turkish yoke, would, in her turn, cede it to Greece. But Cyprus was not Britain's to give away. Turkey had just lost a war with Russia, and Cyprus was part of the bargain for Britain to assist Turkey against possible future Russian encroachment.

When the "Great War" (World War I) broke out, in 1914, the Ottomans sided with Germany. In response, Britain annexed the island, later granting it the title of Crown Colony. Greece, on the other hand, seemed reluctant to participate in the war on the side of Britain, preferring neutrality, in consideration of her king, who was of German descent.

The clamour for Enosis was muted or shelved. It flared up again with a passion after 1918, when the war ended. There were riots in 1931. Stern measures followed; some leaders were deported; it was suppressed—temporarily.

The Second World War found Greece, along with much of Europe, a victim of Hitler's invasion. A sizable regiment of Cypriot volunteers joined the British war effort—to help the Allies win the war while fighting for the liberation of Greece. There was also a Cyprus Volunteer Force for assistance in local defense, as well as local, Air Raid Precaution volunteers, though the War never really came to Cyprus.

But the passion for Enosis had not died out. Church-led youth groups proliferated toward the end of the war and, upon the election of a new archbishop (traditionally referred to as "ethnarch," "national leader") student rallies popped up here and there on weekends in city squares. Demonstrations, peaceful at first, soon escalated into bottle-throwing confrontations with police and British troops. Some arrests were made, but no firearms were discharged.

How could the British Government respond to an "ill-considered" demand by adolescent students—albeit prompted by churchmen— at a time, in the aftermath of a world-shaking war, when people in countries of the region, stretching to the Persian Gulf, were stirred-up with a sense of awakening national identity, despair of economic inadequacy? Greece itself was mired in a bitter civil war with a Communist-led labour movement. In Egypt, where Britain kept tens of thousands of troops, guarding the neutrality of the Suez Canal, and virtually ruling the region with the tacit consent of an unpopular king, there were disturbing grumblings for the abdication of the king and Britain's withdrawal; and in Palestine, a British protectorate, occupied by two opposing claimants: Jews and Arab Palestinians; the Jews pressuring Britain to relinquish and vacate her mandate and allow the two parties to settle the matter between themselves, while the Arab world watched with vexed anticipation for the inevitable, insoluble conflict. In Cyprus, moreover, where the population has, historically, been mainly Greek, there was, at the time, and ever since the Ottoman occupation, a large minority of Turks who would not be happy with the handover of the Island to Greece. (For the record, political demands, protests and civic disturbances, such as being patiently tolerated by the British in Cyprus, are said to have been quickly quelled in the "old days" by decapitating several of the leading churchmen and parading their heads on poles in Greek neighbourhoods.)

Demonstrations and confrontations had become routine weekend affairs, and, finally, in Nicosia, they escalated into a violent riot when the British Council Library was raided and set on fire. Papers and furnishings were thrown out the window into the street.

Shocked by the spectacle of that cultural violence, the administration, it seemed, became aware that appreciation, or love of English, including language, literature and British culture in general, had not been more eagerly encouraged among the populace throughout the years of occupation. An advertisement soon appeared in the press calling for young applicants from whom one person would be selected to be sent to Britain, all expenses paid, to study and train as a teacher in the subject of Shakespeare and Elizabethan drama. Upon completion of the course and return to Cyprus the candidate would make the rounds and introduce the subject into the curriculums of all secondary and higher schools on the Island.

This was about the time when I had been reading Shakespeare religiously, initially as a means of improving my English and, hopefully, patching up some aspect of my deficient schooling, as well as in enjoyment of the literature. This was also the time when, through reading in general, I had become inspired to write. I sent a short story to the weekend magazine of the Cyprus Mail. It was returned, with apologies that they did not want to be judges of original material. But they did publish a full-length column of a letter to the Editor that I later wrote. It was in complaint of a story by a traveling writer-artist (of sorts) whose works were always accompanied by a drawing—very significantly in silhouette: story as well as picture depicting the dark side of all that he saw.

The Council's call for applications concerning the Shakespeare course naturally aroused my interest. But there was a catch to the terms and conditions: the applicant was required to have passed the "Distinction" level of English; whereas, personally, having dropped out of school too soon, my claim to that proficiency was, officially, "Ordinary." To be fair—although the Administration's chief concern may, normally, have been the continual supply of competent clerical manpower to fill the needs of its offices—English was taught at every school, including ethnic elementary schools throughout the island. It was meant to provide a basic knowledge of the language to the public and, at secondary level, also aid prospective applicants seeking entry to the English School in Nicosia. Admittance at the English School was by quota per ethnic segment of the population. My two elder brothers were lucky to have attended the school for two years before threats of war came to disrupt the system, drive many schools out of the city to safer locations, thwarting my own opportunity to apply for admission. The English School was a truly English boys' school, complete with uniform—blue blazer, grey pants, cap and tie; and Anglican—my brothers loved singing at home hymns like "O, God, our aid in ages past..."

The turn and twist of family circumstances and wartime economic dictates saw me and my elder brother, Van, enroll in the American Academy at its emergency location in the mountain town of Lefkara; then, after two years, when the threat of war had subsided, return with the school, together with our mother, to its original base in the coastal town of Larnaca. The Academy was a co-ed school and had no identifying uniform but a badge worn on the clothing. There was also flexibility in the ages of entrants: often older boys, highly educated graduates from college-level Greek schools, would come to the Academy to improve their English conversation—provided they also took a Bible class.

My eldest brother, Kay, naturally bearing some resentment, remained with our father, working on road construction machinery. He became a good mechanic, soon landing a job in a garage in Nicosia, the owner reputed to be the best mechanic on the Island. Kay had, in time, become so well loved and grown so confident at work that once, when his boss was on his accustomed, lengthy lunch break, he "borrowed" a gleaming British sports car he had been working on, and, to impress a new-found girlfriend, drove it to her neighbourhood, never suspecting that his boss also lived in the same area of town. He was seen and was fired. He eventually joined the Royal Navy, cheating slightly on his age, and was posted to Egypt, notifying us by mail.

The family unit came together again in Nicosia when the war ended and Kay returned from the Navy in the mid 1940's. He settled on a routine clerical job in the offices of the Military, similar to what he had been used to in the Navy in Egypt. My brother, Van, was happy with his job as typist-clerk in the Cyprus Mail Daily. With a merely passable English as my only marketable asset, I was happy to be hired as a junior clerk and assistant by a photographer's shop and studio, attending to customers, (mostly British and European tourists) and occasionally retouching portrait negatives.

When an airline company opened in Nicosia, promising better wage prospects, my brother, Van, applied and was hired as the Chief Engineer's secretary. I soon followed as parts and stock-room clerk, later moving into the technical department, apprenticing in the hydraulic and component overhaul shop.

The start of an airline company in Cyprus signified the international importance of the region where the world's power brokers vied for influence. The Arab, or Islamic world, stretching from the North African French colonies, through Egypt, the smaller states of the Middle East, the Persian Gulf and Iran, had begun to stir. The Soviet Union promoted workers' and minorities' rights; the Americans bolstered dictatorships, while Britain, relying on her vast experience of maintaining colonies around the world, sought the wisdom of gradual recognition of colonial maturity, rather than succumb to the ill-considered urgency and abandon of chaotic independence.

(my desperate search for page three)

Members of our Circle who were present at one of our early summer sessions may remember the last story that I read here...or... No! That's not correct! Started to read, I should say...or, perhaps, made an attempt at reading, only to be interrupted when I had read two pages and turned the leaf to read page three. But members present were faster than I was, so that, before I could turn the page, several voices in unison claimed that page three seemed to be an identical copy of page one! "Hah?!...No!...It can't be!" I had "burned the midnight candle" as they say, to write and type and print page after page...until my desk was covered with a mountain of discarded and corrected and re-discarded pages. In the early morning hours, past midnight, after a brief moment of resting my head on the pillow, I printed pages one and two on the same sheet, back-to-back, and grabbed and stapled what I honestly believed to be page three, and rushed to Brock House without breakfast, and was on time for class.

When Pat asked, "Have you something, Jerry?" I proudly said "Yes!" I felt confident...until, to my mortifying embarrassment, I was shown to have made a mess of all my efforts.

At home my search for page three proved futile. I just couldn't find page three—if there ever was one—unless it had already gone into the recycle bin!

I sat down to write anew what should have been page three.

But in the process of doing so I had a revelation. I noted, as I read and re-read the story I had thus far written, that I had hopelessly deviated from the theme I had initially contemplated. My purpose had been—as, I surmised, was that of the Administration initially—to introduce Shakespeare into the Cyprus conflict, perhaps as an image of peacemaker, a figure loved and admired universally by all, a dramatist to compare with the great dramatists of ancient Greece, and, in the process, perhaps ameliorate relations between ruler and colonist.

That would have been the gist of my story. But I found that I had needlessly sidetracked into unrelated family gossip, unnecessary comparison of schools, controversial international relations, unresolved regional conflicts, had inadequate expertise in history, and no business to muddle through.

The Greek students had begun rioting in city squares, and when they set fire to the British Council Library the Administration placed an ad in the newspaper for applicants, from whom one would be selected to be sent to Britain, all expenses paid, to be trained in Shakespearean and Elizabethan drama. The selected applicant would be a young person of a certain age limit, and have attained the "Distinction" level of English.

My claim to that proficiency was "Ordinary" which would rule me out. However, I felt I had an advantage over any "Distinction" claimant in that I had made Shakespeare my "self-study" teacher of English, and felt confident that no one had read Shakespeare or loved the Bard a much as I did. If I could muster the courage to approach the Council and argue my case personally, I thought, I might win the appointment. I had one other advantage as well. The selected candidate, upon returning to the Island, would make the rounds of all secondary and higher schools and introduce the subject into the curriculums of all Greek, Turkish and Armenian Schools. My additional advantage would be that I was neither Greek nor Turkish. I was Armenian, and as such would present a neutral contact between the major ethnic divisions of the populace, whose languages I could speak, rather than pitting a Greek against Turks or a Turk against Greeks, who do not speak each-other's language.

There was already, at the time, a similar case in the Scout movement in Cyprus. An Armenian, of many years a veteran Boy Scout, had been appointed Chief Scout of the Island. His neutral but friendly and enthusiastic relationship with Greek as well as Turkish troops, whose languages he was quite familiar with, had made him very popular on all sides, so much so that he was conferred the title of MBE by the Queen at a Scout Jamboree in London in 1955.

If I had had the courage to appeal to the Council, I might have been able to persuade it and perhaps won the appointment, and...

But all this is water under the bridge, as the saying goes. I don't think anyone answered the call for applications. The situation in Cyprus deteriorated very fast. A boatload of arms was reported to have been smuggled into the Island one night, and the conflict became, overnight, an all-out guerrilla warfare.

Had my dream materialized, I, too, might someday have deserved the honor of an MBE, I dream. Daring Anglophiles were assassinated. I, too might have been marked for the hazard of the post. But, at least, I would have received an education—a formal education—I, who had not graduated from any school. In the words of a famous actor on screen, I would have been "somebody!"

Coiled Message

Mr. Donald James, Chief Engineer of Cyprus Airways Ltd., wanted to know, first thing on Monday morning, what exactly had transpired at the Company's technical site the day before, on Sunday afternoon. A crew of his men had been working in the Airline's newly-built hangar, carrying out extensive repairs and modifications on one of the Company's "Dakota" passenger planes. They had toiled, week in week out, without a weekend's break, through the hot days of a late Cyprus spring. The superintendent engineer in charge of the operations, Mr. Glen Frasier, had telephoned James in the evening and reported that there had been a "mutiny," that the crew had refused to go to work when requested to do so.

James wondered what could have prompted the erratic reaction among the formerly well-behaved workers who provided the local manpower of the Airline. (The supervisory staff was made up of British engineers, licensed in a variety of categories.) No doubt, he thought, the men must have been exhausted, their nerves spent, their disposition edgy. But a foreboding apprehension gnawed at the depth of his thoughts, and he hoped and prayed it would prove not to be true that the politics that prevailed on the Island, a British Colony—and which for the past year or so had acquired an aspect of violence—had finally crept into his workplace.

※ ※ ※

A popular claim for "Enosis"—Union with Greece—long suppressed and dormant through the War years, had resurfaced among the majority native Greek population of Cyprus. For the past several years the movement had found expression in student demonstrations, escalating, over time, into bottle-throwing confrontations with police and troops. Even more violent acts of defiance, such as the burning of the British Institute Library, had shaken the tranquility of the Island. But in general, life had gone on at its normal, easygoing, Mediterranean pace, without much serious disruption of any kind...until a year before. On April 1, 1955, the "Organization" had inaugurated its engagement in acts of terror, with token bombs placed in strategic governmental or military locations.

The worsening conflict called for a greater number of troops, until a force of some 40,000 British soldiers patrolled the towns for suspected bomb-throwers and gunmen, and combed the mountains and villages for guerrilla fighters and their hideouts. Prison camps were set up. Young men and women, many of them students, were rounded up and detained for questioning. Unsuspecting British civilians were shot in the street. Arrests were made. Hanged culprits became heroes of the people. A special constabulary was hurriedly established to assist the local police. But Greek members of the force were reluctant to work against their own people for fear of reprisals. Several high-ranking Greek officers had been assassinated by the secret "Organization."

Turkish Cypriots flocked to the new corps and manned the prisons and concentration camps. This had the effect of setting up historic arch-enemies against each other, further antagonizing the native population in contempt of the Colonial Administration. Horrendous tortures of imprisoned men and women were rumoured. The atmosphere in the Island became tense. Curfews were imposed and there was disruption of business and social life. The Head of the Greek Church, presumed to be the leader of the movement, was exiled. But the guerrilla commander eluded capture. Violence intensified and Administrative Governors replaced one another in quick succession.

It was against this worrisome background, in the early summer of 1956, that James, the Chief Engineer, viewed the report of the alleged "mutiny." But what puzzled him was that the purported leader, the man accused of heading the "insubordination" was cited as Harry, who, in his estimation, was the least likely to engage in an act of defiance. James knew Harry to be a diligent employee, a talented and skillful mechanic, who had studied hard, sat for and recently acquired his Aircraft Engineer's Licence. Besides, thought James, Harry was neither Greek nor Turkish; he was Armenian, a neutral minority in the Island's conflict, which fact relieved, somewhat, his anxiety regarding the seditious overtones of the "mutiny." He had Harry summoned to his office and wanted to hear the local employees' viewpoint.

The story that emerged put James at ease about the political penetration of the workplace, but pointed, at the same time, to the possibility of future repercussions.

ʔ ʔ ʔ

It had been the end of a long, exhausting Sunday in the course of the ongoing overtime-laden labour, Harry told the Chief Engineer. The workers had put their tools away, washed up and changed, and were waiting for the Company's transportation that carried them daily to work and back to the town square. It had always been on time but was running late that day. Yet no one complained. The men were tired but, although they hadn't had a weekend off for a long time, they appreciated the extra income and were in good spirits.

Frasier, the engineer in charge of the job at hand, had been missing all afternoon. His car was parked outside, in the shade of the hangar, but he was nowhere to be found. He must know the whereabouts of the bus, the men surmised, and waited, chatting, unconcerned.

Then they saw him coming. He emerged from the military section of the field that enclosed the Royal Air Force barracks and the Officers' Mess Hall and Lounge. He was accompanied by a stranger, and they appeared, at a distance, to be engaged in gleeful conversation as they walked, at a leisurely pace, across the broad tarmac.

When they entered the hangar Frasier's demeanour changed. He assumed an impatient, aggressive stance.

"What's going on?" he demanded of the men, as though annoyed that they had washed and were ready to go home.

The men were taken by surprise. It was quitting time, they said. They were waiting for transportation.

The bus would not be coming for some time, Frasier told them. He had been informed of the delay. They should not be wasting time idly hanging around.

"Come on!" he ordered them, with a sweeping motion of his hand, his finger pointing. "Back to work! Back to work!" His companion looked on with gleeful anticipation.

There was an embarrassed silence. The workers looked at one another, bewildered. This was not Frasier's usual behaviour, Harry told the Chief Engineer. It seemed, rather, to be a show-off on Frasier's part to impress his friend (who was, apparently, an old-country acquaintance and a newcomer to the Island) as to the authority he could wield on the locals. Ordinarily Frasier's relationship with the locals had been friendly, Harry continued. He had treated them as equals, in most respects, and even helped several of the fitters get ahead through study of the appropriate material.

The men started grumbling. He has no right to do this, they mumbled, though they could see clearly that he must be drunk, as his behaviour, as well as the fact that he and his friend had just emerged from the site of the RAF Officers' Mess Hall, betrayed. They worried that disobedience could lead to disciplinary action. Inadequate knowledge of English—or the total lack of it—denied them the tools or the courage to argue their objection. Harry alone had a fair fluency of the language.

"It's past quitting time, Mr. Frasier," he said, "and we're going home."

"But you can't go home," said Frasier. "There's no transportation."

"That's quite immaterial, Mr. Frasier," said Harry. "We're walking home."

Frasier's face became suddenly very red. His companion made himself scarce in quick steps. The smile had disappeared from his face.

"You can't walk home," said Frasier. "It's too far." But his words sounded deflated and had lost the edge of command. "You will all be reported for insubordination and refusing to obey orders," he said at last, with a tremulous voice, his face a deeper red.

James listened to Harry's story without comment but with an occasional nod.

After he had concluded his report, Harry turned again toward James before taking leave. "May I be so bold as to make an observation, Sir," he said, with some hesitation, and was encouraged by a slight nod from James. "These people pride themselves on the glory of ancient Greek history and culture," Harry told the Chief. "They resent being treated as inferiors, though their basic education has hardly provided them with an elementary knowledge of English. Besides, these are bad times, Sir, and the Island's population is already agitated."

※ ※ ※

James stood for a long time gazing through the window of his ground level office, chain smoking. He surveyed the part of the field that was his Company's domain. To his left, in the old, smaller hangar—the one inherited from the RAF—one of his planes was undergoing routine maintenance. Outside, on the tarmac, another Dakota was being polished and readied for its upcoming flight. Ahead of him, at a short distance, stood the recently constructed hangar where overhaul and renovation of yet another of his fleet was in progress. He had great hopes for the new hangar. It was modern in its facilities and spacious enough to accommodate larger aircraft that the Company contemplated acquiring. Aviation in the Middle East was assuming an importance of indispensable necessity, and James's Company, ideally located in Cyprus, between three continents, would be in the forefront, offering the required services: carrying passengers and freight to and from the great metropolises of the Middle East, the hub cities of the Mediterranean basin and Europe, including Britain. And, most importantly, it would be in a position to provide maintenance facilities to other operators as well...If only the whole dream of the project is not jeopardized by attracting a terrorist's bomb, James reflected, and his heart sank at the thought of that possibility. What could he do to prevent it?

There has to be disciplinary action taken in the wake of yesterday's incident, James decided, and chuckled to himself as his inventive mind settled on a scheme whereby the discipline he had in mind would incorporate the necessary preventive measure as well.

The Chief Engineer was in the process of preparing a memo for

Management's information when a call came through from Head Office. The Managing Director himself was on the line. He said he had just received a complaint from the employees' trade union citing unfair demands made on the workmen over the weekend, followed by unjustified threats of penalty. He asked what James knew and what he was doing about it.

James expounded his assessment of the problem. He said the matter was of more ominous consequence under the prevailing conditions than it would have been otherwise. Frasier might, in all likelihood, be targeted by "terrorists," he opined, and asked the Director to consider, as well, the possibility of an act of sabotage against even the Company itself, such as a bomb in a plane.

"Are you not being an alarmist?" the Director asked.

James said he was being precautionary for Frasier's personal safety, and protective of the Company's prospects. As a preventive measure, he said, it was his conviction that Frasier must go.

"I thought Frasier was one of your best men," the Director said. "He's been a competent, reliable engineer, hasn't he?"

"Frasier has betrayed his trust."

"Are you saying that we harbour terrorists among our local employees?"

"Terrorists don't wear badges," the Chief Engineer said. "Wisdom demands that we give them no cause or invitation. Frasier has made himself a target," he added.

"What do you propose, then? That we fire him, or ask him to resign? His contract isn't up yet, you know. Your solution is easier said than done."

"I am merely suggesting steps for Frasier's own safety, as well as the Company's," James said. "Frasier's removal, besides, may appease the hellhounds that hide in the shadows, and, hopefully, preclude an attack on the Company."

"I caution you, James," said the Director, "not to be a defeatist. I wouldn't talk of appeasement at this stage."

James was not deterred. He was Chief Engineer, he told himself, and it was his responsibility to see to all technical aspects of the Company's operations, including safety of the fleet under maintenance, as well as that of the grounds. He was not going to allow Head Office to trample his authority and bridle his decisions. He was adamant that Frasier must go before a foolhardy act of reprisal should prove tragic for the man and his family, or disastrous for the Company.

⟩⟩⟩

No disciplinary action was taken against the workers, but relations between Frasier and the men had lost the previously held trust and friendliness. It was not strained. Rather, the sentiment was one of awkward self-consciousness on both sides. Early each morning, as was his wont, Frasier would go to his lectern-style desk that stood in a corner of the hangar, open the slanted top, take out the work schedule and blueprints, view the progress of the job and assign new duties to the men.

Half way through the week, the men were quietly changing into their coveralls one day, getting ready to start work, when a loud bang, as of a door being slammed in rage, and a simultaneous terrifying scream—"Aaaah"—tore through the hangar, piercing the early morning stillness.

The sudden jolting sound and Frasier's frightened cry alarmed and startled the men. Frasier had casually opened the cover of his desk, only to slam it shut again instantly and recoil in paralyzing fear. He found a chair and sat to catch his breath, his face ashen, his nerves atremble.

What had happened, the men asked each other? One of them said he thought he had seen, for a brief instant, something like a stick wagging at Frasier's face. From inside the desk-top? Impossible! It wasn't large enough to hide a man—or an animal! But something in there had terrified him. What was it, the men were curious to know?

One of the men, standing to one side of the desk, pried the top with a long lever and lifted it half open. The others looked on cautiously from a safe distance. Though anticipating the unexpected, they were not prepared for the flailing assailant that lunged at the opening, compelling them instinctively to pull back, gasping.

A snake!

The men, taken aback, gasped also with amazement at the sight of the serpent, and were at once plunged into a muddle of perplexing questions.

What dazzled them was the snake's exotic colouring. It had sprung forth from what looked like a squirming profusion of bright reds, blacks, yellows, whites. Its body, writhing and twisting, coil upon contorted coil, took up much of the desktop space.

Repulsed by the sordid method of retaliation against Frasier, someone voiced what was perhaps uppermost in everyone's mind. "Who the devil put it there?"

No one expected an answer. No perpetrator would risk admission.

One of the men, who claimed to know much about local snakes, said he had never seen one so colorful anywhere on the Island. But what was even more puzzling was what struck them as its strange behaviour. The snake had darted forward in a seemingly aggressive thrust, but stopped short at the opening. Bobbing up and down in midair, swaying left and right, it seemed to be surveying its surroundings from its perch in the desktop, as though seeking out its tormentor, focusing on each man in turn. But, strange as it seemed, it held its head at all times bent sharply to the right, apparently viewing only with its left eye. The reason soon became clear to the men. The right side of the snake's head had visibly been crushed, its tongue pinched motionless between its jaws, the eye evidently blinded, its body writhing, probably in pain. It had obviously been intentionally rendered unable to inflict harm, but still capable to terrify.

꿍꿍꿍

James stood at the window of his office and gazed dreamily at his new hangar and the field behind the buildings. He lit a cigarette (while another smoldered in the ashtray), inhaled a puff, and exhaled with a sigh of contentment. He had asserted his authority over the affairs of the Technical Branch; Frasier had been sent home with severance pay; the motive for a terrorist's blow had been removed, and, hopefully, averted. He could now concentrate on expanding the facilities of his Service Department. An ample spread of asphalt blacktop was needed beside the new hangar to park aircraft scheduled for maintenance. There was no lack of space for expansion. The field on his (civilian) side of the taxiway, across the RAF barracks, was vacant and stretched for miles as far as the eye could see. It was a barren wasteland; flat and barren. Claimed to have been the bottom of the sea millions of years ago. You could see fossils of seashells if you chipped the bedrock, exposed at places. Very little topsoil. Only a few inches deep. But enough to sustain a twinkling of anemones in the Spring. They were long gone now. All he could see now were clusters of scraggly, sun-browned bushes here and there. What were they capable of sustaining? Insects and spiders, surely. Birds, perhaps? Sparrows fluttered about in the hangars, but skylarks, which he had heard occasionally, probably dove down and nestled on the heath somewhere. Lizards, too. And...snakes!? James thought he saw a tiny wiggle on the cement walk outside. It disappeared under a small rock by the grass. He quickly found a little box and went outside, lifted the rock, and, sure enough, a baby snake, probably newly hatched, about three inches long, wiggled out. James held the box in the snake's path, trapped it and taped the box to take it home.

He sat late, in bed, that evening, writing a letter to his two young sons. They had gone "home" with their mother for school registration in England. Unable to bear the loneliness and isolation of an expatriate in a foreign culture and language; the tension of rising hostility in the land; the neglect of a husband dedicated to his work, and, not least, the stench of his cigarettes that permeated the house as well as his own person, his wife had taken the children and flown home to Britain. James lived alone now. Though never too expressive, he did miss his boys. And tonight he had good reason to write them. "P.S." he wrote, leaving to the end the main occasion that had inspired his letter. "Today I trapped a little 'wiggler,' a local baby snake, and brought it home to add to your collection. It's only three inches long. Nothing exotic, perhaps, but will be grown a little by the time you come over. Then we'll know its kind and colour.
"The weather is really warming up here. It will be good sailing and swimming season when you come, soon, on your holidays. Love, Dad."

It had been a gratifying day. He felt fulfilled. The radio hummed gently. He was ready to go to sleep. An hour past midnight. He stretched to silence the radio before reaching for the light switch.

He hadn't yet touched the knob when the music was suddenly cut off at mid-song. James stopped short and waited. A newscaster's formal sounding voice came on the air.

"We interrupt this program for a special bulletin" began the announcer's voice.

Just then the bedside telephone rang. James picked up the receiver at once and held it away from his ear. He did not want the ringing or the call to interfere with the message on the radio. (With the time-zone difference in their favour, it was not unusual for his family to call from Britain at such late hours.)

"Hello! Donny Jim?"

Though holding the receiver at arm's length, James recognized the caller's voice as that of the Company's General Manager. That doesn't bode well at this late hour, he thought to himself.

"Some twenty-five minutes ago," the radio announcer continued, "at approximately 12:45 a.m., an explosion in a passenger plane owned by Cyprus Airways Limited..."

"Hello! Donny Jim? Are you there, Donny Jim?"

"*...blew a hole in the front end of the fuselage...*"

"You were right, Donny Jim. We should have paid better attention to your concerns. Can you hear me Donny Jim? Are you there?"

"*...There were no casualties. The plane was parked for the night at the technical tarmac and would have been prepared for service in the morning, a spokesman for the Company said...*"

"This has to be the work of a madman, Donny Jim, perhaps an employee of ours, frustrated at having lost his intended target. Good thing we sent the poor fellow home."

"*...The damage is said to be light, but the spokesman we contacted said the Company's security has been compromised and it may affect the jobs of all local employees.*"

"Anyway, I've arranged for Scotland Yard to conduct the investigation. They'll be at the site in the morning to interview all local workers. We'll get to the bottom of this! Donny Jim? Can you hear me, Donny Jim? Donny Jim? Are you there? Donny Jim? Donny Jim?..."

My Brother K

I was informed by telephone that my eldest brother, K, had had surgery for stomach cancer a year before, and that the information had been kept from me.

I spent frustrating hours trying to contact him and was met with what seemed to be intentional resistance. There was no answer from his home. After much evasiveness and feigning ignorance of my brother's whereabouts, his secretary at the office relented and gave me a number I could call. I finally located him in his yacht at the Sheraton marina on the Limassol waterfront in Cyprus. His wife was reluctant at first to let me talk to him but when she saw that I would pay a personal visit anyway, she gave in, and I at last had my brother on the telephone.

I immediately made arrangements to fly over and see him. It had been a long time.

He was hospitalized—apparently, yet again—by the time I reached him. He was wasted to a skeleton and looked nothing like the athletic soccer player I remembered. I visited with him every day for several weeks, staying at a seaside apartment he owned and driving to the clinic in the car that he lent me. On the last morning of my visit I was told he had died the night before. He had been delirious as I held him at parting and kissed his forehead, yet the announcement came as though I should not have expected it.

I sat at a service station waiting for my brother's car to be washed and filled up before I left the Island for home. And as I reflected on the past, my brother's life seemed to unfold, scene after scene, in my mind's eye.

He had had little schooling. After two years in the only English school on the Island, my father had taken him away to earn money attending to road construction machines. He was only fourteen then.

A master mechanic who owned a garage hired him as an apprentice. My brother, K, learned the trade fast. He had finished servicing a shiny British sports car one day, and, seeing that the boss was not in, thought he'd take it out on a test drive and show off to a girl that he had set his eyes on. The boss saw him driving through the narrow streets of Nicosia. He was fired.

Frustrated with his life, he ran away from home and joined the Royal Navy. Notwithstanding his scant knowledge of English, he attained the position of Petty Officer, serving in the Suez Canal Zone. Upon his discharge he worked as a clerk at a British military base in Cyprus. At the same time, he was making inroads into the world of business. When he felt fairly established financially he also invested in real estate. In time, he became very wealthy and finally had the fulfillment of his lifelong dream—a luxury yacht, custom built. It cut an imposing figure at the marina, moored alongside an array of sleek pleasure craft. He had asked me to go and see it while he lay in hospital.

How he had loved that boat, I thought, as I sat musing now, and wondered whether it had also, perhaps, contributed to his demise. He had it designed by British naval architects, and yet had it built by a local Greek boat builder in Limassol. The result—though he sang its praises, as well as bemoaning its faults—was that the boat ended up looking, in my opinion—though I never mentioned it, to save his feelings—more like an old eastern Mediterranean cargo vessel than a modern pleasure craft.

I was engrossed in these thoughts when a man in a Jaguar pulled up to the gas pump. He got off and walked toward me.

"Are you K's brother?" he asked. "You look like him. I am his lawyer," he said. "This car used to belong to him." (I found out later that my brother had made a gift of the Jaguar to his lawyer.)

"My condolences," the lawyer repeated at parting. "He was a miracle of a man! A miracle of a man!"

Mediterranean Crossing

Mistaken Identity

In 1956, when a terrorist's bomb blew a hole in one of the airplanes of the Company where I worked in Cyprus, all local employees of the technical department were put through questioning by Scotland Yard first thing the next morning, and all but a few were summarily suspended. I, along with three other men of varied expertise, was kept on temporarily at a rented shop in town, pending optimistically anticipated cessation of hostilities. But when there seemed to be no longer any hope of a political settlement with the rebels, we were given compensation and finally let go.

I sought employment in nearby Beirut, Lebanon, and was accepted as inspector of the hydraulic component overhaul shop. My new employer, Middle East Airlines, was owned by Arab sheiks, in a sort of partnership, I believe, with British Overseas Airways Corporation.

The technical branch, or service department of Middle East Airlines, had its own separate corporate identity and was called Mid-East Aircraft Service Company, commonly known by its acronym as MASCO.

On the weekend before I was expected to start work, I took the Middle East Airlines plane for which I had been issued a ticket, and with my wife and two-year-old son, flew to Beirut. It was nighttime and I was a little bewildered in a country where I did not speak the language. I wondered whether the Company, which had hired me and arranged for my arrival, would have someone meet me. I felt reassured at the sight of a young woman dressed in Company uniform, welcoming the passengers. When she came near I told her I was with MASCO and asked if she knew whether anyone was meeting me.

"Let's go find out," she said, and became, suddenly very deferential, treating my wife and myself with special attention. As we walked toward the terminal building, she said she hadn't noticed anyone from the embassy and asked whether they had been notified.

"Embassy?" I said, puzzled. I was coming from a British colony—

Cyprus—and wondered whether the British Embassy in Beirut would be informed about or have anything to do with my arrival. But then, I wasn't an experienced traveler, and thought anything might be possible in the organized system of crossing borders with passports. "Well," I said, hesitating, "I don't think so."

"Well," she said. "We'll see. If there's no one waiting, then we'll phone the Soviet Embassy and tell them you're here!"

"Soviet Embassy?" I said, more confused now than ever. "Why the Soviet Embassy?"

"You said you're from Moscow," she said. "Aren't you?"

Lebanese Transactions

The Greek revolt in Cyprus had disrupted my career in the field of aircraft inspection. I was, therefore, thrilled to secure an enviable position in the maintenance department of Middle East Airlines, a Beirut based company, a half hour's flight from Cyprus. I moved to that hub city of the eastern Mediterranean, the "Paris of the Middle East," with my wife and two-year-old son, in March of 1958. We did not speak the language of the land—Arabic—and were even less aware of its politics. A respectable, long-established business contact of a close relative of ours reassured us. The constitution of Lebanon, he maintained, provided for such harmony among its diverse population that unrest, such as we had experienced in Cyprus, could not even be dreamed of as a possibility. He even lent us one of his employees to act as our interpreter as we went searching for an apartment to rent. A third-floor unit in a newly constructed building in the suburbs seemed suitable and well located. It afforded a view of the mountains and a glimpse of the sea. Our interpreter bargained long and hard with the owner, a Lebanese Arab who had made his wealth in Brazil. Then, after a brief whispered exchange with the owner and several furtive glances our way, he asked us whether we understood Arabic. Having ascertained that we had no idea what they had been arguing about, he told us that the owner would make no concession from his original asking price, and that he wanted a full year's rent in advance. This, he assured us, was the indisputable practice of the land.

We had to borrow the money from our interpreter's employer and for better or for worse began settling, unpacking our effects, buying essential furniture and appliances. With the help of an acquaintance who had recently sojourned in Cyprus, we met a number of friendly Armenians and, through the benefit of a common language, were introduced to shopping facilities in the neighbourhood. (Armenians, constituting sizeable minorities in countries of the Middle East, are descendants of survivors of the Genocide committed during the upheaval of the First World War, who were subsequently driven out of their historic homeland by Turkey.)

My wife, Alice, was directed to an Armenian butcher shop. Though fascinated with the unusual method of marketing meat, she found it, at the same time, frustrating and annoying. Lacking powered refrigeration in a sub-tropical climate, the small neighbourhood butcher had no option but to sell his inventory—usually a single carcass—before the day warmed up. Which meant, if you wanted a particular cut, you had to be there early.

On the day Alice went to buy meat it was early enough. Or so she thought. There was a group of elderly women, apparently local acquaintances all, sitting on chairs and benches along the walls, waiting patiently, drinking Turkish (Armenian) coffee, and gossiping—in Turkish. (That had been the enforced common language of their usurped Armenian homeland.) A waiter from a coffee shop nearby popped in occasionally to reclaim emptied demitasses, or take further orders. The butcher, an elderly man, was busy mincing meat on his wood block with a pair of sharp knives. He welcomed my wife, a young, new customer, and asked what cut she wanted.

"Tenderloin," my wife said. The move to a new country, and the change in environment had disrupted our routine, and our two-year-old son had not been eating well.

"Tenderloin?" The butcher sank into deep, calculating thought. "That's a rare and expensive cut," he said. My wife gazed at him in surprise. But a more unexpected shock greeted her when the man asked what she was cooking that day.

"It's none of your business," she said. "I'll make whatever I want with the meat."

The butcher obviously surmised that his new patron was not familiar with the customary practice of the community.

"Some of these women here will make lahmajoon (Armenian pizza) and keofteh (meat balls) he explained. "I'm mincing the meat for them. It takes a cheaper cut, and I have plenty of that. It's a pity to use the tender cuts, and it tastes just as good."

Upon further reflection on our family's diet, we concluded that, in our preoccupation with the trials of settling, our nutritional intake had fallen short of the traditional health-restoring chicken soup. It was not easy, in those days, in Cyprus or in Beirut, for city dwellers to have chicken for a meal. Live poultry was available in the central public market, but the hardships of carrying it home discouraged purchase. Some households in the outskirts of town, in Cyprus, kept a few domestic fowl in their backyards for fresh eggs and the occasional "boiler." Frequently a hawker from a village would cover sections of the town, on foot, with a bunch of the birds—their legs tied together—suspended from each hand. The householder would call him over, make a selection from the panic-stricken, shrill-throated, rackety squawkers, and have the hawker himself execute the killing, away from delicate nerves, faint hearts and sensitive eyes.

I made inquiries regarding the Lebanese procedure of procuring chicken. The customary option for the city dweller, I found out, was the live poultry "warehouse," across from the fish market, in the area of the central bazaar.

The invasive stench guided me to the general vicinity, but I could not avoid the narrow, smelly alley of the seafood market. It was paved with cobblestones and lined, on both sides, with shallow gutters in which, surprisingly, clear water flowed constantly, though at a sluggish pace. Discarded fish lay here and there in the gutters, but the flowing water was not plentiful enough to wash them or the stench away. They were, apparently, meant for the cats, which seemed to be too well fed to bother.

The poultry market, such as it was, was housed in an oversized shed, detached from other buildings, with high, galvanized roof and raised concrete floor. I climbed up two or three steps into a cavernous, poorly lit, gaping hall. It looked as if it had been built as a warehouse, though it contained no merchandise, except for a few cages of birds in a gloomy corner to the right. The attendant, a short, balding, middle-aged man, seemed surprised at seeing me. He appeared to have woken on hearing me come in. There was a sense of isolation to the place. I was the only customer in sight.

To the question apparent in his greeting as well as his countenance, I answered, "Poulet," in a single word, resorting to my scant knowledge of French, and indicated with gestures that I wanted it plucked.

(Lebanon and Syria, having been French mandates following the First World War, maintain some familiarity with the language among the citizenry.) The man nodded comprehension, walked over to the corner, selected a young hen from a cage, brought it over and held it high for my approval.

I had hardly signaled consent when, shocked into a state of confusion, I felt the gloomy hall transform into a magician's stage. I couldn't tell whether the man, in a sleight-of-hand maneuver, had tossed the bird upward, or whether it had escaped his grip and taken flight, flapping its wings helter-skelter, in the scare of its life. What seemed to deepen the hypnotic perplexity of the erupting commotion was the unnatural silence of the bird, the sudden ending of its noisy racket. Was I losing my hearing in a hysterical spell of black magic? I could hear the flapping of its wings! It flew with vigorous effort, yet directionless, in erratic pattern. It could not maintain altitude. Its body weight forced it down. Bouncing off the floor, it took off again. It came down again, and bounced up yet again—not as high, but again, and again. Then down...all spent...and could not rise again. Blood gushed a last spurt where the fowl's head should have been. I caught a glimpse of its red comb in the beheader's hand. He noticed my horror. "Halaal," he said, explaining the ritual. The Arabic escaped my grasp. I understood halaal. There would be atonement. The executioner would be forgiven. Blood must drain to the last drop. There will be no grudge left.

I understood why the floor had looked dark and dirty when I came in.

I returned home with a chicken in my bag, plucked, gutted, wrapped in brown paper.

Grocers in the suburb carried most staples and dry goods in plenty but did not stock fruits and vegetables in adequate quantities or varieties. It was occasionally necessary, therefore, to take a taxi "service" to the central bazaar in town.

After getting off at the main square, as you walked the few blocks toward the marketplace, you would become aware of a distant din that would gradually resemble the strains of a complicated chorus, sung in a kaleidoscopic variety of voices. As you entered the open market and walked past the stalls, you would be accosted by every single vendor, chanting, at the top of his voice and in full volume, the praises of his wares.

I approached a young lad of thirteen or fourteen selling bananas. The price was marked at 75 piastres a kilo. I handed him a ten-lira bill. I had nothing smaller. He gave me change for five and heartily resumed his banana song. I spoke to him in English, gesturing and indicating that he owed me five more liras. He pretended not to understand. Worse still, he ignored me completely, as if I weren't even there, and kept on chanting, holding a bunch of bananas high above his head.

Argument is useless when truth is ignored. So are gestures and sign language as aids to the verbal brand. I bent over the lad's barrier and reached into the box where, I had noticed, he stashed his proceeds. He immediately stopped his chanting, grabbed my wrist, picked out a five-lira bill from the box and held it out for me, without even so much as a flicker of change in his expression, dismissing me with a sweep of his hand. His demeanor calm and unruffled, as though nothing unusual had happened, he picked up where he had left off his rhythmic paean of the banana, and, waving aloft a fresh bunch, rejoined the chorus that blared from the bizarre bazaar of Beirut.

Civil Disorder Comes to Beirut

Within weeks of our move to Beirut, shopping for food as well as commuting to work, as trying as they had been in the new, somewhat alien environment, became, overnight, more difficult, even dangerous, and, in time, almost impossible. The brand of political turmoil we had experienced in Cyprus and which we had been assured could not happen in Beirut, began to show its ominous face through the veil of perceived tranquility, plunging the city into disarray and our lives into a state of confusion.

The unrest, in the spring of 1958—as I gleaned at first from colleagues engaged in agitated conversation in Arabic—started with discontent among parties opposed to the President. As far as I could deduce from scraps of information, the constitution of the country called for a Christian president and a Moslem prime minister, corresponding to the proportions of the diverse population. The rule had worked well since the declaration of the country as a republic in the early 1940's, when France relinquished the mandate she had assumed in the aftermath of World War I. But there had been murmurs, of late, among the Moslem community, that the balance had not remained the same, and that it was now time for a reassessment. Complicating the issue, there were, at the time, over 100,000 Palestinian Moslem refugees camped in the country, clamouring for recognition as well as repatriation, though constituting no part of the country's official population count.

Soon it became apparent that the matter was more than political rivalry between the religious factions. The disgruntlement, we soon learned, had been simmering for the past two years, instigated by external influences: President Nasser of Egypt, who had aligned his country with the Soviet Bloc and nationalized the Suez Canal, urged and expected neighbouring states to break relations with the West and condemn, as an act of aggression, the British and French attempt at recapturing the Seaway.

Lebanon's Christian, pro-Western President refused to do so, ignoring Nasser's bidding. Moreover, he proclaimed his endorsement of the Baghdad Pact—a West-led treaty of alliance for the defense of member countries of the region against Soviet encroachment.

The Moslem Prime Minister, on the other hand, yielded to Nasser's demand. He rebelled and broke away from the Government, thus provoking a complex of divergent allegiances, not only between the religious communities, but also rousing dormant rivalries between "Right" and "Left" in the prevailing "Cold War" politics.

Further aggravating tensions in the region, Nasser had, in recent weeks (about the time of our arrival in Beirut, early in 1958) also formed a political union between Egypt and Syria, called the "United Arab Republic" (of which, our sources of information on local politics were themselves probably not yet aware) and strove to coerce other Arab states, including Lebanon, into joining.

The dissident Prime Minister had now found a popular cause for his rebellion. He declared his readiness to join the UAR and, to confound the government, called a general strike, enforced by shadowy gunmen of his militia.

Daring shopkeepers of our suburb carried on stealthily behind closed doors. Idled tradesmen began selling groceries on secluded street corners. We soon ran low on staples and searched the neighbourhood for supplies. My wife found a young man selling potatoes. She watched him place a number of them in a bucket and slap the stuff on his scale. She asked him whether he was charging her the weight of the bucket as well. The man was taken by "surprise" and went into a litany of apologies. He said he was a shoemaker who had lost his job to the strike, and knew nothing about selling potatoes.

The airport shuttle that had, to my convenience, begun making its first station of the day in our vicinity, stopped serving our suburb. I had to rise early, find a taxi with a daring yet cautious driver who would defy the strike, and hope to catch the shuttle at its main post in the City Square.

On my first venture at the new arrangement the taxi dropped me off about half a block from the shuttle—a comfortable coach of German manufacture—stationed on the periphery of the Square.

As I made my way on the sidewalk, alone, in the cool of the early morning, with a paper bag in my hand holding my sandwich for the day, a strange sense of silence and solitude seized me. The absence of the usual hustle and bustle of Beirut: the jumble of law-defying traffic, the noise of car horns blaring, and human voices at their tops shouting abuse at some offender, punctuating the cacophonous din; the sudden removal of all that racket, and the emptiness of the reigning hush, was eerily uncharacteristric of the city.

The City Centre surrounding the Square—office buildings and edifices housing company headquarters, foreign embassies and international connections: the throbbing heart of the country's commerce and finance—had been placed under the protection of the army. Tanks guarded points of entry into the plaza. Converging streets had been sandbagged, restricting vehicular traffic, and were patrolled by armed soldiers. Sandbags were also piled here and there around the tanks in the Square, and watchful soldiers moved about, as though in slow motion, with guns on the ready, apparently in case of a surprise assault.

Something uncharacteristic was being forced on Beirut. Rumours we had been hearing about armed Syrians infiltrating the border to join with the Prime Minister's rebels must be true! The very success of the enforcement of the strike was an indication that the man was a force to contend with. The Government had already begun taking action against him. We had heard the sounds of gunfire and seen from our balcony Government fighter planes strafing what we were told was the Prime Minister's mountain stronghold. But how decisive or effective could that be? A few tanks and small planes would not be enough if hostile, larger neighbours overran the border. Lebanon was not a warring country. It had thrived for millennia with its ingenious trading population.

There was now talk of the native Christian Maronites preparing to rise against the Moslem followers of the Prime Minister. That would mean civil war!

So...what on earth are we doing here, then, I kept asking myself as I walked toward the shuttle bus.

I had learned, since adolescence—perhaps as a survival strategy—to view events from a detached standpoint, as though rising above the waves, unperturbed by the turmoil of life. "Savour the experience," I would tell myself at a later, more ambitious age, "no matter how upsetting it might be; you may write a story about it someday," (which, too, may have been a game plan for weathering the storm).

The irony of our situation—'Out of the frying pan into the fire'—didn't escape me, nevertheless, and, as painful as it was to dwell on, hung on my conscience heavily. I felt myself in a quandary: Despite the initial difficulties of adjusting to the new environment, I had begun making an impact in my position at work. Within the few short months since I started, I had prepared a complete set of simplified overhaul instructions for all the hydraulic components of newly acquired British airplanes, easy for the local technicians to follow. I had gained the respect of my colleagues and seniors, and even learned a few words of Arabic. But could I carry on under the prevailing circumstances? I felt I had no right to subject my wife and child to a life of uncertainties.

I had been absorbed in these reflections as I walked along, when I was startled at the sudden appearance of a scruffy-looking young man a few paces ahead. He was standing snug, in a niche of some structure on the kerb—perhaps a kiosk, no longer in use, due to the strike—hiding, it seemed, from view of the soldiers in the square. He held a jackknife in one hand and rubbed the blade in the palm of the other in a honing motion. My heart leapt instinctively, and started pounding.

Words of wise counsel I had heard, or read, immediately came to mind and, having no time for hesitation, I instantly, consciously, put them to the test. 'Never look a barking or growling dog in the eye,' was one that I had often proved to be sound. Another was my uncle's frequent admonition to "walk like a soldier!"

I quickly stiffened my back and walked upright, shoulders squared, looking straight ahead, past the man, as though he weren't even there...my ear bursting the while with the thumping of my heart. I could read, in secondary vision as I passed by, the frustration of defeat in his face. He folded the knife with a grunt, put it in his pocket, and walked away, muttering.

Shots rang out as our vehicle rode past a stretch of shrubbery lining the shoulder at one section of the road to the airport, though the daily drive had, so far, been uneventful, despite the strike. A horse and its rider sporting a handgun suddenly emerged from the brush with a shuffle and galloped away through the fields into the distance where, the men said, there was a Palestinian refugee camp. Our driver got off to inspect for any damage, declared it negligible, then drove on.

The Prime Minister's mountain home must have been closer to the airport than to our apartment, for I could hear much more loudly, to my annoyance, the roll of the fighter planes and the ratatat of their guns strafing the village, periodically, all day.

There was a letter from the British Embassy in the mail that day.

Escape From Beirut

The letter from the British Embassy in Beirut advised that we pack the bare necessities we could carry, including wide-brim hats and sunglasses, and be ready for evacuation on short notice.

The summons for an emergency evacuation would rule out, as far as we were concerned, the proposal of returning to an already deteriorated state of affairs. It would mean, for us, a permanent departure. We would not want to come back. It would, furthermore, be too costly financially, and especially exhausting physically – with a two-year-old child to take care of.

I had only recently - perhaps three months before - moved from Cyprus with my wife and child, assumed my duties as Service Inspector with Middle East Airlines, settled in a new apartment in the suburbs (with a year's rent paid in advance - a customary practice of the land, we were informed), and had just completed furnishing it when civil unrest broke out in the country. A general strike was called by the "rebels"; stores and offices were closed, or carried on business behind closed doors; shopping for food became difficult and commuting to work dangerous. Ignorance of the language of the land (Arabic), above all, hampered communication and made us, newcomers, feel isolated and in the dark as to the why and the wherefore of the turmoil.

It was the Summer of 1958 and, as we later were to learn , Colonel Nasser of Egypt, who had become alienated from the West over the Suez crisis of 1956, and formed the United Arab Republic, in alliance with Syria, was now, apparently, trying to coerce Lebanon into joining the fold.

We reviewed our situation and weighed our prospects. Commuting to work had become difficult, let alone risky, and lately almost impossible. (Some of the men would take rides with a few who had cars. I had been urged to buy a car myself, and become independent. But I had only recently learned to drive – in the left lane, in Cyprus, a British colony – and would never be reconciled to right lane driving in the chaotic traffic of Beirut, where lane sides and traffic lights appeared to be held in disdain and were rarely obeyed. I was, also, not ready for another major expense at this stage of my employment.) The hardships and restrictions imposed upon our lives (not the least of which was the fact that we were strangers and did not speak the language of the land) had become intolerable. Stores and offices were kept closed in fearful compliance of the strike enforced by the rebels. Snipers took shots at people suspected of shopping or going to work. Transportation and other services, which at the best of times were scarce in the suburbs, had now become almost non-existent. Under these unbearable conditions, with my wife and child confined and stranded in the fourth-floor walk-up apartment, I too was now forced to stay at home. I had hinted as much at work, and had also intimated that, at times, I had even considered leaving the country.

Our predicament called for a quick resolution. The option of an emergency evacuation would be too costly, financially, and probably too exhausting, physically. We decided to sell or dispose of whatever we could – furnishings that we had bought only a few months before, as well as a whole year's rent paid in advance – at a sacrifice if necessary, and go … where? … back to Cyprus? The Cyprus hostilities had been the very cause of our flight to Beirut in the first place. And the present situation in our homeland – whose relinquishment we were now so agonizingly considering – was no more reassuring than it had been. It was perhaps even more dangerous now than Lebanon, in as much as the conflict had become further embroiled by the arousal of the Turkish community. Moreover, we could not dream of imposing ourselves upon the hospitality and welcome of relatives. For all we knew, their sense of permanence on the Island may itself have become shaken by the turmoil. As well, we could not expect any change in the employment situation to facilitate our resettlement, for which, we felt, we had lost the fervour. An inquiring call to a kinsman seemed to confirm our reserve.

A young, close relative had, of late, emigrated to Canada, having spent some time in Britain, and was now in the process of settling in Vancouver. However, though Canada might remain a remote option, we were not inclined to follow suit. The distance daunted us. We had not intended our departure from Cyprus to be a permanent goodbye.

We learned that another young relative who had been studying in Britain had his parents visiting him there as we spoke. They were the closest of kin, and would be more than willing to make arrangements for our initial accommodation in London. We realized that whatever move we were to make we would be stepping into the unknown and an uncertain future. That too was daunting. But Britain was, at least, closer to "home" and, though we had not been in Britain before, I surmised that we would be no strangers there, thanks to our knowledge of the language, our British citizenship, and my close association with British engineers in the workplace for some years in Cyprus.

All things considered, the scales tipped toward migrating to England. Our mind was made up. We must arrange for a passage to London. But first, liquidate as best and as fast as we could, our lease on the apartment, and all locally acquired furnishings.

We had hardly communicated our plans to acquaintances in the neighbourhood when a young couple came knocking. They were returning to their home country of Lebanon following the expiration of a teaching contract in Cyprus, and were thrilled to find all immediate necessities in a well-located, brand new apartment, and all at half price, to boot. That major concern so effortlessly taken care of, we now concentrated on a search for a shipping agent, and packing up for our journey.

The shop foreman, my colleague at the workplace, came calling and tried to dissuade us from leaving. He said the situation with the rebels could not continue the way it was. The Western Powers would not allow it. America already had battleships in the vicinity, and would, without a doubt, land troops any day now. He urged me to hang in just a little longer. Peace and normalcy would be restored soon. But it was too late. We were already committed on the transfer of the apartment and were in the process of packing and arranging for our passage.

Under the prevailing emergency conditions, with air travel endangered or suspended, our only choice was to make an exit by sea.

My inquiries led me to a shipping agent that had a vessel scheduled to depart within a week or two. That would allow us the opportunity to finish packing and be ready to board on the appointed day. We considered it a lucky break, in view of the emergency restraints, the scarcity of sailings and rumoured controls on travel. I found the agent's office in a part of town past the City Square, which was being patrolled by tanks. An aura of desolation and abandonment seemed to emanate from the place, whereas in normal times it would be buzzing with commerce and industry. Barricades of sandbags, here and there, blocked off some streets. The door opened stealthily to my knock; I was hastily ushered in and was asked whether anyone had followed me. I had hardly time to say no, when shots rang outside. The clerk immediately dropped himself flat on the floor and asked me to do the same. Finally, we were able to rise and I booked our passage - the last available space, in third class - in the only available room on board the S/S Aeolia, a Greek freighter/passenger steamship: Beirut to Marseilles, then by rail and ferry, via Paris and Dover to London - a journey that would take no less than two weeks.

The vessel had not yet arrived for me to see what I would be paying for. I was told first- and second-class accommodations were fully booked. A cabin with four bunk beds, in third class, the sole space remaining on board, was the only choice offered. Take it or leave it. There was no other option, except to wait for the next sailing, which luxury we could not afford. I had to take the offer so I booked our passage.

We boarded the ship on July 7, 1958. The dock was crammed with a multitude of passengers, many obviously fleeing the Middle East. My promising position with Mideast Aircraft Service Company had been short-lived – a little over three months. Our emotions, as we ascended the gangway, were a mixture of excitement in anticipation of our very first sea voyage – mixed with a tinge of trepidation the very thought implied; a sense of liberation from the bondage inflicted by the rebellion; and the sobering dread of having taken a blindfold step of finality in the dark.

Our first impression upon boarding and going through the

purser's office was quite elevating, however, and seemed to dispel any misgivings nagging our thoughts. We could not help but feel a sense of importance as smartly uniformed, clean-cut, courteous officers took our passports and put us through the registration process. Temporarily forgetting our worries, we were filled with hopeful anticipation of a pleasant, once-in-a-lifetime journey.

Then began our descent. We were guided down several flights of stairs to lower levels where the sky was no longer visible. With each drop down to a lower deck our hearts also sank a notch. Through a long, dimly lit corridor we were marched toward the fore end, then down to what seemed the very bottom of the ship – the third-class dining "salon." "Salon?" It should have had a different name. There seemed to be no ventilation. The air was hot and hard to breathe, and a suffocating smell of greasy food, emanating from the galley, permeated the area. Aside from two or three portholes, which could not be opened, there was hardly any décor to lighten the spirit. Walls of charcoal grey were on all sides and the steel floor seemed buckled in places.

A flight of narrow and steep stairs led us down to yet another deck, and we were shown to our "cabin" at the extreme fore end of the vessel, where the side of the hull tapered sharply toward the keel. It was a triangular-shaped space, measuring no more than six feet at the wider, entry end, and no longer than the length of the slender bunk beds that lined the two sides as you squeezed through the door. A peculiar whiff, suggestive of oily tools or rags having been previously kept there, greeted our nose as we entered the room. A pile of lifejackets had been randomly shoved under one of the bunks. The single porthole bobbed above and below the waterline in gentle undulations while at dock. At sea it shot up into the sky then dove below into dark, foamy froth.

At one point in the journey, crossing the Mediterranean northward, the sea was in a strange turmoil. Against an ominous, misty background that seemed to blend sky and horizon in a darkening, grey mass, mountainous "towers" of water, covering the whole surface of the visible ocean, rose heavenward and fell flat, in unending repetition, their crests exploding in the gale-force wind into fluid "bullets", battering and noisily bombarding the side of the ship. Our "cabin" shot up and dipped below in quick succession, violently swinging and rocking, all the while, from side to side. It became impossible and dangerous to remain in the cabin, knocking about from wall to wall, trapped in the torturous spiral of a mighty "corkscrew", with a two-year-old child to take care of, not to mention the agony of sea-sickness. The steward came at midnight and helped us to the dining salon where the vibration was claimed to be less pronounced. Groaning passengers were there, clinging to tables and other fixtures.

I recently learned the specific word that applies to the space of our confinement. It is called a "cuddy". The Random House Dictionary defines cuddy as a small cabin in the bow or stern of a vessel. It also means, according to the Dictionary, a stupid fellow.

Don't get me wrong! I am not complaining or apologizing. The little cuddy served its purpose very well, thank you very much. I feel honour-bound, however, to repeat: It was the last remaining space on the only available transport on our escape from revolution-bound Beirut in the Spring of 1958. There was nothing to do but accept what we could not change, look for positive aspects, and enjoy the trip as best we could.

The city of Beirut and the Lebanese mountains gradually disappeared, dancing on the horizon as in a mirage. The sea, the Blue Mediterranean, acquired a deeper, almost inky hue as the ship moved farther and farther away from land and made for Egypt in the south. On our starboard the sun slowly sank, aflame at the end of a golden highway paved over a shimmering sea. In the morning we woke to find the ship anchored in glassy waters off the city of Port Saïd.

Port Saïd

A motorboat, packed with a crowd of Egyptians, putt-putting in the cool of the early morning stillness, headed, at an imperceptible pace, from the shores of Port Saïd toward our ship. At length a multitude of peddlers and hawkers scrambled up the side of the vessel and, before the Egyptian sun had warmed to a scorching heat, started hurriedly making the rounds of all the decks, laden with armfuls of merchandise: leather goods, woven cloths, brassware, items of crafted wood inlaid with mother-of-pearl, and other trinkets and souvenirs.

A good-sized leather tote bag imprinted with Egyptian motifs interested us, mainly as a practical necessity for the trip, but also as a souvenir of the country. It was nothing fancy, such as the heavier, embossed leathers we had seen in Beirut; but large enough to carry our child's as well as our own daily necessities, yet compact enough not to be cumbersome on the trip.

The vendor, a young man in his twenties, placed the bag at our feet and gave us a lengthy sales pitch in Arabic, enhanced with generous gestures of his arms, and interspersed with an occasional "very good" as a verbal translation. We needed no persuasion but could not afford the initial asking price: twenty-five U.S. dollars, the favourite currency of exchange.

Haggling, a confirmed tradition in the Middle East in general, seems honed to an extreme dramatic art in the Arabic countries. Both parties in a transaction relish the opportunity to pit their skills against each other, as in a contest, and upon mutually satisfactory culmination of the tug-of-war they each come out the winner.

I was a reluctant participant in the performance. The vendor asked for my offer, but I would not risk offending the man with the low figure I thought I could afford. After all, we were not tourists hunting for souvenirs.

The man scaled his price down in five-dollar gradients, embarking at each drop, upon a long, angry tirade, and went into an agonizing confession of final concession, calling upon Allah as his witness. A gradient at a time he dropped his price, finally to five dollars and still would not give up.

I regretted having expressed an interest in the article at all, and almost wished that he would pack up and leave and find a better, more willing customer. How much profit would the poor man show for all his time and effort?

He was quiet now, but seemed angry and frustrated at the prospect of losing the battle. The whole game was spoiled before having reached a conclusion. The drama was interrupted without a denouement. He made as if to pack up and withdraw. Then, as a last-ditch effort, he suddenly placed the bag on my lap and, masking concession of defeat behind a frown and glaring eyes, asked, in an angry tone, what I could afford to pay. I said three dollars. Suddenly his face lit up into a victorious smile of satisfaction. He thanked me profusely and wished us the blessing of Allah for the rest of our journey.

Alexandria

Our ship, the S/S Aeolia, was the only vessel at dockside in Alexandria. Marine traffic calling at Egyptian ports had severely dwindled in the wake of the "Suez Crisis" of 1956: Antagonized by the United States and Britain over their refusal to finance the Country's proposed Aswan Dam Project, President Gamal Abdel Nasser had nationalized the Suez Canal, ostensibly as a source of revenue to pay for the massive undertaking. He had, moreover, soon after assuming power in 1954, entered into an arms deal and friendly relations with countries of the Soviet Bloc, as well as embracing a system of socialism in his native land.

But Nasser had not stopped there. Self-proclaimed leader of Arab nationalism, he had abolished the monarchy, sent King Farouk into exile; ruled invalid the long-rooted agreement whereby the British had concentrated a great number of armed forces in Egypt, and exacted a concession to have the troops evacuated within a specified short period of time.

The canal, built by the French, had been incorporated in Egypt, with Egyptian participation. Not long after its completion in 1869 the Egyptian Ottoman Governor sold his majority interest to the British who thus became principal shareholders in the Suez Canal Company.

Acclaimed as an indispensable global gateway that drastically shortened distances between continents, the waterway was declared neutral territory by a multi-national treaty signed in 1888. It guaranteed free passage to all in time of peace and war. A British military presence was sanctioned to defend the canal and maintain its neutrality. British troops had occupied Egypt in 1882, though nominally the country was under Ottoman sovereignty. In 1914, when Turkey sided with Germany in WWI, Egypt became a protectorate of Britain. Thus Britain had, in effect, ruled the country throughout the first half of the 20th Century, and by the early 1950's had some 80,000 troops stationed along the Suez Canal alone.

Nevertheless, international agreements notwithstanding, Nasser had now obtained a concession, no matter how extracted, for the removal of the troops. In compliance, therefore—though the Canal still ran under management of a joint British and French concern—all British defense forces had been duly evacuated at the time of Nasser's defiant, strong-arm takeover in July of 1956.

With a view to recapturing the waterway and preventing the hardships and obstacles to international shipping that were sure to be imposed by a totalitarian (and now unfriendly) regime, Britain and France, with an alibi provided by Israel, attacked Egypt. (The British government realized that it had been a mistake to accede to the evacuation of the troops. France, on the other hand, was faced with a revolt in her colony of Algeria, and hoped, somehow, to silence or neutralize Nasser whom she blamed for encouraging the rebels.) The attack, however, was strongly opposed by the United States and the United Nations, who viewed it as provoking Soviet intervention and threatening world peace. It was soon aborted, but not before the Egyptians had scuttled a vessel and blocked the seaway. Shipping had been diverted around the continent of Africa, avoiding and isolating Egypt, crippling her economy, and plunging Europe, to boot, into an alarming shortage of oil and other imports.

The "Crisis" was settled through United Nations arbitration, averting a global conflagration between rivals in the Cold War, but not without touching off a number of international repercussions, such as (a) the rise of Arab nationalism throughout the world and the shift of the Israeli-Palestinian dispute into an Israeli-Arab conflict; (b) the ruthless suppression of the closely-coincidental Hungarian Revolution by Khrushchev (whose vilification of Stalin had fanned the fervour for freedom in Eastern Europe in the first place) while the Western Powers were tangled in the sticky situation of their own creation; (c) the assumption of leadership by the U.S. in affairs of the oil-rich Middle East, stepping into the void of influence resulting from Britain's entanglement in the "Crisis;" and (d) the determination of European leaders to seriously pursue the concept of a European Union and aim for an independent and more effective voice in their own affairs, avoiding superpower interference.

〉〉〉

We had tied up at dawn and would set sail again around midnight. No peddlers invaded the vessel here. Rather, there seemed to be a tacit anticipation to have the passengers go ashore. Ours was not a crowd of vacationers, but any amount of money spent in town, it seemed, would be gratefully welcomed. The dockside plaza had a deserted appearance. A handful of men in civilian apparel ambled idly, gazing with expectant expressions, smiling at the passengers lined up along the ship's railing. There was, however, an entertainer—a man, kneeling on a mat, shuffling coconut shells, providing distraction for the onlookers.

Little by little an unhurried line of passengers trickled down the gangplank and almost hesitantly proceeded toward the customs building.

Could we follow suit? As we lingered by the gangway, with our two-year-old child in my arms, my wife, Alice, and I contemplated the temptation of celebrating our escape from Beirut with a brief sightseeing diversion. It would also be a respite from the stressful confinement of our miserable accommodation on board. As well, we would, for what it was worth, be stepping ashore, for the very first and...perhaps only time in our life, on the soil of this most distinguished land of antiquity. A sudden pain pierced my heart, as though at the sinking loss, beyond retrieval, of a priceless treasure. I had been an employee of airline companies, with the privilege of free travel that I had never used. That opportunity had now been lost, and who could tell if we would ever return to tread this path again and pick up the thread of our interrupted life.

In other considerations, we were also debating the wisdom of stepping off the ship at all. We would be entering a country that had recently alienated itself from the Western Powers, struck up a pact with the Soviet Union and embraced socialism. More worrying was the fact that we hailed from Cyprus and carried British passports. It had only been two years since Britain and France had waged an air attack on Egypt, with planes taking off from Cyprus. How would the Egyptians react to our presence? Could they, perhaps, detain us on some pretext, just for spite?

A couple and their young son, somewhat older than ourselves, who had apparently heard us talking, approached and greeted us in our native tongue. They were an Armenian family, the man a tailor, from Tehran, Iran, (traveling, obviously, in the luxury of First Class) and though they spoke the eastern dialect of the language, we had little difficulty communicating. They too had been thinking of going ashore, and encouraged us to join them. Their suggestion that we could hire a horse-drawn carriage on a sightseeing tour and reduce the expense by sharing the fare seemed to be the stimulus we needed.

Cameras slung over shoulders we walked to the customs shed. Inside, probably prompted by what he had observed in the activity ahead in the lineup, our companion stealthily stuffed his camera and a near-bursting wallet into the narrow pockets of a light jacket he wore. He thought it wiser, apparently, not to declare them, and considered his shrewdness justified when we came through at the other end without a hassle—even though my declaration of camera and cash had produced no adverse effect.

We had, naturally, made no previous study of noteworthy sights to see nor had we been concerned about details of our itinerary. The planning of our brief, casual ride had been left entirely to the judgment of our coachman-guide. He deemed the Alexandria palace of the deposed King Farouk to be the most appropriate limited-time, single-destination tour, and that is where we headed. The ancient monuments of Egypt would remain a remote and, possibly, inaccessible dream. Yet in Alexandria we would at least be stepping on Egyptian soil, albeit for a few short hours.

Alexander the Great, as the name implies, founded the City in 331BC, then went on after further conquest. Sadly, the celebrated Greek Ruler did not live to return for a second look at his handiwork.

Referred to by coveting monarchs as the "shining pearl of the Mediterranean," Alexandria remained the capital city of Egypt until the Muslim, or Arab occupation in AD641. Other aspirants after empire in the interval, such as the Romans, Persians, and Byzantines, invaded Egypt and held Alexandria for varying periods of time.

Napoleon's troops stormed the city in 1798, followed by the British entry in 1801. Alexandria has, ever since, boasted a cosmopolitan population, with large communities of Greek, Italian, Jewish and other expatriate minorities.

Many Armenians—survivors of the Genocide and the dispossessed of their usurped native land—have also made their home in Alexandria, as well as Cairo since the early years of the 20th Century, in the aftermath of WWI. Egypt became one of the major centres in the region where a few dreamers among the survivors—teachers, poets, college graduates—who had clung to an unfading vision of hope, took up the torch and put their shoulders to the work of salvaging the endangered culture, the history, and a generation from being totally wiped out (when all known intellectuals, artists, teachers and clergy of the homeland and of Constantinople had been rounded up and summarily murdered.)

Moreover, prior to that barbaric onslaught on the nation, there had been a prosperous Armenian presence in Cairo and Alexandria that counted wealthy leaders of commerce and industry, as well as high-ranking members of government in the Ottoman administration of Egypt. Among the latter the name of Boghos Nubar Pasha is held in great regard and gratitude. Son of a finance and foreign minister of Egypt, Boghos, himself once the director of the Egyptian State Railways, lent his initiative to the creation of the "Armenian Legion," a corps of volunteers gathered from the Diaspora in Europe and the Americas, to serve under the French colours in the campaign against Turkey.

Upon the conclusion of the war—with Turkey defeated—when Armenian historic territories had been liberated—with the participation of the Volunteers in the common cause—Boghos Pasha worked tirelessly, expending all his influence and energy at the Paris Peace Conference, as well as constantly shuttling between Paris and London, in urgent pursuit of the promised official recognition of Armenian liberation and independence, and the proposed American mandate over Armenia.

All to no avail; caught in the confusion of the rising adverse international conditions in the prolonged wavering interim, the victorious nations were blinded to the possibility of any advantage in awarding justice to a potential though smaller ally. Turning also a deaf ear to the popular outcry of a multitude of prominent international voices from Europe and America clamouring for the long-hoped-for "justice for Armenia," they took the path of seeming economic and strategic gain, and allowed the defeated perpetrator the opportunity to resume and carry out to the end its original genocidal objective.

Of the wealthy magnates of industry, the memory of two tobacco baron brothers of Cairo is still cherished today for the technical and educational institute they established, on vast grounds, in the then British Colony of Cyprus, where thousands of Armenian orphans and deserving poor have received their training and scholarship and gone to become leaders in their respective communities in the Diaspora.

❧ ❧ ❧

The route to and from King Farouk's palace, which happened to be located in an outlying desert district, afforded us no glimpse of the Big City. Not quite palatial in appearance, the residence was described as one of the king's summer retreats where, it was rumoured, he entertained his mistresses. Its park-like setting may have been impressive when in use, but it appeared run down and neglected, due, likely, to the scarcity of water. Of the interior of the palace, the gold-plated plumbing—gone dry—was a sad reminder of a not-too-long-past decadence.

Our brief excursion of the day thus yielded little of Alexandria to speak of. But, betraying the general situation in Egypt, the lack of vehicular traffic and the absence of tourists seemed significant; though, admittedly, tourists would be more likely to frequent the more popular archaeological sites of the country.

One scene, observed on our way back, however, has left a lasting impression: As our carriage plied its course in the sleepy heat of the midday sun, a lumpish object, that clearly did not belong in the landscape of the well-groomed, wide boulevard, came obtrusively into view at a distance. It broke the monotony of the all-pervading colour of the sand that had seemed to deepen the drowsiness of the hour. Heaped under one of the tall date palms lining the sides of the highway that ran straight as an arrow for miles through desert country, was what at closer range appeared like a young fellah, wearing dark glasses, resting where the crown of the palm's branches cast its shade directly below, surrounding the slender trunk.

When we came close enough for a clearer view of the solitary figure stretched on the roadside, it became apparent that what he wore on his face were not sunglasses, but swarms of black flies covering his eyes in a solid mass. By whatever means, and for whatever purpose the poor wretch had found himself where he lay, it had been only to languish in neglected solitude, miles from human habitation. He lay motionless, dead to the world, unacknowledged by the driver, eliciting a subdued gasp from the passengers in the carriage, as the vehicle drove past in silence, with even the clip-clop of the ponies' hooves muffled in the sound-absorbing vastness of the desert sand, of which a fine cushioning film had also settled on the paved highway.

We had lunch—a serving of delicious lamb shish kebab—under a thatched awning at a rustic restaurant by the sea, where for the first time we were among a small crowd of people. Uncharacteristic of the occasion or the setting, conversation at the tables seemed to be cautiously subdued, which made us surmise that perhaps the rest of the diners were also passengers from our ship.

Our compatriot companion from Iran, promising to reimburse me, asked me to pay for the meal, since he hadn't declared his money and didn't want the driver, who also ate with us, to see it. On our return to the ship I also paid the driver.

As we entered and walked through the customs-house I noticed the driver approach a couple of officials and whisper to them briefly. Whereupon the officers arrested our friend, the Armenian tailor from Tehran, and led him through a door, leaving his wife and son frightened, and us shaken, but not surprised.

Northward to Greece

Our excursion in Alexandria had ended on a sour note. I kept an eye for our compatriot from Tehran while we spent the rest of the daylight hours strolling in the open on the promenade deck, but did not see him come back on board by suppertime when we had to retire to the confinement of our quarters down below. I surmised that he would have paid a penalty and been released from custody, and that he would not come looking for me, in Third Class, to pay his share of our expenses of the tour. On the other hand, I probably would have difficulty tracing him, in First Class, since I didn't know his full name and could not even remember his first. I would have to take the initiative, I concluded, and use the next opportunity to confront him where he might be relaxing in a deck chair on an upper floor.

The ship set sail northward for Piraeus around midnight, hardly drawing attention to the stir, its gentle motion in glassy waters lulling us, rather, into deep sleep—but for a nagging thought of having been cheated of indispensable cash by a stranger we shouldn't have trusted.

We must have been in motion for perhaps two hours on the journey when the ship's smooth course began to get ruffled. It seemed as if we were heading into rough weather. It started with a gradual increase in the range of the bow's rise and fall. And soon, the almost-imperceptible gliding undulation of the ship began to feel more like a ride over an interminable chain of rolling billows, dipping and soaring, heaving and rocking at a rapid pace. Before long, it had become a wild and shaky seesaw, making it all but impossible to hang on to our positions in the bunks. Our cabin, in the very front end of the hull, would tear skyward, like a runaway rocket, then plunge hurtling down, well below the waterline, churning our stomachs on its way as in a sickening roller coaster. The ship's structure creaked and groaned with each stroke, while heavy volleys of what sounded like hailstones pelted the side of the hull in mighty gusts of howling wind. The pace of the seesaw accelerated to an alarming degree, and strange side forces, it seemed, began adding a wobbly tremor to the teetering totter.

Voices could be heard outside our cabin, and soon the steward came knocking and helped us, with our two-and-a-half-year-old son, to the dining hall. Centrally located, the hall was deemed and truly proved to be less susceptible to the extremes of the bounce. A small crowd of bewildered-looking passengers, already gathered there, sat in pyjamas or housecoats, on benches along the wall, quietly moaning. One or two knelt doubled up on the floor, pressing their stomachs. A few, perhaps catching up on sleep, rested their heads on their elbows at the large common dining table. Hardly any appeared to be in deep agony of seasickness. The air in the dining hall, engulfed in strong smells emanating from the open kitchen, was hot and hard to breathe.

It was our second night at sea, and the gathering over a shared predicament provided an occasion to meet some of our fellow passengers: There were two young women, each with a daughter of four or five, escaping home to Barcelona. Their husbands, flamenco guitarists both, had remained behind to fulfill their contracts with a luxury hotel in Beirut. An elderly man and his wife, ethnic Greeks from Alexandria, had packed their essential possessions in one suitcase and were escaping Nasser's Egypt. The husband had long been a productive manufacturer of footwear, until Nasser had decided to nationalize all businesses. They had decided to spend their retirement in Greece. They expressed no complaint. Patience seemed to be their motto. The man didn't speak much. The woman, too, was mostly quiet, but kept exhorting the moaning younger folk to have patience.

"Patience, mon enfant, patience," she kept repeating calmly, in French, the lingua franca in the region of her time, her snow-white hair and unruffled, smooth face commanding the respect her words inspired.

The fury of the sea raged on at daybreak. The pattern of reaction it transmitted into the ship's course had not changed. I was curious to know what kind of wave or marine upheaval would impose the subtle yet unsettling sideways tremor, or 'wobble' we had been experiencing in our cabin at the fore end of the hull, in addition to the violent up-and-down bounce. I also wanted to know whether it had been raining all night, or whether hailstones had truly been pelting the side of the ship—in the middle of summer, in the Mediterranean? I went up into the superstructure to the level of the promenade deck and watched the scene through the glass protection. It was a rare and exciting sight and my good fortune to witness. I had not been at sea before, though had seen movies of ships being tossed about in stormy seas, battling giant waves, but could never have imagined the surface of the ocean capable of breaking up into such chaotic, convulsive agitation as had been whipping us about all night.

There were no undulating or rolling waves of any size or description. Our ship, though seesawing up-and-down, was not rolling. The weather was clear and the sun shone brightly. The sea, a sun-drenched panorama as far in all directions as the eye could see, was feverishly astir with thousands upon thousands of giant, crystalline ghosts, dancing a frenzied dance of madmen, leaping skyward, as though intent on leaving their watery world: massive pillars or towers, churned out of water, popping out of the surface unexpectedly, gushing upward to great heights, glistening in the sun for a brief moment, then being sucked back into the surface without a stir, as though they had never been there. But not before the mighty East Wind (the 'levanter?') had captured their sparkling crowns of a dozen crystal globes and flung them into the roiling splash and spray, or thrust them toward a moving target, bombarding the side of our ship, crashing on the hull like a ton of cannonballs.

By breakfast time the temper of the sea had all but spent itself. The wind had died down, the sea was calm again, and peace and tranquility prevailed. Soon after breakfast the whole crowd of passengers on our level was out strolling on the promenade deck, enjoying the sunshine and fresh air, exchanging friendly smiles with each other, happy to have survived, as though set free from the bondage of prison.

The "promenade deck," we soon learned, was no seaside mall. Although it provided an area for us to walk about and stretch our legs in the open air, it was not free from impediments; it apparently also served as partial cargo deck and even included a hatch that covered a hold for passengers' freight. As well, our vessel, a steamship, was also equipped with deck gear that functioned with steam power, we painfully learned when our son, who had been playing with the other, newly-discovered children, sat for a moment on a hatch cover and jumped screaming, having burned the back of his leg on a steam conduit that ran alongside.

Photos

Jerry in the center, the youngest son of Genocide Survivors, Mesrob and Sirarpi (née Levonian) Shekerdemian.

With his older brothers Vahé and Kaloust c.1935

With his sport bike. Jerry was one of the first people on the Island to have a sport bike, which he even rode from Limassol to Nicoscia (84kms), considered a long distance by car at the time.

With Alice and Haig, Nicoscia, Cyprus.

With son Haig in 1957.

With his family 6 years after immigrating to Vancouver, Canada, 1965. Son Haig, Jerry, 3-year-old-daughter Linda, and beloved wife Alice.

In Sweden 1967, to train at Hagglunds Headquarters as a Marine Crane Specialist.

The Renaissance Man.

Immigration

Coming Into The Unknown
The Importance of Where You Come From

The mention of my birthplace, Cyprus, may remind some Canadians—if the memory of it is not altogether wiped away from their minds—of our peace-keeping years in a small island republic, its population engulfed in ethnic conflict. Older people may even remember the guerrilla warfare, frequently reported in the media of the time, which the majority element of the population waged against the British administration, in the late 1950's, when the Island was still a British colony. No particular emotion may be aroused by the remembrance among Canadians, except perhaps in our peace-keeping soldiers who may think it a pity that a beautiful island, reputed to be the mythical birthplace of Aphrodite, the Greek goddess of beauty and love, should be so charged with hatred as to depend on an army of foreign soldiers to keep the peace among the populace.

The past, one might think, is hardly remembered today when European and British tourists by the millions throng the Mediterranean Island's warm beaches, cool mountains and ancient monuments, in all seasons of the year. (And yet, flags of rival communities across a no-man's-land in a divided country, and walls of sandbags blocking streets in the capital city, are grim reminders of an unresolved conflict, despite a half-century of peacekeeping action by the United Nations. Hostilities between the warring factions, Greeks and Turks, culminated in an invasion and occupation of half the island by Turkey.)

Older Britons, on the other hand, may recall the years of upheaval and terror, and how, towards the end, the nationalist movement deteriorated into senseless murder of British civilians, including women, in city streets. This turn of events naturally bred intense hatred and justified anger in the British public against anyone and anything from Cyprus. It was in this hostile atmosphere that I found myself arriving in London with my wife and child, without a job, in June 1958, my career in aircraft engineering having been cut short as a result of the foolhardiness of a misguided fanatic who succeeded in blowing a hole in a civilian passenger plane.

I called on the secretary of the Society of Licensed Aircraft Engineers, of which I was a member. He was a tall, courteous man of impressive presence. He asked about the origin of my name. "Ah!" he said, with a pleasant smile. "My mother also is Armenian." The Society was not a trade union or employment agency, but the secretary gave me some useful advice and warned that I might experience difficulties.

Prejudice, understandably, prevailed. Airline companies in particular would rather not take a risk. Most I applied to had no openings, but politely promised to keep my application "on file." British European Airways, a coveted company to work for, advertised a vacancy in my exact line of experience. The personnel manager, a Scotsman with a heavy accent, approved my qualifications. "It seems that we have finally found someone to fill the position," he said, with a sigh of satisfaction. Then, after some hesitation, "Let me send you down to the foreman," he suggested, "and get his opinion as well."

The foreman, a stern, unsmiling, military type, asked me many questions and listened without comment. He made notes on my application form, replaced it in the envelope and handed it to me to return to the office.

"It sounds all right," was the personnel manager's immediate comment, but there was a hint of uncertainty in his expression. "'Technically satisfactory,'" he read from the foreman's notes. "I don't understand," he said, frowning. "He's heavily underlined 'Technically.' What does he mean? I better call him and find out." His only response, as he listened to the foreman on the telephone, was, "I see...I see...I see." Then, turning to me, "It looks like we'll have to let you know by mail," he said.

I did not have to be told the gist of his conversation with the foreman. Several previous applications for work and other experiences had prepared me for the nature of the response. Having met with disappointment in the aircraft industry I had tried my chances in the field of general machinery. Following a satisfactory interview, one machine shop hired me. The manager bade me start work on the following Monday. I thanked him and was on my way out, when, on a sudden impulse, apparently prompted by my accent, "By the way," he said; "I didn't ask you. Where do you come from?" Upon hearing Cyprus, his reaction was, "Oh, my God! Well," he said, "it's too late now. I've already hired you. But the first sign of trouble, and out you go!"

There would have been no occasion to justify the man's fears, which I could understand. I did not try to explain. I cursed my lot, and never went back to be engaged under a cloud of suspicion.

My birthplace, it seemed, was no matter for concern where I next applied for work. I was hired as fitter's assistant in the machine shop of the "X" appliance factory near London. Though its distance, at the start, and the shift work it entailed, presented inconveniences (especially to my wife and two-year-old child, who were confined to a single "furnished" room hastily rented by a young relative studying in London) and I considered it a compromise, yet it was a fairly interesting position, in that it offered new challenges to my limited experience in machine shop practice. Above all, it provided a livelihood.

My immediate superiors on the job were three machine fitters responsible for maintenance of the hydraulic die-cast presses. I alternated among them on three shifts. I remember few traits and hardly any details of my morning and afternoon shift leaders. The one of the morning shift was a small, bespectacled elderly man who had lived all his life in the suburb where the factory was located, but had never been to London proper, and never set eyes on the historic, fascinating sights of the Great City.

The man's omission was not unusual, of course, nor to be scoffed at. Native dwellers of the land often overlook their historic or natural heritage, with the ill-considered assumption that the opportunity will present itself "some day." I have found, in my own experience, that circumstances occasionally so dictate. I had lived all my life in a small island—smaller in area, certainly, than the expanse of Greater London itself—yet had seen or visited but few of the sites where conquerors and saints, ancient and more recent, from near and far had trod, their surviving monuments now crumbling walls, gaping arches, and toppled columns of marble. And further, I, who, as an employee of an airline company operating in the Middle East, had been privileged to travel free of charge, yet never took advantage of the benefit, and forever fled the region without having visited any of the great cities of Athens, Constantinople, Jerusalem, Baghdad or Cairo.

The afternoon shift leader was a middle-aged man who spoke in what I surmised was a regional dialect. He was a quiet man and did not fancy making much idle talk. I soon learned to muddle through his accent as well as vocabulary, and we got along well.

The youngest of the fitters I was assigned to appeared to be of somewhat misguided ambition, bent on getting ahead in life by outwitting the powers that provided him with a living. He had managed to buy himself a small, much-used car and always drove to work, happy to do the night shift on a regular basis—for a reason, I found out in time. The factory was mostly empty and quiet at night, except for the shift of the die-cast press operators on the ground floor. We, of the maintenance staff, though stationed in the machine shop on the third floor, made our regular rounds through the sweltering foundry and were, when occasion arose, called on to inspect or rectify some problem that involved hydraulics, our "expertise."

My superior of the night shift often extended our route beyond the regular beat and paid a visit to the locked stock room to which he had a key. (We had to have access in case of any requirements.) He would ask me to wait outside while he went in to "check a few things." I once peeked in and saw that he had lowered the top part of his coveralls and was wrapping his body with yards and yards of green felt material—the type used on billiard tables—which he kept pulling and unwinding from a big bolt that sat on the floor. I also learned where he spent his time when he sometimes went on the beat by himself and disappeared for an hour or more. He had discovered an isolated spot on the top landing of a grated steel stairway where he would take a snooze when things were quiet and the boring hours of the night dragged on. The stairwell lay in the path of a stream of warm air that wafted up the shaft, emanating from some vent in the boiler room down below. On one sleepy occasion, induced by the same drowsy hours of the night, I myself enjoyed a catnap there, courtesy of my leader. I lay on the rough, serrated grate of the landing, and quickly drifted into a blissful state of oblivion, unburdened of an ever-haunting past of dashed hopes; heedless to the phantom of a looming bleak future; lulled, nay, hypnotized by the ceaseless hum, or drone, like that of a bagpipe, that seems to be inherent to all factories; cradled in the caressing embrace of the warm updraft; transported, in reverie, to a familiar Mediterranean beach of sun-baked, surf-swept sand, the jagged grate a goose-down cushion on my back.

He had allowed me a glimpse of his unlawful exploits, but my leader of the night shift showed no sign of regret for having done so. On the contrary, he seemed emboldened to take me along on his surveillance rounds, and even reckless enough to let me in further on his ingenious method of smuggling his loot. Often, he would go on his walks through the die-cast shop when the press operators had gone for tea and the place was virtually abandoned. The workers left useful tools lying around, he said, and looked for things he could easily hide on his person. He once was elated when he saw a small electric drill someone had left on the floor, presumably on a job interrupted, to be resumed after tea. He chopped off the wire with a pair of side-cutters he carried, and slipped the drill in his ample coverall's pocket. I asked him how he could safely pass through security on his way out at the gate. He said he had built a secret compartment under the floor of his car, which he always parked at a dark spot in the yard.

I felt a certain uneasiness about my reluctantly gained knowledge of my shift leader's secret life. Why was he being so open, almost boastful, about it? Did he not care that I could report him? Perhaps he hoped to manipulate me into an accomplice by weaving a web I would be trapped in. Or—and the thought was even more troubling—

was he preparing a scapegoat, in case of exposure?

❯❯❯

The technology of hydraulics had made great progress in all branches of industry, and yet no standard graphic rendering of its specific applications had been devised as a tool to aid engineers design systems or technicians trace faults. A case in point presented itself at the factory where a brand-new die-cast press was being installed when I began my employment there. When installation was completed the machine malfunctioned and did not serve its purpose for many weeks. The manufacturer's technicians and engineers came and went, stared at it helplessly day after day, switched the machine on and off, put it through trial runs, again and again, taking shots in the dark, and then, finally, after many days, hit upon the culprit, which turned out to be a regulator valve that had been installed in reverse.

A method of diagrammatic portrayal of hydraulic systems, using an array of symbols representing every conceivable component was developed and universally adopted by industry in the ensuing years, facilitating the work of the design engineer as well as that of the field technician. But this breakthrough was to impact industry several years in the future. In the meantime, at the factory, whenever any of the presses broke down, fitters—not technicians, but fitters—were called in on the job, and it resulted in a tremendous amount of down time while attempts were made to trace the problem, the faulty component removed, sent out for repair, or a replacement ordered, while the machine sat idle for days.

It occurred to me, watching the process, that if the Company were to adopt a system of "progressive maintenance"—which had always been in use in the aircraft industry, and with which I had become familiar in my previous incarnation—a great deal of down-time would be avoided, the department would function more efficiently, and a lot of money would be saved. (Airlines cannot afford to wait for a functional failure before "attempting" a remedy.) If this idea were adapted to the present "industrial" situation, I thought, it would serve a similar purpose in forestalling costly breakdowns. I put my ideas on paper and dropped it in the "Suggestions Box" that hung beside the Chief Engineer's office door, in our Department.

I was summoned to the Chief's office in due course. He showed obvious interest in the proposals and seemed somewhat amused, I thought, that the presenter was a shy young man with a foreign accent and a strange, unpronounceable name—a recently engaged junior employee, besides.

The adoption of the program would initially call for a spare set of components for every machine. A schedule would have to be drawn up and a time period of serviceability assigned to each part. Upon the termination of its assigned service life, the unit would be replaced with a new or reconditioned one. And this process would be an ongoing cycle, so that no machine would ever be encumbered with a time-expired component. This procedure would, thus, theoretically, eliminate the risk of unexpected breakdowns during critical times of operation. The "used" or "expired" components, meantime, would be sent to the manufacturers or a reliable repair shop, reconditioned and replaced in stock.

Toward the end of our meeting the Chief Engineer had assumed a thoughtful expression and a somewhat indifferent attitude. The interest he had shown in the beginning appeared to have waned. The program might work for airlines, he said, but didn't think it practical in the manufacturing industry.

Sometime shortly after my meeting with the Chief Engineer I began sensing a concerted effort on the part of Management to make my stay in the Company uncomfortable. The foreman called me to his office more than once and made vague allegations of not having the Company's interest at heart. I expressed surprise and wanted to know of any specific offence. There was none, in particular; just that I seemed to have lost interest in the Company's welfare, which claim surprised me even more.

But what had brought about this unexpected attitude? Something must have occurred, it seemed to me, that made Management wish me gone; something that prompted them to, unobtrusively, quietly, nudge me out. If there had been real cause for complaint I would be called to answer questions and dismissed, without a doubt. Had my night-shift charge-hand been trying to cover up his own crime by planting false seeds of suspicion against me? But then, if believed, that would be a chargeable offence deserving investigation, and reason for dismissal. There was no suggestion of that.

There must be a more subtle reason, I thought, baffled, why Management would want me to disappear—without a fight.

In an effort to find an answer I began reviewing my position and relationship among co-workers—machinists, electricians and other specialists—with whom we shared the machine shop, as a base or workshop, during my daytime shifts. I met them in the shop at tea breaks, and during lunch in the cafeteria. I had known that the English regarded their tea as almost a sacred ritual. My observation at the factory seemed to confirm my belief. It was a quiet period. Conversation was subdued, and everyone seemed absorbed reading, a newspaper or a book, while relaxing with tea and perhaps a biscuit or a sandwich. I had also observed that, along with his tea, the Englishman is also dedicated to his newspaper. Most of the men read the Daily Mirror, or another similar tabloid. The paper I took to work, to the men's unspoken curiosity, I think, was the Daily Telegraph—and it wasn't the daily news I cared about. (I once picked up a Penguin paperback that had been lying, seemingly neglected, on one of the workbenches. It turned out to be an autobiographical memoir/essay by George Moore, Irish man of letters. I quickly became so engrossed in it, and read with such rapt interest that I must have caught one man's notice. I heard him tell another, sitting nearby—who, I believe, was the original owner of the book—that he had tried reading it himself, but found it so boring and beyond his grasp that he couldn't bear more than a page or two of it. "What does he find so interesting?" I heard him say; "and he's not even English." "Well, that's right," the other explained, "he's an intellectual." Flattering though the comment was, it was also humbling, in that, it made me painfully conscious of how lacking I was in proper education.)

Based on my association with coworkers, I had come to regain my high regard of the Englishman's sense of reserve and decency. Though in contacts outside I had been made to feel guilty concerning the situation in Cyprus, and despite the fact that the papers carried sensational headlines with reference to the crisis almost every day, the men at the factory never ever mentioned it, though they knew where I came from, and I was made to feel no different from them. On the other hand, although I was satisfied that the discontent expressed by the foreman, such as it was, had not originated with the working staff, I now, to my chagrin, found myself having misgivings that it may, in all likelihood, have been contrived at the Management level, though my night shift leader's behavior still nibbled in the depths of my thoughts.

In my early days of employment with the airline company in Cyprus, one of the first chores I was assigned as an apprentice in the component shop was to restore to spreadable consistency small tins of gasket cement that had hardened in storage. The method I was shown to follow appeared rather primitive: I would add a few squirts of deicer alcohol as the thinning medium and, with a slim tool through the screw-top neck of the can, stir the stuff until a density of heavy molasses was achieved. I have always had great patience with work that is worth doing and strive to do it well, though it may take a long time. But this procedure seemed silly, to say the least, and I found it extremely boring. After giving it some thought, I fabricated a special tool, consisting of a tiny wheel, or propeller, attached to the end of a slender machine screw. Clamped into the chuck of a drill press, it became a power tool and cut down the time that it had taken to do the job from many hours of manual tedium to minutes operating the control lever. When my superior, who was a Scotsman, saw what I had made, he said if I had been in Britain, the company I would be working for would reward me for the invention, for the time-saving idea that it was. Well, I wasn't in Britain, and I wasn't rewarded. Nor did I think of exploiting the idea for gain in any way. It never occurred to me, and I wouldn't know how to go about it. But someone else must have patented it, some years later. If you want to see the idea in use, next time you notice a house being painted, find out how the craftsman mixes his bucket of paint.

The suggestions I had given the Chief Engineer at the factory were not a mechanical invention, but they were an idea that would help avoid countless hours of wasted time, and, I was convinced, save the Company a great deal of money. It should therefore deserve a reward. But if a sense of guilt or inadequacy could be instilled into my consciousness, as the foreman had attempted to do, and have me bid farewell without a fuss, then...the idea could be claimed by... the Chief Engineer himself? He had already tried to discourage me by declaring the idea to be impractical for industrial use, though I was sure he had shown genuine interest at first.

Had I decided to put up a fight for what I considered to be my claim, how would I go about it? Complain to the trade union, or some Government agency? I didn't know whom, where or how to contact them, or even who the shop steward was. And what would I tell them? That the Chief Engineer had stolen my idea? Preposterous! He had done no such thing. Not yet, that I could prove, anyway. He had simply rejected my idea. That was his prerogative. Who could tell what he would do in the near or far future? I wouldn't wait around to find out.

Maybe the foreman was right. Maybe I was losing interest in the Company. Homesickness may have been setting in. Perhaps nostalgia, more than homesickness. The last position I had held (under sunnier skies) was that of Shop Inspector, with Middle East Airlines in Beirut. In the few short months that I had been with them — before political turmoil had necessitated my hasty departure — I had prepared a full set of overhaul schedules for every component of the hydraulic system in a newly purchased British airplane. My interest in writing too, besides my technical skills, had thus found an outlet of some kind. In my capacity of Shop Inspector, I had been licensed to certify components for airworthiness. I could also amply provide for my family. My job at the factory was no substitute, and showed no possibility of any degree of compensation. Though more than a year had since elapsed, my licence as well as my membership in the Society of Licenced Aircraft Engineers were still valid, and I still received the Society's periodic communications.

But nostalgia could not feed my family. The further pursuit of my lost love would be frustrating and could prove disappointing and economically damaging. I had also ruled out going back to

Beirut, even though the Airline's Personnel department tracked me in London and asked me to consider returning, now that the "Americans had landed, the revolution had died down, and things were even better than before." I knew my wife would not be happy there, but neither would I; and Beirut's chaotic traffic was the least of my dreads.

To outgrow the pangs of homesickness is, doubtless, a validation of the maturing process, I kept telling myself, even though I knew that I would forever regret having left my loved ones in Cyprus without a parting farewell. I also knew that I would cherish forever memories of familiar places, faces and experiences that marked my growing years. But life must go forward, though the path we have trod may glow in the setting sun, and the road ahead blur in the gloom of the twilight before sunrise.

What, then, was my option? I would stay in London, where I could pursue my long-held aspiration of becoming a writer, while attending school, part time, to make up for my deficient education. But I learned that it had been a dream, an inspired dream, nevertheless, whose accomplishment demanded an unencumbered, dogged and tireless campaign; and I was awakened to the done deed that in my youthful, starry-eyed wisdom I had misread the road signs, and taken the turn that filled my life, too soon, with priorities that superceded the dream.

What remained to be done? Should I probe the source of the foreman's reproof; or the Chief Engineer's intentions of exploiting my suggestions? Should I care? I was in no position to yield to that egocentric vanity, or to thrust my family into the futile grind.

A member of my wife's family had immigrated to Canada and beckoned.

The future would be no less uncertain than it already was, and it would be much farther from "home," but the adventure of a fresh beginning in a new, hopefully unbiased country challenged.

I opted for Canada.

London Drizzle

Harutune Kasparian—Harry, as he was conveniently nicknamed in the workplace—waited alone in the early morning drizzle at the bus stop outside the factory in the London suburb where he had found work.

The job was not strictly in his line of experience. He had hoped it would be a temporary arrangement. But judging by the cautious welcome he had encountered at prospective employers' interviews, he could tell he was in for some uphill, even hopeless struggle. The way they regarded him it was as if he were a marked man. He was branded, he felt, through no fault of his own. How could he make them understand?

His name was foreign and difficult for the English to pronounce. But that didn't inconvenience anyone. Even if he changed his name it would make no difference. They called him Harry at work and he could get by with that. The problem was not his name.

The problem was his homeland, his insignificant little island of a birthplace: Cyprus, a British colony, in the far corner of the Mediterranean Sea; historically Greek, where nationalist segments of the majority native population had been in rebellion against British rule for the past several years. The conflict had become ugly and violent since its outbreak in the spring of 1955. Guerrilla warfare was waged on the mountains. Shootings and clashes took place in towns and villages. Curfews were imposed and searches carried out. A special constabulary of Turkish conscripts manned prison camps filled with Greek students. Hideous tortures of female detainees were rumoured. Horrible atrocities, committed on both sides, were frequently reported in the British press and promptly aired on radio. Pictures of black-robed churchmen, alleged to be leaders of the "terrorist" revolt, appeared regularly on television, on front pages of tabloids and periodicals.

The British were attached to their dailies, Harry had observed. They read them in trains and buses and carried them to their workplace.

Surely, he presumed, his workmates had read the latest shocking news. The public was up in arms over the recent cold-blooded shooting of a civilian Englishwoman while she shopped on a Cyprus street.

If the men at work ever discussed the Cyprus excesses among themselves, Harry had not become aware of it. They treated him, in the shop or the cafeteria, with unaffected civility, even friendliness. He was amazed at their reserve and marveled at their restraint. In the region of the world where he came from people customarily vented their agitation and displeasure over even lesser issues in vociferous arguments, huddled on street corners or in coffee shops.

And yet this latest murder had revolted and filled British citizens with disgust, suspicion and hatred against even the name of the "cursed" Island. That's where Harry was born. That's where he came from. He could not change or hide that.

The problem was also the nature of work he was seeking. Official documents in his résumé defined him as a "Licenced Aircraft Engineer." Compelled by the necessity to make up for an inadequate formal schooling (which had been disrupted during the War years), he had embarked on a fumbling, self-driven endeavour to improve his English by reading works of literature. Then, through apprenticeship and the help of correspondence courses, he had qualified for an aircraft inspector's licence. The establishment of an airline company and maintenance facility in Cyprus had provided the initial opening for employment as well as the opportunity for advancement. He married, settled in a comfortable apartment in a suburb and kept on with his studies for additional categories of his license.

Harry's enjoyment of the benefits of his promotion was short-lived.

An ill-advised fanatic placed a bomb in one of the Company's planes. As a repercussion of that reckless, self-ruinous attack, all local employees were barred from the airport. When hopes for an end of the rebellion were dashed, prospects of aviation's future in Cyprus also foundered, and the men—including Harry—were finally all let go.

An airline company based in Lebanon, a country deemed to be politically more stable in the region, began to show signs of gaining prominence in the fields of both air transport and aircraft service and repairs. Harry secured a position as "Shop Inspector" with the company and moved, with his wife and two-year-old child, in early spring of 1958, to nearby Beirut, a half hour's flight from Cyprus.

But soon signs of an ill-defined discontent that had, apparently, long lain dormant throughout the whole Middle East, began bubbling to the surface, like a fermenting brew gone sour.

Harry had been in the country for hardly two months, paid a whole year's lease for an apartment—customary practice, he was told—bought furniture and appliances, and settled to a challenging job with high hopes, when indistinct demands of a politico-socio-religious nature began stirring among mutinous factions of the population.

Stores and offices were closed in fearful compliance with a general boycott proclaimed by the rebels. Government planes shelled and strafed rebellious mountain villages. Tanks patrolled city squares; sandbags blocked streets. Provisions were unobtainable or sold surreptitiously in "safe" corners in the suburbs. Garbage piled up on sidewalks. Rumours of infectious diseases spread. Normal life was disrupted. Daily survival became a hectic struggle for Harry and his family. (It would be less distressing, thought Harry, if he could only speak or understand Arabic, the language of the land, and learn what the turmoil was all about.) Going to work proved dangerous. Snipers twice fired at the Company transport Harry rode to the airport. His child's health presented a major concern. And when a communiqué from the British Embassy advised to be prepared for evacuation, Harry decided it was time to seriously consider their choices.

The move to Beirut in pursuit of his budding vocation had appealed to Harry for the timeliness of the job opening as well as its closeness to home. But now, although in moments of weakness and homesickness the option of returning to Cyprus seemed tempting, he dreaded the thought that it would mean the abandonment of his hard-earned choice of a career which, though still of short duration, had already begun weaving its spell around his heartstrings.

And now his accomplishment, that would have been a qualification to sustain him for life and open doors throughout the world, had become a repellant that signaled caution and kept prospective employers on guard. His work had entailed inspection and certification of specific areas of aircraft maintenance. Now, on his present quest for employment in this new environment, he had answered many advertisements and applied personally at airline operators and aircraft manufacturers. Every one of them, without exception, had balked at the mention of his country of birth. They had politely said they would keep his name on file, though not hiding the fact that they considered him a security risk.

It was a cold, damp and grey autumn morning.

Harry pulled his cap down closer to his ears, raised the lapel of his raincoat around his neck, and skipped on the sidewalk, alternating his feet in the manner of a dance, to keep warm. He had just ended the midnight-to-seven, "graveyard" shift, and waited, sleepy-eyed, for the bus that would take him to the Underground station where he would catch a train for Earl's Court. The whole trip would take about two hours, provided he caught the bus on time and did not fall asleep on the train.

His wife and young child, confined to a musty, "furnished" room that a young relative studying in London had hastily rented for them before their arrival in England, would be up and waiting for him. She would want to discuss their future plans while serving him breakfast. His child—who had started wheezing from the fumes and smoke that choked London on Guy Fawkes Day—would want to climb onto his lap and implore him, between gasps, with what had become a pining for almost a year of his young life: "Let's go home, Papa." But Harry would be too tired and sleepy to answer either of them. He would gulp down a hot cup of tea, snuggle into a cold bed, and hope that his wife had not run out of pennies for the gas meter.

A sense of isolation and abandonment crept into Harry's consciousness, as he stood alone, under the lamp, by the edge of the awakening highway, in the gloom of the grey twilight. The heavy fog of the previous night had lifted, though the streetlights were still veiled in the haze of the misty drizzle. And that peculiar "industrial" smell of London, that seems to drift with the fog, still permeated the air. He was cognizant that his mind, unconstrained by reasoned deliberations, had begun again dwelling obsessively on the sequence of events that had led him to London. This reminiscence, this futile exercise in retrospection, had become the constant preoccupation of all his waking hours. The move, to the Country of his citizenship—British—across a continent, unplanned and unprepared, at an unpropitious moment in history when he was viewed as a hostile colonial, had been an upheaval, a disruption of life, fraught with heartache and disappointment. And yet, the destination of the move—London—was one aspect of it that, at an earlier, impressionable stage of his youth, would have been welcomed as the fulfillment of a dream, but had ever remained an unattainable longing.

There was conflict in his head. His sentiments were at odds. He felt angry, on the one hand, at the political turmoil and popular revolt, in two countries, that had cut short a hard-earned, evolving career, and driven him half a world away from his native, sunny Mediterranean.

On the other hand, he was amazed at the pranks and contrivances of fate that had handed him, on a platter—too late—a situation he had once longed for, but, engrossed with more immediate concerns, he had deemed impractical, and, in time, consigned to oblivion.

Vancouver-Bound

The westbound train reduced speed, rolled gently into a glade, whistled a signal, and crept to a stop at a viewpoint in Jasper National Park. There was no station or building marking the site: a clearing on a ridge in the rolling Rocky Mountain range, described, on a map, cast in metal, indicating directions and distances of major cities and landmarks, as the highest elevation on the railway line. The balance of the journey would be a steady descent toward the sea, southwest, to the final destination: Vancouver. Passengers were allowed thirty minutes to take in the view and stretch their legs in the cool of the early morning mountain air.

Harry, who, with his wife and child, had boarded in Montreal three days earlier, having arrived there by sea from Britain, and though still weary from the week-long ocean crossing, had not been able to sleep much all night. The whistle of the train, which he had hardly noticed during two or three days across flat country through the Prairies, had become more frequent on the winding mountain climb. But it wasn't the loudness or the frequency of the whistle that had kept Harry awake. It was the evocative character of the sound that disturbed his thoughts, especially now that his journey was nearing its end. Reverberating at times in a crescendo, or fading to an almost plaintive whimper, as the engine, far ahead of Harry's car, rounded the folds and creases of the range, it made his heart leap, as though on a shaky roller-coaster, now into precarious heights, then plunge into depths of despair. There was something forlorn, a hint of desolation, in the 'howling' of the whistle, Harry thought. It seemed to wrench him away farther and farther from something—or somewhere—that was close to his heart, and that he would rather be closer to.

The spectacular panorama of the Rockies that Harry stood gazing at was an exhilarating change of scene after the seemingly interminable, unvarying, though awesome vastness of the Prairies. A landscape of undulating hills and snow-capped peaks spread ahead into the distance, like a boundless canvas, until, at the very far end, it seemed to blend into the blue of the sky. Forested slopes all around and in valleys below, already speckled with autumnal tones, shades of yellow and brown among the green, sparkled in the bright, late September sun.

The mountain air was crisp, crystalline and chilly. Harry and his wife were warmly dressed in woolens and scarves. Their child, too, seemed comfortable in his brand-new English duffel coat. Despite what a young man in the train had told them about not needing such heavy clothing in Canada, Harry's wife said they had been wise to have shopped as well as they had in London, before departure. They were well prepared for a country reputed for severe winters.

Harry beheld the scenery with distanced emotion. He grasped the grandeur of it, but as though on an anesthetized level of consciousness, cerebrally, without passion. For the past several years, trapped in a tidal wave of events, he had learned to view life and judge all experience—the good as well as the bad—with resignation and detachment. Uprooted by insurrection in his birthplace; then further dislodged by turmoil in the neighbouring region of the world, he had finally migrated to his country of citizenship, Britain, for which he had always felt an intellectual affinity. But he had soon found that an identity, with which he had, apparently, only circumstantially been labeled, had preceded him. (The native element of the population of Cyprus, a British colony at the time, were at guerrilla warfare with the Administration.) Faced with hostility and prejudice; barred from employment in his chosen field, his hopes of salvaging his prospects of a future foundered; all his past efforts, his studies and training were frustrated and had come to naught. No longer sure of himself, he had opted to migrate yet one more time. Hard knocks had taught him that Fate—'The Writing On One's Forehead,' as his old folks used to say—had no regard to the individual's efforts at betterment or change in life's fortunes. "There is a Divinity that shapes our ends," Harry recalled reading in some sage's work—was it not Shakespeare, his first discovery in his self-taught English literature? How true it rang! Here he was, still roving across the oceans, now in a new continent, surrendered to the whims of whatever 'Divinity' or 'Force' it was that blew his shattered boat adrift in an aimless sea.

A contrasting adage he also remembered reading caused Harry to chuckle at the presumptuousness of the author. "I am the master of my fate; I am the captain of my soul," the poet boasted. It is very well, Harry thought, if you have managed to escape the notice of Fate (or Divinity, for that matter); avoided becoming their plaything, and found the wind always in your favour. What was the use of accomplishment—of building the boat of your dreams and setting out on an unpredictable ocean—if in the next rolling billow, against which you were powerless, your boat were dashed to pieces?

Harry pondered, as he gazed at the wonders of the vast land that was to be his new home. The platitude had once inspired him to defy Fate's verdict; prevail over obstacles and rise above his inadequacies. Was he now becoming a defeatist? His reach, he felt, had, of late, fallen short of his goals. Fate, as if at war with a dissident, had torn down his accomplishments and was now throwing him a tougher challenge to repeat the struggle, against new obstacles, and rise anew, if he could. Why could he not? He had already made a fresh start, by coming to an unspoilt, young country. And it was beautiful. I must allow it to inspire me with new hope, Harry told himself; to undo the negative spell of the recent past. Surely there must be healing in the serenity of the mountains, he thought, as he gazed across the colourful peaks into the distant blue. And Harry found himself filling his lungs with a deep breath of fresh air, deeper than he had been able to breathe for a long time. He felt a fog lifting in his inner vision; and though he could, as yet, not see what was in store for the days to come, the dark shadow of the recent years seemed to be receding, and the light of his former accomplishments cast a glimmer of hope onto the road that lay ahead.

Immigrant Story

Harry returned from the lavatory of the train and sat beside his wife. His three-year-old son clung to his knee and, with some effort—his brand-new duffel coat restricting his movements—climbed onto his lap.

"Are we going home, Papa?" asked the child, in a language that was not native to the land they were traversing.

Harry did not answer. He breathed a deep sigh and gazed absently through the window. He had been asked the question many times over half the child's young life, a question he had found difficult to answer truthfully and had given up trying. He felt as though his life had ceased to be his to plan.

Bitterness and frustration over a past of dashed hopes; a glimmer of initial success come to naught, efforts interrupted and plans destroyed by events beyond his control had begun to shake his faith in his ability to provide a happy environment for his young family.

It was not for lack of trying or want of ambition, Harry mused.

Though of modest means and limited schooling, yet through hard work and study he had attained an impressive technical qualification in aircraft service that could have opened exciting opportunities throughout the world, with prospects of further advancement. He married the girl he had long had eyes for.

They had scarcely celebrated his achievement when the fabric of their dreams began to crumble.

Civic rebellion, terrorism and revolution in one region of the world, where he came from, followed by prejudice—undeserved—in another, where he would have preferred to remain, had forced them to move from country to country, and seek to establish a new home three times in two years.

Their child, in the strenuous interim, confined in restrictive rented apartments, had longed for the freedom he had opened his eyes to, and the love and attention he had enjoyed of aunts, uncles and grandparents. It was no wonder, thought Harry, that every time they boarded a vehicle, were it a bus, a ship or a train, the child would ask to know whether they were going home.

Would this new land provide an answer? Harry wondered. Would it prove to be a place he could finally, truthfully call home?

He gazed with imperceptive eyes at the thickly forested skyline and the diversity of autumnal colours mirrored in the still waters of lake after countless lake, men in waders fly-fishing in rivers wider and more abundant than he had ever seen or imagined, and knew deep down that he ought to be exhilarated at the sight. Pessimism had begun taking hold, he reflected, and was sapping his manliness. Relatives, in a show of helpfulness (perhaps resentful of his ambitions, Harry thought) had begun making inadequate and unsuitable offers. The future had seemed dark and bleak.

He must shake off the web of despair that had been paralyzing his will, Harry chided himself, and allow the beauty of this new land to rekindle the resolve that had driven him to his achievement not long ago. He knew, above all, that the child needed an answer—very soon.

"This is going to be our new home," he said, at last.

"Is Grandma going to be there?"

The question stirred other memories and emotions. Harry's original quest for employment had been centred in neighbouring countries close to his birthplace where he could pay frequent visits. Now they had come too far away and he felt their move was in the nature of a pioneering step and implied a completely new beginning.

"No," he said after a long pause. "But there will be an uncle here," he added quickly, ameliorating the child's sense of loss. "A new uncle you haven't seen before."

An alarming suspicion suddenly grabbed Harry in a paralyzing twinge. Drops of perspiration formed on his forehead. He brought his hand down casually to his side and felt his hip pocket. His wallet was gone. He put the child down from his lap and hurried to the lavatory, his ears throbbing, his heart leaping to his throat, his breathing constricted. The lavatory was occupied. He waited. The occupant came out. He was lightly dressed. He didn't appear to be hiding anything. Harry looked inside. It wasn't there. He broke into a sweat. His knees felt weak. He felt he had to sit down. He managed to totter back to his seat.

His wife eyed him with a concerned expression.

"Are you feeling sick?" she asked.

"It's too hot in the train," he said, avoiding her eyes and wiping his brow. To lend credence to his claim, he pulled the loose-fitting, brand new turtleneck sweater that he wore off his back.

He sat, unable to plan a course of action. He stared at people down the aisle, interpreting suspicious movements. Someone had taken his wallet.

A uniformed railway attendant appeared at the far end of the car. Harry considered reporting his loss but was uneasy at the thought of making a fool of himself. The man kept advancing slowly and appeared to be scrutinizing passengers on both sides of the aisle. He came and stood finally before Harry. He put his hand in his pocket and took out a wallet.

"Is this yours?" he asked.

Lost for words, Harry was struck dumb. "Yes," he blurted out, embarrassed, his voice hardly audible to himself. His wife, witnessing the unfolding story, urged him to offer the man a reward.

"It isn't necessary," said the attendant. "Next time be more careful."

The unexpected relief from that moment of deep anxiety left Harry suddenly exhausted and weak. The scenery they were going through assumed the nature of a stretching dream, and with the rhythmic chugging of the train, he became drowsy and found it difficult to keep awake.

His wife had her eyes closed and appeared asleep. She had her overcoat unbuttoned and her face and yellow sweater were lit up in the ray from the window. Harry watched her and it seemed to him that he had not looked at her like this for a long time. Lines that had begun showing around her eyes and brow seemed gone and she looked completely relaxed. And though himself uncertain of what awaited him in this country, his wife's face betrayed no reservations regarding the future but reflected perfect contentment, and he was happy for her. Their son was also asleep in her lap, his duffel coat over his legs.

They were passing through a dense forest, where close-packed colonnades of fir trees, their trunks de-branched, paraded on both sides of the train. The endless flow of the perfectly straight, uniform trunks frantically racing past at close range had a hypnotic effect. Harry gazed, mesmerized, at the rushing scene and wished that the speeding procession would, in some mystic way, pick up one end of his confused thoughts, unravel the tangle, sort out and soothe the jumble of his memories. And as the train chugged along with the steady clatter of steel rolling upon steel he gradually became oblivious of all sounds and soon felt as if he were floating in space, devoid of all physical sensation…And he found himself re-living a scene, stamped indelibly in the bank of his memory, that had haunted him every time he closed his eyes of late.

He was among a group of passengers being tossed about on board an old ship crossing the Mediterranean on a stormy summer night. The aging ship creaked and groaned as she climbed and dipped, rocking and rolling. Third class passengers had gathered in their dining hall, at mid-section. All were in the throes of seasickness and all were fleeing the revolution-bound Middle East.

But the image that loomed largest and more vividly in Harry's vision was the calm and composed face of an elderly Greek woman from Alexandria who, with her husband, sat on a bench against the wall. They were fleeing Egypt with only their suitcases, their thriving manufacturing business having been nationalized by Nasser's socialist government. The woman made no sounds of discontent and sat unperturbed amid the turmoil. Her elegant lined face, capped with snow-white hair, grew closer and larger before Harry's eyes until all other figures faded out of the scene and only her transparent face filled the sky, like a formation of cloud against the blue, and all he could see were her reassuring eyes and her moving lips, and he could hear her words, spoken in French, repeating over and over, "Patience, mon enfant, patience…"

(Note: Submitted to CBC Short Story Contest, Oct. 31, 2012)

Immigration and Employment Office Interview

Perhaps more than a year had elapsed since my arrival in Canada with my wife and child, in 1959, before I decided to present myself at the Immigration and Employment Office in Vancouver. I had existed in a daze in the interim and had not been able to shake myself free of the quandary into which I had been drifted by circumstances I could not control.

The clerk took down details from my British passport and immigration documents.

"'Citizen of the United Kingdom and Colonies,'" he read from the cover of the passport. "You're a British citizen, I see," he said, casting a surveying glance at my features.

"Yes. Cyprus, my birthplace, is a British Colony; though it's in turmoil these days. I was born a British subject."

"What nationality is your name?"

"It's an Armenian name."

I waited for his reaction, but he probed no further into the origin of my name. I had learned, thanks to recent experience and observation, that few people had more than a passing grasp of world geography; fewer less of history, and that the average man in the street had not even heard the name of my people's homeland, Armenia. Most confused it with Albania or Rumania. The odd person, of an older generation, remembered a story by Stephen Leacock—early 20th Century Canadian humorist—titled "Helping the Armenians," while some few vaguely recalled being admonished in childhood to finish their dinner and bear in mind the "starving Armenians," but had forgotten, or knew nothing of the events that had given rise to the epithet.

The clerk kept taking notes as a matter of course, and I felt gratified thinking that here was a knowledgeable man for whom I

145

did not represent an obscure specimen. I was not looking forward to the unpleasant task of reciting agonizing details of the barbaric decimation of my ancestors and the loss or usurpation of their homeland. To my relief, the clerk stuck to the business at hand.

"What has been your work experience?" he asked, leafing through a file on his desk. "What kind of work are you looking for?"

"I am a Licensed Aircraft Engineer," I said, handing him the certifying document, which was still valid, though I hadn't been employed in the profession for the past two years. "That's, under the British system," I expounded. "I understand they're called mechanics here."

"Category 'A'! You shouldn't have much trouble finding a job with that qualification."

"Well...the problem is the difference between the British and the Canadian licences. The Canadian Category 'A' covers engine as well as airframe, whereas the British 'A' covers only airframe, which includes the hydraulic system. A separate licence, Category 'C,' is required for engines. My main duties were in the hydraulic shop. For a brief period I held the position of Shop Inspector with Middle East Airlines, in Beirut, certifying overhauled components for airworthiness."

"I see. Well, all you need to do, then, is sit for a Canadian licence."

"Well...yes. But I don't have engine experience, you see. To gain experience I need to land a job. And to get a job, it seems I'll need a Canadian licence."

A wry smile twitched on the clerk's face as he bobbed his head in understanding.

"I see you spent some time in England before coming to Canada. How did you fare in England?"

"The airline industry was closed to Cypriots."

"Why was that?"

"Because of the guerrilla campaign the Greeks—the major, native population of the island—were...are waging for 'Enosis,' or 'Union with Greece.'"

"Oh, yes. We see the news coverage on TV, don't we? But you're not Greek!"

"No. But they wouldn't understand that in Britain. They had

become incensed—justifiably incensed—at a recent chain of killings of innocent British civilians. Emotions block the course of reason. And, what is worse, the struggle had deteriorated and sidetracked into ethnic conflict between Greeks and Turks, so that Armenians, a small minority on the Island and co-religionists with the Greeks, were assumed, by the uninformed British public, to be in sympathy with the Greeks in their struggle with Britain." I found myself, reluctantly, having to chronicle yet again the events of a disturbing past. But I did not want now to leave an impression that could be misconstrued. And my listener appeared interested. "If we seemed to be in sympathy with the Greeks," I pointed out, "it was in relation to our mutual historic conflict with the Turks; not with the British. My parents' generation had come to Cyprus as refugees from the Turkish Genocide, and they were eternally grateful to the British for taking them in."

Unsure now how much I was taxing my listener's tolerance, or whether he was in fact interested at all, I felt uncomfortable recounting what I thought sounded, perhaps, like a litany of my personal woes. I was, therefore, greatly relieved when the clerk resumed his concern with the business at hand.

"I see you arrived in Canada almost a year ago," he observed. "What took you so long to come and see us?"

"I had a ready-made job—with a promise of partnership—waiting," I said, after some hesitation. The clerk stared at me, expecting further clarification. "I washed dishes at an Old Country friend's coffee shop," I confessed. "It's not an episode of my life I want to remember with joy."

"It didn't work out?"

"It didn't get beyond minimum wage." The clerk bobbed his head again and kept leafing through his files. "I quit and have been trying other work unrelated to my past experience," I further explained, "like direct sales, door-to-door, or by appointment."

We sat in silence while the clerk scanned his list of jobs. "I was wondering," I ventured, "if your office could help me enroll in some aircraft mechanics course. I could then sit for a Canadian licence and hopefully find a job in my line of former training."

The clerk's response was curt and abrupt.

"No way!" he shot back, bluntly.

I was slightly shaken and felt myself assume a somewhat defensive stance.

"We may do that for people with no skills," he explained, in an effort to soften my initial reaction. "You have hydraulics experience besides aircraft. Some opening is bound to come up in that line."

He sat, sunk in thought for a moment, leafing through his books; then, as though he had just remembered something, he hurriedly picked up a new file and turned a few pages. His face lit up.

"Jordan's!" he beamed, with an air of having had a revelation. "Jordan's Interiors has an opening for a carpet salesman!" He faced me gleefully, obviously expecting a positive reaction.

I was quite aware of the popularly held, and perhaps well-founded view linking Armenians with the carpet trade, but was not fast enough to take it as a jest and laugh at the humor of it. I just could see no connection between my work expertise and his new discovery. We stared at each other blankly for a moment as his enthusiasm waned.

"I thought you said you were Armenian," he mumbled, head hung at my gaping bewilderment. "Didn't you?"

Canada

A Fistful of Diamonds

I had hardly put down roots in Vancouver, in the early 1960's, when I received an unexpected telephone call from a young man with whom I'd had a remote acquaintance in the Old Country, C. He had preceded me to Canada by a few years, but had settled in Toronto. He had somehow learned of my whereabouts. People who come from small communities eventually learn where each one has emigrated, whom they have married, whether they are dead or still kicking around.

"Hallo! Who is this?"

"This is Andy."

"Andy?"

"Andy K. Don't you remember me from C?"

"Oh, yes. You were from a different town; though I went to school there. But, yes. I know you. Where are you calling from?"

"I am in Vancouver. I won a prize for a weekend's holiday. I am staying at the Hotel Vancouver. I was wondering if we could meet. Old Country friends, you know?"

In those early days of my arrival in Canada I had not yet managed to find steady employment in my line of training. Although I was struggling with various selling jobs in an effort to provide a living for my family, I was not tied down by the clock, or under anyone's supervision. I was, therefore, not inclined to refuse the man's offer of "friendship."

I checked the gas and oil in the much-used, second hand Hillman, which I had acquired at an affordable price, and went to meet my newfound Old Country compatriot.

From scant observation in past years, I remembered him as somewhat of a simpleton, a naïve and rather unsophisticated teenager, though his family was known to be well to do. He was a tall and lanky youth, with fair skin and blondish hair. But the most significant feature that I recalled was his eyes. They were a motley blue-green in colour, wide and peering, and appeared, oddly, out of focus. When he looked at you, you felt as if his gaze converged on the backside of your head, or that he saw through and beyond your body mass, and made you feel as though he were looking at a ghost.

I entered the hotel lobby at the Georgia Street entrance and found Andy seated, in a rigid posture, his feet and knees held stiffly close together, his hands resting on the arms of the bulky lounge chair. The expression in his eyes was as I remembered it. Moreover, he looked as if he had been gazing at a ghost even before my arrival. There seemed to be an anxiety, an aspect of fear in his countenance.

"Jerry," he said, without rising or even so much as moving an eyebrow, "don't look now, but you'll see a couple of men pacing the floor behind me. I think they have been tailing me and are waiting for a chance to get me as soon as I go out."

I took a casual glance and did, indeed, see two men in seemingly confidential conversation, walking back and forth near the Burrard Street entrance.

"I see them," I said, "but they are at the far end of the hall. It looks as if they are waiting for a bus or taxi. Why would they be following you?"

"I'll tell you when we go out," he said. "Stand behind me so they don't see me getting up."

I did as he asked, and we were soon safely outside.

"Diamonds!" said Andy as we entered my car. "I have diamonds in my pocket. Take me to your house and I'll show them to you." He said they had been entrusted to him by a distributor in Toronto for delivery to a jeweler in Vancouver.

I had had misgivings about the man's sanity, and his statement seemed to confirm my suspicion. But then, who was I to know about the ordeals of handling diamonds?

In our humble Kitsilano basement suite I introduced Andy to my wife and, after coffee, he produced, from his pocket, a handkerchief, knotted into a little bundle. He laid it on the coffee table and, kneeling before it, carefully undid the knots. He spread the handkerchief flat on the table and laid bare a glitter of diamonds.

"Have you ever seen so many diamonds in all your life?" he exclaimed, almost shouting with glee, and with a jerky swing of his hand swept several of the stones onto the floor.

"Ah! Ah!" he moaned. He searched our little Persian carpet on his hands and knees and found three of the gems. Red faced, his brow showering perspiration, he started counting.

He counted fifteen stones of various sizes. Some were as large as a man's small fingernail. How many were there supposed to be? He had forgotten. Frantically he fumbled in his pockets. He had it written somewhere. Where had he hidden that damned piece of paper? He sat sweating profusely, a faraway stare of dismay in his eyes.

His face was suddenly transformed into a happy smile. He remembered! It was in his wallet! My wife handed him a towel to wipe his brow. With a sigh of satisfaction he opened his wallet and found the piece of paper. He had written "16" in large numerals. He carefully counted the stones again. There were only fifteen on the handkerchief. He started sweating again. And now, my wife and I joined him in his search of the floor beyond the carpet. We turned all the lights on. I shone my flashlight around the room and in all corners. There was a sudden, momentary glint. Where had it come from? I swung the flashlight from side to side and finally located the lost sparkler. It had lodged in one of the narrow slits of the heat register on the floor. It was just large enough not to fall in.

His emotions rising and sinking, Andy bundled the diamonds again and, his nerves spent, sat down to catch his breath. We offered him a glass of cold lemonade to soothe his nerves. He drank in pensive silence. He was relaxed. There was even a flicker of a smile in his eyes.

On our return trip to his hotel I took Andy through Stanley Park, stopping briefly at key points to show him the sights. While getting back into the car at Prospect Point he was seized by a sudden panic.

"My wedding band!" he cried. "How did it get there?" and started furiously digging his fingers into the rubber floor mat of the car.

I hadn't been aware before, but was amused to learn then, that the mats in my old Hillman were held down with brass studs whose topsides looked almost exactly like gold rings.

"Good thing I remembered my ring!" exclaimed Andy, rummaging in his pockets. He found his ring, which he had apparently hidden for the duration of his holiday, put it on his finger and stepped out of the car. He handed me his camera and posed for a picture, his left elbow leaning on the fence, his hand hanging over to show his ring.

"I think God is taking care of me," he said, as we neared the hotel. "My pursuers didn't catch me, I found the lost diamond, and I remembered to have my picture taken with my ring on, to show my wife as proof that I had never taken it off."

A Trigger Of Memory

I experienced a strange phenomenon the other day when I entered a shopping mall in Burnaby. A vivid image of my grandmother appeared in my mind's eye as I walked past the first corner. Then, after a few paces, it just as spontaneously disappeared. I was intrigued.

I went back to the same corner, and there was her smiling face again!

What had so powerfully projected an image from the bank of my memory of someone who had been dead for fifty years? I lingered in the area and discovered that the image appeared when I was near a cinnamon rolls bakery. My grandmother's baking did not include cinnamon rolls, but I concluded that it must be the smell that evoked the picture from the past. Still, I could not make a connection.

I went back again. There was a woman at the counter, this time, talking to the owner. I heard the man say, apparently in answer to her question, "I must confess to you, ma'am. We boil it." That solved my mystery!

Whenever my grandmother came to stay with us she would be up at daybreak to make tea for our breakfast. It was her method of making tea. She would put the tea leaves in a strainer, boil water in a pan with half a stick of cinnamon in it, then pour it through for a sparkling glass of orange-red tea, the aroma permeating the whole house for hours.

Lured by Sirens at Deep Cove

"What kind of car do you drive?" "Where did you go on the weekend?" How many miles did you put in?"

Those were some of the questions that assailed us co-workers every Monday morning at the industrial establishment in Vancouver where I had found work in the early 1960's. The degree to which you could keep up with the Joneses was an unquestioned measure of social integration. But if you were a recently arrived immigrant, such as I and my family were, it made you uncomfortably conscious that you really didn't measure up.

To begin with, you had to have a car. And the newer and bigger your car the higher your prestige with the Joneses. You were then expected to go somewhere on the weekend. The farther you drove or the greater mileage you logged the higher you scored with the boys. Or, even on shorter trips closer to home, some uncommon personal exploit or outing that you could talk about on Monday morning would win you acceptance and make you feel a part of the group.

My wife and child, on the other hand, were bored to tears all week and were pining to be set free from their domestic confinement on Saturdays and Sundays. We were new in the Country. We knew no one. Except for one relative—a single young man—we had no circle of friends.

And so...we bought a car. Nothing like the big Chevvies or Buicks or other American V-8s that some of the boys drove. Ours was a humble, small, much-used, four-cylinder, British Hillman. Standard transmission. Very stiff clutch. It bequeathed me a serious case of sciatica before we parted company. But, at least, we now had a car and began enjoying life and going places around Vancouver.

One of the first destinations I contemplated was Mount Seymour. But, wisely, before overheating on the steep climb, I abandoned the idea and went to Deep Cove, just below, instead. (Though, I doubted whether I would have much to brag about with the boys on Monday).

A mystic aura seemed to pervade the atmosphere at Deep Cove.

Mighty, forbidding peaks, densely covered in black forest, hung over the encircled body of water and mirrored in the sunless, sleepy surface below. Rusty-brown cliffs, sheer and jagged, dipped into the gloomy depths of the bottomless cove. And the eerie silence, the solitude and tranquility of the surroundings seemed to lend the site a bewitching, ominous character. I don't remember what time of year it was, but we seemed to be the only sightseers in the place. Perhaps it was too early in the day. A souvenir and gift shop was not yet open, but a coffeehouse next-door was. The attendant also managed a small marina of light aluminum boats moored in a little recess down the ramp.

What fun, what diversion it would provide my wife and child, I thought, if I could take them on a boat ride! Could I manage it? Although, in the process of our migrations, we had crossed oceans on ships, we had never been in a small boat. But what could go wrong in such calm waters? I surveyed again the idle and quiet surroundings and described in my mind the short round trip I would make, for not longer than a half-hour, and, with a sudden chill in my spine, had sense of an awakening revelation, which I promptly ignored and suppressed. I understood why, in folk legends, Nature is often cloaked in human personality. It was as though a thousand pairs of invisible little hands, along the water's edge that lapped the mossy, dripping cliffs, waved and beckoned, and soft murmurs, blending with the wash, whispered tenderly, in chorus with the mythical song of the siren, "Come! Come! Silence the nagging caution and come!"

The attendant showed me how to start and operate the little outboard motor and threw three lifejackets into the boat as he pushed it into open water. "You won't need these," he said, "but just in case!"

I slid the boat smoothly out of the cove and, with a sense of great accomplishment and fun, turned into the larger expanse of the inlet, keeping a safe distance from the threatening cliffs. Here too the water was calm and the sailing smooth, though the scenery was dull. No sea craft of any description — large or small, pleasure or commercial — adorned this section of the inlet, and industrial sites across the water seemed uninteresting and were idle on the weekend.

Just as I thought of turning back, a magnificent large fishing vessel emerged from behind the headland, puffing and purring. Newly painted in impressive lines and colours, she was a thing of beauty to behold as she darted proudly past, her masts waving a victor's salute to the skies. The scenery became alive all of a sudden. She had seemed so close to our boat that, instinctively, I veered away closer to the cliffs. And now, as she receded into the distance, I became aware of a picturesque imprint that with a single magic pass she had left in her path. An array of undulations was set in motion, fanning out, enlivening the sleepy face of the water.

My reverie of admiration was abruptly ended, however, when, within the space of a split second I came to a series of sudden realizations: that the traveling undulations were actually waves of considerable size; that they were rising higher than they would have because of the containment of the water against the cliffs; that they were fast moving towards us, the first one dangerously close; and that if I tried to run away from them I would be heading into a dead-end trap, they would surely catch up and tip my boat or batter it against the cliffs. My whole family was at stake. I was already trapped. There was only one option, risky as it seemed: plunge ahead into the coming onslaught! There was no time to lose. I ordered my wife and child to quickly wrap the lifejackets around their shoulders and lie low in the fore end of the hull. I took a firm grip of the control, accelerated the motor and aimed the boat directly into the advancing waves. I couldn't tell whether I was making any progress but I had my motor at full throttle and rode the waves at "full speed," riding the waves up and down, mounting and dipping, worrying the while that my wife and child might be tossed out with the next shaking. It was perhaps the scariest time of my life, but I could not afford to lose control, and deep down I had a sense that I had been guided by instinct to do the right thing.

Gradually, their energy spent, the waves subsided, and I could return to the cove. I brought my family safely home and have been wiser to the song of the sirens ever since.

A Letter To Burl Ives

Dear Mr. Burl Ives,

If only I had written to you when I could still hope for the possibility of a reply! But, no matter. It is not the expectation of a reply that prompts me. I am writing because I owe you an apology. An apology which, I am ashamed to admit, is forty years overdue. This delinquency has weighed upon me for too long, and now, for peace of conscience, I have decided to go through this ritual of confession and...well...a process of self-exoneration. I feel certain, as well—if I have been a good judge of character—that you too would not deny me your kind forgiveness.

You must wonder what offence a total stranger could have committed that he should feel compelled to apologize after so many years. Someone you have not even met, you might think. Well...that's not entirely true. You see, we have met. We stood side by side on the sidewalk of a deserted Vancouver street one night, forty years ago. And it has been my deep regret, ever since, that we parted as strangers...well...without an introduction. Without a word, even. Without so much as a hello and good-bye. Perhaps you don't remember the occasion—in any case, it is mostly my memory of it that troubles me. Because, you see, Mr. Ives, we really weren't strangers at all! I mean, we were not both strangers to each other. I was the stranger. You didn't know me. But you were not a stranger to me. I used to be—always was and still am—a great fan of yours. My brother played the guitar and we sang the songs that you had made famous.

But I am getting ahead of myself.

Do you remember when you were in Vancouver, some forty years ago—in the early 1960's? It wasn't customary in those days, as it is today, for films to be made in Vancouver. Perhaps you had come on a lecture tour, or a fishing and hunting trip. Whatever the reason for your visit, you were in town, and you were interviewed on CBC Radio. It was a Sunday night. After the interview—if I may conjecture—you picked up a parcel that had arrived for you at the Hotel desk (CBC Radio had its studios in Hotel Vancouver at the time) and decided to take a leisurely walk in the surrounding downtown area, before retiring to your room. The weather was fine and exceptionally mild. (It doesn't always rain in Vancouver, you know; although it often seems so.)

Swinging your parcel by the twine that bound it, you walked several aimless blocks and found yourself on Granville Street. If you had never before been in Vancouver on a Sunday night, you probably felt as though you had just stepped into a ghost-town. How the empty street echoed to the scraping of your heels on the sidewalk! All business establishments—bars, restaurants, coffee-shops—were closed, and there seemed to be not a single soul about. It felt uncomfortable pacing the lifeless street at night.

Just when you thought there was no point in walking any further, you noticed a man standing before a lighted window in the middle of the next block. Another solitary fellow-human, you probably thought. Maybe a stranger in town, like yourself. It gave you an incentive to walk a little further and see for yourself what one man found so absorbing in a lonely street.

The young stranger stood looking at the display in the window of a bookstore. You came along and also stood gazing at the titles. Your parcel had your name on it, distinctly hand-printed in black ink. And you probably sensed that the young man saw it. He then took a furtive glance at your face, but turned quickly and continued gazing blankly at the books. Not a word was spoken by either party. After a moment the man turned abruptly, and though he seemed about to say something, hesitated for just a brief instant, then walked hurriedly across the street to his car and drove away.

The incident may not have stayed in your memory for any length of time. Perhaps you paid no attention to it or to the stranger at all. You may, however, have assumed that the man did not recognize you. If so, your assumption was not correct. If, on the other hand, you judged him to be ill-mannered and perhaps even stupid, your conclusion would be well-founded. Because, you see, Mr. Ives, that idiot was none other than myself.

My behaviour must have seemed abrupt, awkward, and even

rude. I cannot justify it but can only try to explain it. Earlier that evening, I had attended, in West Vancouver, a performance of William Saroyan's "My Name Is Aram," a one-man show by an American actor. His rendition of an old Armenian's English was so well done, his accent so authentic, that I had to congratulate him after the show. He said he had spent two weeks among Saroyan's relatives in Fresno to perfect it. Saroyan had been one of my early models in my ambition to be a writer. Part of the reason was that, like myself, he had had little formal schooling, but had acquired his education in libraries. I loved his humour and his philosophy. And his style seemed so simple and unsophisticated that it made you think anyone could write short stories. I was encouraged, with conviction and faith, that if he could, then so could I!

But ambition seems to spawn frustration. And, to me, Vancouver, on a Sunday night, in the early 1960's, symbolized the collective causes of my frustration. Life's circumstances, and impositions of historic events—including migration that involved four countries and three continents—had thwarted my ambitions. Other obligations and priorities claimed precedence over the necessity to devote time for the pursuit of the Muse, or draw inspiration from surroundings. In my unschooled and starry-eyed concept of the gift of writing, I had also found Vancouver boring and lacking in cultural stimulation—as compared to London, where I had stayed briefly. I longed for the bustling crowds where one could watch people and study characters for stories. I longed for the creative magic that, I felt, must emanate from monuments of antiquity with connections to historic and literary figures.

I don't mean to bore you with a narration of my woes and failings, Mr. Ives, but I want to convey to you the state of mind I was in when you came and stood beside me on that sidewalk. There was, also, another reason why I was taken by surprise and was rendered gaping speechless. I had been listening to the radio in my car, and there you were, giving your interview! I parked and listened to the end of the program. You can't imagine the memories it evoked! Years before, back home ("home" was Cyprus, in the Eastern Mediterranean), my brother, Van, and I used to sing your songs: "Big Rock Candy Mountain," "Blue-tail Fly," "Hand Me Down My Walking Cane," and so many more! They were our favourites. Van played the guitar and spent his summer holidays in the cool mountain camp of the American Academy, entertaining the children of the missionaries who came from countries of the region.

I was in a complex mental state of nostalgia, mixed with frustration, as I stood on that sidewalk, that night, ostensibly absorbed in the display of books in the window, when I heard someone with idle, scraping footsteps, approaching. I was in no mood to be accosted by a panhandler, or any other kind of bum. I had a mind to make a quick exit. But I wasn't going to be chased away. I decided to assume a stance of aloofness and leave, upon my own decision, but without giving him a chance to engage in dialogue. I was also aware, at the same time, that here was an opportunity, perhaps, for character study; that I might be able to write a story about the man, some day. Just then, your parcel began swinging right under my nose, so to speak. I couldn't avoid seeing your name on it: "BURL IVES." Were my eyes playing a trick on my mind? Or my mind on my eyes? I had been hearing your voice just a few minutes before! I looked through the corner of my eye; and, sure enough, there was your familiar bearded face. My heart began racing. A million thoughts jammed my mind...and it went blank. I was aware of an urge to say hello! I know you. I am a fan of yours. But language betrayed me—not the choice of words, but the faculty of speech abandoned me. I had read somewhere that you had been fond of spending hours with your friend, Carl Sandburg, the poet and biographer of Abraham Lincoln, exchanging Lincoln anecdotes. Having read a short biography myself, I, too had become an admirer of the former President. I thought, vaguely, of driving you to my house. Although the family would be sleeping, we could sit in the kitchen and, I knew of a thousand things we could talk about over coffee and cakes. I turned around, and...I could not utter a single word. I just managed to teeter to my car and drive away.

I regret having missed a great opportunity at making your personal acquaintance, but I do thank you for allowing me to tell my (your) story.

I remain, forever, your most devoted fan.

Jerry Shekerdemian

Real Canadian? One Man's Question of Identity

"What is your nationality?"

I had become accustomed to anticipating the question ever since my departure from my native Mediterranean homeland. The inquirer this time was the elderly wife of the retiring Chief Engineer on board a British cargo ship.

The freighter had lain idle on a remote expanse of the Mississippi, some miles north of New Orleans, her anchor inextricably stuck in the gummy riverbed. The hydraulic winch had lost power and, as a member of the manufacturer's team of service technicians, I had been called to effect repairs and pull the anchor in.

My job successfully completed, I had showered, packed my bag and had the Radio Officer order a water taxi to take me ashore where I would be given a lift to New Orleans Airport to catch a return flight home to Vancouver.

I was in the Chief Engineer's office waiting to obtain his signature on my time and service report. He was not in, but his wife graciously offered me a chair and, while I waited, we engaged in idle conversation. She had accompanied her husband on this his last voyage before retirement and they were now preparing to return home, by air, to Edinburgh.

She may have become intrigued by my accent of English and possibly also by my sun-touched complexion when she asked to know my nationality. I could have given her a straightforward answer. But her question immediately crowded my mind with memories of the countless occasions of endless and agonizing explanations I had endured ever since arriving in Canada some twenty-five years earlier. Whether it were in business or social contacts, applying for work or meeting would-be clients in the various sales jobs I had attempted, the same question would inevitably pop up upon introducing myself, prompted by the strangeness of my name and perhaps the accent of its delivery.

"What is your nationality?" people would ask before I even had a chance to present the products I hoped would provide me with a meagre living.

"Armenian," I would reply. I had been taught to be proud of my ancient heritage.

They would stare at me blankly for a moment. "Rumanian!" they would exclaim, as if a light bulb had suddenly been turned on in their head.

"No, not Rumanian. Armenian." I would enunciate clearly.

Their eyes would narrow into a squint and, delving deeper into their knowledge of geography, "Albanian!" they would beam with a victorious smile, as though congratulating themselves for having won in a quiz program.

"No. Not Albanian either. Ar-men-ian."

"Is that a country?" They would relent now and ask to be informed on an aspect of world lore that would add little of significance to their basic education.

"It used to be a country," I would explain, and, not to appear rude or abrupt, would try to satisfy their assumed curiosity by reciting the three-thousand-year-old history. "The land is now occupied—has been, since the Middle Ages—by invading hordes from Central Asia. What survives to-day as a country is a tiny speck in the Soviet Union."

The lesson in history over, we would now start a session in geography, mixed with a smattering of Biblical lore about Noah's Ark and Mount Ararat. "The Sacred Mountain of the Armenian people is in the part of Turkey which used to be Armenia."

I was not sure whether my lectures enhanced my prospective customers' knowledge of history and geography, or whether they cared at all, but at the end of the day I would go home wondering where the next meal for my family would come from. And I was every time painfully reminded how right Hitler was when, upon revealing his plans to "cleanse" Europe of races he considered inferior, to allay the fears and concerns of his aides as to world opinion and possible retribution, he said, "Who nowadays remembers the

Armenians?" That was barely twenty years after the Genocide that decimated their numbers by half and robbed the Armenian people of their homeland.

These thoughts raced through my mind when the good lady asked to know my nationality. I knew what she meant. But this was not, I thought, the time, the place or the audience for a lecture. I was anxious, above all, to save myself the agony. We were in American waters and as far as she was concerned, I reasoned, I could have been an American. I therefore deliberately interpreted nationality to mean citizenship.

"Canadian!" I declared, with a hint of pride in my adopted country — the kind of patriotic pride with which any American, I had observed, would proclaim his or her citizenship.

I immediately regretted my evasiveness. The woman's brow knitted, betraying her displeasure, and she turned her head away slightly to one side. A charge of icy silence gripped the atmosphere.

"But you're not a real Canadian, are you?" she said, after what seemed a long, embarrassing moment, looking through the corner of her narrowed eye.

It was a bitter, cutting comment. But still, I foolishly continued avoiding the answer her question demanded, beating around the bush, about being a citizen, not native-born, until, finally defeated, I owned to my identity of origin.

"Armenian. Born a British subject in the former Colony of Cyprus. No, never been to Armenia. My parents came from there. It is now known as Turkey. No, I wouldn't go for a visit. No Armenians were left there. They were marched into the desert to fry to death, or butchered and dumped into the Euphrates. My parents were among the scanty survivors. It's a long story. I wish I had more time to go into the delightful details."

This parting experience tormented me on the long flight home. I would suddenly wake from moments of drowsiness hating myself. My asinine evasiveness, ruffling the old lady, was unforgivable and unnecessary. My regret was compounded, however, as I mulled over the incident, by a greater conflict of emotions, of anger and indignation at the necessity to identify myself in relation to the tragic history inflicted upon my people. Then, as fatigue bore down, I gradually felt consoled, remembering, in a state of reverie, the words of a wise man I had heard at a lecture given by Simon Wiesenthal, commemorating the Jewish Holocaust, to the effect that those who forget the past are condemned to have it repeated.

But while it seemed, in a drowsy moment, that my mind was on the verge of attaining resolution, the true monster that lay at the bottom of my mental conflict pushed its sinister head through the surface, disturbing the deceptive tranquility. As the plane approached the Canadian border the epithet assigned to my adopted identity vexed my soul and plagued me like an obsession that would not be dismissed. "You're not a real Canadian, are you?" The question echoed in my head over and over through the rest of the flight home until it ceased to be the opinion of one foreign national. Memories of past incidents, discriminatory attitudes and snide remarks I had met with in my adopted Country, as well as official pronouncements of political convenience, now acquired a new meaning that seemed to lend confirmation to what the words implied.

What if the woman was right, I thought as I presented my Canadian passport at the gate of entry?

Am I a real Canadian?

What does it take to be one?

Union Meeting

The stimulus to join a union had its initial brewing at Friday evening beer drinking sessions at the neighborhood Canadian Veterans' Legion Hall. A group of mechanics from the small industrial repair shop nearby had made it their weekly routine to congregate at the crowded hall, drink a few rounds of beer, and wind down the tensions of the week, before heading home.

The practice had started upon the instigation of Brad Welke, an energetic, younger member of the group. "Shooting the breeze," Brad had termed the purpose of the "get-together," and the idea had appealed to the men. It had become a sort of weekly "social," bonding the group together as friends with a singularity of purpose in certain aspects of their employment.

They would sit close together around a small table and talk with raised voices in order to hear each other above the cacophonous hum permeating the packed hall. The conversation, in the early days, did not have a specific aim. They would start with new jokes they had heard, loosen up further after a round of beer, then talk randomly about their cars and plans for the weekend, discuss field projects some of them were involved in, gossip about the girls in the office, and, above all, vent their exasperations with the abusive foreman, and, generally, try to relax.

Some of the men would take leave after the first round of drinks. They were strictly expected to be home for dinner. A few, who had been working on field projects, used the alibi to miss dinner at home, ordered some "grub" and persisted in drinking. Others would go home with an untimely "hangover." Everyone's take-home pay was, thus, more or less, diminished at the end of the day. One or two of the group, it was rumored, tried to make up for "lost" wages at gambling tables elsewhere; which led to a falling out with their wives.

But the experience of the "Circle" meetings did have its beneficial results. To set the record straight, the Royal Canadian Legion Hall was not your run-of-the-mill "beer parlor." Among its positive aspects was its demand for a measure of formality and discipline.

"Sir! You, Sir! Will you, please remove your headgear, Sir! And watch your language! You're in the presence of the Queen here. You lads are not veterans, are you? You must consider it a privilege to be allowed in here as guests. So behave accordingly."

As well, contact with others in similar fields of employment had lent further depth to the group's knowledge of labor relations in general.

"Hey! Buddy! What Union you belong to?"

"None. We're not unionized."

"Wha'd'ya mean you're not unionized? You allow the boss to exploit your talents and get rich on your backs? You got rights, man! You need a union to uphold your rights and defend you when you have demands and problems. Find a union you can fit in and apply to join. And do it soon!"

No sooner had they joined a suitable union, received their membership cards and started paying union dues, than the handful of workmen of the small repair shop were summoned, along with the collective membership, to a General Meeting. The purpose of the "Extraordinary" meeting was to have members vote on a single vital motion that would determine the "future of the Union."

A fairly large banquet hall had been rented for the occasion, and all members, from various branches of industry, had been pressed to attend. Brad Welke, now Shop Steward, met outside with his few colleagues. They entered the hall as a group so as they could be seated close together.

Greeting members at the door was a giant of a man, very likely a trained body-builder, perhaps a wrestler or "bouncer." He wore tight jeans and a sleeveless black T-shirt, his head shaven, his massive muscles bulging at his bare shoulders and powerful arms. "Welcome, Brother," he would repeat in an assertive, commanding voice, inspecting every entrant's membership card, admitting each one with an iron handclasp.

The hall filled close to capacity, and members waited with anticipation to learn the "extraordinary" agenda that had necessitated the meeting. Conversation among the audience, before the meeting began, was, strangely, subdued. A sense of caution and awe seemed to restrict the crowd that, many, voicing their opinions in whispers, thought should have been more boisterous under normal circumstances. The confrontation with the strongman at the door seemed to be uppermost in everyone's thought. It seemed as though it had been meant to intimidate the crowd into a docile flock of sheep before herding them into the fold.

But why?

The meeting was called to order before the murmur could magnify to the level of vocalized discontent. The Regional Secretary, chairing the meeting, thanked those present for their attendance in such numbers, welcomed new "brothers," and stressed the importance of the motion to be put to the vote, for which the full membership had been summoned.

"Your vote tonight will decide whether you want your Union to continue on its glorious course...or not. A simple 'Yes' or 'No.' That is all that is required of you. Naturally, your answer will be 'Yes.' I don't have to remind you, Brothers. You know it very well yourselves that your Union is one of the most highly regarded in the World! It enjoys the respect of both Labor and Management. And that, Brothers, does not happen by chance! It is earned by the wise application of rare and hard-to-come-by negotiating skills. And that is a talent, a gift that not many are endowed with. And when an organization is so blessed as to be led by a gifted person of such unique talent, it will do all in its power to retain and not lose that person.

"Such a person, Brothers, is our International Secretary, who sits at the International Headquarters of the Union. But Headquarters, today, finds itself face to face with a crisis, Brothers. A crisis which could become paralyzing if we don't act on it without delay. Other organizations—wealthy organizations—are trying to take away our Secretary from us by offering him a greater salary. We don't want to let him go! We can't afford to let him go! Such talent is impossible to replace!"

"Motion! Motion! Let's have a motion!" There were shouts coming from men seated in the front rows.

"I hear calls to present the question as a formal motion," said the Chairman. "But, let me warn you, Gentlemen; we're not talking peanuts here! Our Secretary receives, at present, a salary of $150,000 a year. You can't keep such talent at such pittance these days, Gentlemen! Not these days, when we have crossed the half-way mark of the Twentieth Century, Gentlemen! We're already in the Glorious 1960's! The increase must be substantial enough to reflect our times as well as befit the exceptional qualifications and competency of the man!"

"I move that the Secretary's salary be doubled!" a forceful voice called from somewhere in the front rows.

"I move that it be tripled!" a louder voice quickly rang in.

"I second the motion to triple!" a familiar voice bellowed from the very front row. It was that of the big muscleman everyone had met at the front door. He rose to his feet and stood tall, his fist held high for all to see, and repeated his endorsement, "I second the motion to triple!"

"We have a motion, Gentlemen!" the Chairman joined in. "It is moved and seconded that the present salary of our International Secretary be tripled. Our next step, then, is to put the motion to the vote."

"An open vote! An open vote! Let's have a show of hands!" a chorus of assertive voices shouted from the front rows.

The Chairman scratched his head, gazing left and right at the audience. "All those in favor of an open vote," he directed, after a brief moment of seeming hesitation, "please raise your hands!"

A forest of hands rose above the crowd's heads.

"Very well, then. All those in favor of the motion to triple the Secretary's salary, please raise your hands!" From his elevated position on the stage the Chairman surveyed a denser forest of hands that had risen even higher the second time. "All those 'against'?"

A few hands, hardly visible, dared rise no higher than their owners' chins.

"We have a unanimous decision, Brothers!" an elated Chairman announced from the stage. "You can rest assured that Headquarters will receive the news with deep appreciation and great admiration for a mature membership that is guided by wisdom. You make us proud, Brothers! Thank you, and Good Night!"

Christmas Bonus

Harry did not tell his wife what had transpired at his workplace on the day before Christmas. He, along with his fellow workers, had tidied up the shop, received their wages soon after lunch and, as was customary, been allowed to go home early for the festive occasion. Christmas had fallen on a Saturday that year and they had been given ten days' vacation, combining the weekends and days off for the holidays.

A relentless anxiety dogged Harry in the interim, gnawing at his insides, tying up his stomach in knots. He went through the festivities putting on an appearance of normalcy. There were few parties and dinners, for Harry and his family were relative newcomers to the Country and had as yet not many intimate acquaintances: Besides his wife and two small children, a young brother-in-law with his girl-friend, and recently-befriended elderly couple made the party for New Years Eve. The children must be made happy, thought Harry. The show must go on. He had some experience on the amateur stage and considered himself a fairly good actor. A real-life situation now demanded he utilize his talents, he convinced himself and proceeded putting on an act. He took part in setting up and decorating the tree, blowing balloons, wrapping and upwrapping gifts, pretending to be surprised, assembling new toys and playing with the children, hugging and kissing Merry Christmas, Happy New Year.

Though he was ever conscious of the need to cover up his true state of mind and perturbed emotions, yet, at times, he seemed to lose his concentration and was afraid his anxiety would be revealed, betraying a perceived weakness in leadership. His wife, Helen, wanted to go shopping on Boxing Day. They nearly had an accident when Harry ran a red light. On coming out of the store he forgot where he had parked the car.

It was after New Year's when Helen confronted him. "What's been bothering you?" she asked. Harry knew he had been irritable at times, through the effort to hide his distraction. His heart sank and he hated himself for his ignorance of a woman's instinct to see through the charade.

"You have been avoiding me," his wife said. "Don't think you can fool me."

Harry did not respond but shook his head, dismissing any implied accusation.

"It feels like the early days when we had newly come to this Country," Helen went on. "You were not happy in Vancouver. For more than a year you kept saying you would go back to England. Things didn't turn out the way we had hoped, I know. I wouldn't want to live through those days again. We went through nearly three years of argument and accusations before you landed this job you have now.

"You've been at this job for almost two years now," Helen continued after a moment of stressful silence. "I realize it was not exactly in line with your experience and training, but...Are you not happy with it?"

"I am not complaining," Harry said, not wishing to engage in the argument, afraid that his silence would betray the truth of his wife's observation. "I'm just tired, I guess."

It was January 4 when Harry went back to the shop. An unusual blizzard had piled two feet of snow on the city. Harry's old Hillman miraculously made it through the slippery side streets. With a sigh of relief he plowed at last into a space in the snow-bank, about a block's distance from the shop. He walked, with a sinking spirit, through the trodden path in the snowbank, and stepped with trepidation into the poorly-lit, cavernous shop, a sickening tightness gripping his stomach. He wondered if the feeling was confined to himself alone, for he thought he sensed an uneasy tension permeating the place as he approached his work bench. Some of the men cast furtive glances at him as they changed into their coveralls. Only the man closest to his bench murmured a subdued "Good morning." Harry thought perhaps the men also felt as he was feeling under the circumstances and doubted whether any of them would greet him with a "Happy New Year."

A grinding-stone that had been running in a darker corner behind a concrete post when Harry entered the shop stopped its grating whine. "You needn't bother putting your coveralls on," a voice said, approaching Harry from behind.

Harry's heart started racing. His ears throbbed. He had hoped he would not hear those words when he came back to work, yet he had been afraid he would. He took a deep breath and turned around. It was the shop foreman. He held a knife in one hand and menacingly stroked the eight-inch blade with the other, as though testing it for sharpness. He knew the foreman always sharpened his gutting knife after a fishing holiday and was not concerned though he had seen him use it before as an intimidating gesture.

"You might as well pack up your tools and go home," said the foreman.

Harry had decided he would not argue. He breathed deeply, trying to control his nerves and glanced briefly into the man's face. The foreman was of less than average height but of stocky build. His large abdomen protruded conspicuously, straining the buttons of his smock. His pipe, an almost permanent fixture on his face, hung by its curved stem from a corner of his mouth, saliva drooling down his chin as he spoke. The constant smoke from his pipe and occasional cigarettes had turned the colour of his bristly moustache into orange. His hair, a greenish blond and of average length, was uncharacteristically well groomed. Harry was intrigued by the foreman's eyes. A cold blue-grey behind thick spectacles, they reflected fear and anxiety, or even hatred, Harry thought, rather than anger.

"I told you last week," said the foreman, gesticulating with the knife in his hand. "You're fired!"

ꣾ ꣾ ꣾ

Harry placed his coveralls in a pile on his bench. He was tempted to counter with the foreman and tell him what he thought of him. A surge of emotion, accompanying the beating in his chest, seemed to be rising to his head, blurring his reason. He felt his hand twitching. Could the conflict be confined to words alone? He was vaguely aware that it might deteriorate into an irremediable situation. A vision of his little daughter's pretty face flashed before his eyes and he was suddenly reminded of family responsibilities. Reason seemed to return. He was able to take a deep breath and get his nerves under control. He grabbed his coat and thought the sooner he lost sight of the foreman's contemptible face the wiser it would be and the better he would feel.

"I'll have to speak to Walter about this, first," he said, his voice shaking as he pushed his way out through the heavy sliding door.

"You don't have to speak to no management," the foreman shouted after him. "I am foreman here. I do the hiring and the firing."

It would be several hours before Walter, the technical manager, was due at his office. Harry could not possibly hang around on the premises. The foreman would not allow him, anyway. And even if he managed to sneak into the front office, the atmosphere would be too tense for comfort.

He stepped out into the cold street. The snow was piled high at the curbs, but a path had already been packed on the sidewalk. Instinctively he turned and started walking towards Broadway. From his workplace on False Creek it would be a distance of nine or ten blocks up a fair incline. But Harry was not in a calculating frame of mind. If he walked far enough, he felt, he would find a warm place to sit and wait. He trudged along in his rubber boots and was well protected from the cold in his heavy parka and wool hat. He dismissed thoughts of taking his car. It would be too risky to tackle the snow-bound streets and impossible to find another parking spot.

Though he walked in the trodden path with firm and steady steps, Harry was not conscious of his progress or his surroundings. The street around him, rather, seemed to be gliding past. He was just a mindless automaton pounding the icy conveyor belt. His ears registered no sounds, but a million thoughts, like so many voices vying with each other, hammered on his brain, jarring his nerves, as though thundering a persistent cacophonous rumble. Casual thoughts would come into focus, as though in passing, then fade out and give way to another.

One thought rose, obsessively, to the fore and, like a fixation that could not be shaken off, dominated the jumbled confusion in Harry's head. At the end of a quiz show he has watched on New Year's Eve the host had asked each member of the Panel for his or her definition of happiness. "Happiness is when you can tell the boss to go to hell," Gordon Sinclair had said. "Go to hell! Go to hell!" Harry mentally repeated, involuntarily, at each step. Until the impracticability of the sentiment overtook his consciousness. "Damn!" he thought, in frustration. It was easy enough for Gordon Sinclair but how could Harry say it? What was he going to tell his wife? I told the boss to go to hell? But...no...really! What was he going to tell his wife?

Harry was drenched in perspiration when he reached Broadway. The exercise had calmed his nerves and the cold air on his seemed to have cleared his head. He came upon a coffee shop near Cambie Street, shook off the snow from his boots, went inside, removed his parka and wool hat and sat down.

"What can I get you, love?" said the waitress as she stood close and poured him his first cup of coffee. She must be English, thought Harry. For a brief magic moment he felt he was back in England and wished he had never left London. He felt oddly comforted by her attention. Was it a nostalgic sentiment, because he had taken her to be English? Or was it being called love by an attractive, fortyish woman? Harry felt relaxed and could view his situation objectively. He was in Vancouver and he must face reality.

He would tell Walter his side of the story. But would management mete out justice? Or would they, rather, stand by their foreman and thus lend confirmation to his firing? In that case Harry would not only be fired but he would not want to work for the Company. What then? How would he break the news to his wife? After years of struggle, I had this satisfactory job and, Honey, I just got myself fired! Not to worry! Surely there must be another job waiting for him somewhere! He was a Licensed Aircraft Engineer. Had been! A glorified title the British system had given him. They called them mechanics here. Licensed aircraft mechanics. They didn't recognize his license, though. You have to obtain a Canadian license, they said. How? Gain Canadian experience! Get a job on aircraft! Sorry! You must have a license to get a job in the first place!

Harry had almost given up. An ad in the paper for a component repairman at a major airline company had seemed like a godsend. A cute Oriental girl at the front counter had taken his application with a smile. Yes, she said. They're hiring in this same category. I think you have a good chance. She took the paper in to the personnel manager. He rushed out almost immediately, with an inquisitive expression on his face. He looked about, as if expecting to see someone other than Harry. But there was no one besides Harry. The man approached him with some hesitation, as if he was not sure what to say. Sorry, he said, avoiding Harry's eyes. We are not hiring in this category. The cute Oriental girl appeared shocked. She had almost been sure. But one look at the name on the application and the man's mind was made up. He had come out looking for a darker face, Harry thought. Name sounded like Chacravardi, or something. Harry had given up. He had tried selling: Vacuum cleaners, brushes, auto parts, and some intangibles. Until he landed this job. What now?

᠈ ᠈ ᠈

"More coffee, love?" The waitress eyed him with a searching look as she filled his cup. Aren't you going to eat anything?"
"Oh...Yeah...Something...Anything."
"How about a piece of pie? Apple pie's fresh."

Harry had not noticed. There was no one else left in the little restaurant now. Working people had had their coffee and breakfast and gone to their jobs. Cigarette smoke had cleared, although the smell was still strong in the air.
"Has Santa been good to you for Christmas?" the waitress said as she placed a wedge of pie before Harry.
Harry stared up at her as if trying to wake from a dream. "Oh...Yeah...Very good...I got a special bonus."
"You wanna tell me about it?" It was not a question. She pulled the chair across from Harry and sat at his table as though it were her profession to listen to people's problems.

"What good would it do me to tell you?" Harry was not eager to reveal his personal affairs to a stranger. He was a private person. And yet there was something casual about her manner, something disarming that made Harry feel at ease.

"Well," she said. "I certainly can't change whatever your situation is. But talking about it might clean the cobwebs and you can see your way through without the obstacles. Maybe I can hold your hand," she added after a moment's pause, reaching her hand across the table, offering Harry a cigarette, touching his hand.

Customers started drifting in from the cold. It must be close to lunch time, thought Harry. He had been telling his troubles to a total stranger, oblivious of the time.

"It's on the house, love," the woman said when Harry rose to pay. "You didn't have much. And it's been nice talking to you," she added as he left.

A peculiar emotion overwhelmed Harry on his way. He ought to be regretting, he thought, having laid open his personal affairs before a stranger. And yet, on the contrary, he was surprised at the curious sense of elation he felt, as though he had been talking to a long-time friend and confidant.

Waste no time! Start applying for a job as soon as possible, Harry told himself. And his mind drifted into a daydream that seemed to pamper his ego. He would come upon and be snapped up by a prospective employer who had been searching for a man with just his qualifications. He would avoid all the heartache in the interim and be able to tell his wife he had taken Gordon Sinclair's advice and told the boss to go to hell.

The elation soon waned and Harry was faced again with bitter reality. Past experience reminded Harry that he was daydreaming. It wasn't that easy. Memories of agonizing hours waiting in long line-ups at the Employment Office flashed through his mind. He shuddered at the prospect of the torture that lay ahead and felt a twinge as if the sharp end of a needle pricked his heart.

There was no other way...Of course he would talk to Walter at Management first...Walter was a sensible man but...If Management stood by their foreman then he would have to start looking for another job. It would be an emotional storm again but not a new experience for his family...

What if prospective employers asked him why he was leaving his present job? What would he tell them? I had a fight with the foreman? Oh, yeah? You are a recent immigrant to this Country. Is that accepted practice where you come from? It wasn't my fault. He was picking on me. On Christmas Eve!

Well, whatever. We don't want any trouble in our workplace...

Harry felt stigmatized. Would any employer want to listen to him? His best chance would be to see Walter in the office and tell him all that had happened...He was embarrassed at the thought of reciting in detail the absurd causes of the predicament he found himself in. Not that Walter would not believe him, but...Where do I start...?

"It was Christmas Eve. We had swept and tidied up the shop immediately after lunch, waiting to receive our pay-cheques and go home early for the holidays. The men were gathered in a group talking and laughing, in a merry mood. The foreman had gone out for lunch—something he had never done before. But...It was Christmas and it seemed he had decided to treat himself. Suddenly he barged in through the door. He looked different. As though he were angry at something. He was panting. His normally bulging abdomen seemed filled to bursting capacity. He made some factious remark, as though we did not deserve to go home early. Huffing noisily he dashed over to his cubicle then went to the office. We could tell he had been drinking. Why not, we thought. He had started celebrating a little early.

"Holding a number of envelopes in his hand he came back to the shop but before handing them to the men he made the rounds of the shop to see if it had been swept to his satisfaction.

"Harry!" He called in a snarly voice. "There's metal shavings under the lathe. I want you to sweep it up."

"Why don't you ask the machinist?" I said. "It's his machine. I don't do any work there."

"I am asking you to do it," he said. "Are you defying my order?"

"Oh, no!" I said. "Heck. It's Christmas. I'll do anything you say. Peace on Earth and goodwill among men," I said and grabbed the broom and shovel. When I came back he still had not given out the envelopes. The men stood around looking cautious and whispering nervously.

The foreman went inspecting again. "Harry!" he called again. "You haven't done a good job. There's still shavings under the lathe." I felt harassed. He was purposely trying to provoke a reaction. My heart started beating fast. I again reminded myself of the festive motto. "Peace," I told myself and went to see. Sure enough! There was a pile of shavings where I had swept clean before. He had dug into the corners of the drip-tray and dumped a handful on the floor.

Trying to control my nerves I swept the spot a second time and returned to the waiting group. The men stood frozen now in apprehensive silence. The machinist, who was the only person who ever used the lathe, was standing, with a smirk on his face, beside the foreman, at a distance from the rest.

"Harry!" called the foreman a third time, after another round of inspection. "You still haven't swept properly. I want the damned spot cleaned thoroughly." That is when I lost my temper. I could feel my heart hammering in my throat. My hands were shaking. I must have lost concern for consequences.

"Why don't you sweep it yourself," I said and flung the broom and shovel at his feet. I didn't hit him or anything. But I gave him the pretext he was looking for.

"That's insubordination!" he cried. "You're fired."

Walter listened to Harry's story sympathetically, but seemed to make excuses for the foreman. "He may have his character flaws," he said, "but our foreman is a competent technician. We can't just take your word against his and defy his decision."

"Is that, then, approval of his unreasonable behavior, a confirmation of his decision? Are you asking me to pack up my tools and go home?"

"I am not asking you to do anything of the sort," Walter said. "You men have recently joined a union. I'd advise you to see your representative. They may take it up with the Labour Relations Board. I suggest you go through the process and see what comes of it."

Harry sat contemplating in silence and felt his spirits sinking. "I might as well start looking for a job," he said, after a long moment, lost in thought, as he stood and walked, dejectedly, toward the door.

"I wouldn't do that just yet," Walter said. "We can't step over our foreman," he continued, motioning Harry to his seat again. "But we don't want to lose you, either. I've been looking through your file and I see you have other qualifications we may be able to use. You've taken some courses that may be useful. Drafting. Right now, we need a draftsman in the Engineering department. And I see you've done a couple of acclaimed sales courses," Walter said, with a smile of amused astonishment. "We may even be able to combine our talents...I'd advise you to hang tight and be patient for a while."

Harry felt somewhat relieved and sat in silence pondering Walter's implied proposals.

"There's another possibility," Walter said after a long pause. "It is still very confidential at the moment and I trust you will keep it as such. We are being offered representation for an exciting European product and will need a man with your qualifications to take charge of it. The job will involve a great deal of foreign travel and your knowledge of languages will certainly be an advantage."

When Harry went to his car, he found he had left the lights on. The battery was dead. He didn't' care. He hailed a taxi and rode home with a smile in his heart, stopping on the way to buy a bouquet of flowers for his wife.

Hail Vancouver

"Tourists from around the world hail Vancouver for its world-class setting.
If they want civilization, they go to London or
New York or Montreal."
Paul Sullivan
The Globe and Mail, Aug. 4, 2003

We, Vancouverites, who love our city, would be naturally inclined to ask Mr. Sullivan the obvious question: What do they have that you think we don't? But since we cannot engage him personally to present his justification for the claim, we'll try and see if we can come up with some answers of our own.

What attributes of a city, aside from its natural setting, would tourists from around the world be looking for in their quest for "civilization?" What properties distinguish London, New York or Montreal that, as Mr. Sullivan seems to suggest, Vancouver falls short of? One obvious answer might be their ages. Any city, anywhere, that, in the opinion of Mr. Sullivan, has the capacity to cater to the tourists' preference for civilization would, almost certainly, be older or longer established than Vancouver. Another undisputed difference could be size. The three metropolises cited by Mr. Sullivan are and have always been (with the possible exception of Montreal), vastly more populous than Vancouver is today.

But before we become any further absorbed in our discussion, we must determine our interpretation of civilization, and, specifically, the aspect of civilization that tourists in general gravitate to. There is perhaps always a substantial number of professional or amateur students of specialized lore, such as archaeology and anthropology, who will seek out and travel to the most obscure ends of the world to study the remains of an ancient civilization, or the life of a tribe of humans isolated on an island or in a jungle that have remained stuck in a "primitive" state of civilization. But these specialists do not comprise the type of tourists under discussion, though the latter too may appreciate such curiosities of exploration, if included in the package of their itinerary.

Let me also confess at this stage of our inquiry that I do not pretend to speak from extensive experience as a globetrotting man of leisure, but rather from personal observation, as well as travel that has come my way by a twist of fate or the demands and benefits of employment.

I spent my younger years in my birthplace of Cyprus, a small island in the eastern Mediterranean. In my later teens I held a job for a year or so as a photo shop assistant and receptionist. That exposure gave me the opportunity to meet many tourists from around the world first-hand, especially in seasons when the Island was teeming with visitors, and learn about the particular interests that had drawn them there. Whether the sunny beaches or the cool, pine-forested mountains were the enticement of their holiday for some, all took a keen interest in visiting the sites, with guidebook in hand.

Whereas in more celebrated, greater cities notable quarries of touristic pursuit may be concentrated in museums, theatres and art galleries, the points of interest in Cyprus are scattered throughout the island, which is probably smaller in area than the spread of the city of London. Historic eras of the land jostle one another, and tourists enjoy the sights—the natural setting of the Island—as they hop from site to site: from prehistoric, regional artifacts, or Greek statues (in various degrees of wholeness) in the archaeological museum, to Roman columns—some with Biblical connections, many toppled by earthquake, lying in the sand; from antique churches and monasteries clinging to jagged cliffs on mountaintops, or nestled in densely wooded valleys, each one a virtual depository of Byzantine icons and treasures, to remains of Crusader castles: lookout posts of the warrior knights, erected on uppermost elevations of the northern mountain range, precariously perched on precipitous rocky ridges, with a wide view of the sea far below; from the cathedral of St. Sophia, a magnificent specimen of medieval Gothic architecture, still standing (built over two centuries, initiated by the French Lusignans, carried to near completion by the Venetians of Othello's time, captured and converted to a mosque by the invading Ottoman

Turks, before the inhabitants had a chance to hold their first service in it), to the Venetian walls surrounding Old Nicosia, the capital city; and, finally, the stone-built Anglican Church and government offices reminiscent of Tudor style architecture, Westernizing symbols of the British Colonial Administration.

I sojourned in London for over a year, which, for a job-and-accommodation hunting immigrant (or any traveler, for that matter) is too short a time to even pay cursory visits to all that London has to offer. A tourist will find, gathered and displayed in the countless museums and galleries of London, treasures—models, specimens and originals, unearthed, discovered, invented or created—from all fields of endeavour, to meet his or her interest, whether in the sciences, technology or the arts, through which civilization has served mankind.

London, of course, is much more than museums and galleries. Architectural wonders of ageless beauty: palaces, castles and cathedrals designed by engineers of immortal fame; monuments, and sculpture depicting historic figures or events; parks with neatly landscaped grounds, and sites with connections to literary or historic giants, wow the visitors at every step of the tour, and they throng to them in great numbers.

Music and theatre in all their varieties are offered at many venues. Shopping to suit all pockets in districts bustling with people attract tourist and resident alike in all seasons of the year; and for visitors who prefer to observe the population at close range, London affords the leisure to loll about among the crowds in city squares, park corners, railway or transport stations throbbing with multitudes of people at all times.

New York and Montreal may boast of similar outlets for tourists as London, though certainly in lesser degrees concerning aspects of age and history. One attribute common to all three that must be borne in mind, however, is cosmopolitanism. Which brings us to a comparison with Vancouver.

Vancouver, as already admitted, far excels many cities in the beauty of its natural setting, as well as the many bonuses that come with that endowment, such as boating, sailing, water sports, fishing, skiing, golfing, etc.; not to mention the milder winters of our temperate climate; or basking on countless sunny beaches around English Bay on many a summer day.

A glance at the history of Vancouver may surprise you to learn how young the city is. To develop and maintain what Mr. Sullivan seems to refer to as "civilization" takes time and money, requisites that go hand in hand with the growth of an appreciative citizenry. Vancouver has taken great strides over the past fifty or sixty years in the realm of "civilization," whether in arts, entertainment or the sciences. We see it growing and wish and pray that her citizens may grow and mature in pace with her growth.

The Big Rock Mountain Ship Registry of Vancouver Island

Newly launched from her Swedish shipyards, Motor Vessel Euro-Can Forest had neared the first destination of her maiden voyage virtually trouble-free. She had come through the Panama Canal, bunkered at Long Beach, California—where the deck-crane manufacturer's technical representative had also been picked up—and was now in Canadian waters, on course toward her next port of call. She was expected to dock at Gold River Pulp Mill on Vancouver Island early the next morning for her initial loading of cargo.

Young Second Officer, Lars-Erik Johansson sat at the controls of the foremost crane, on his final day of instruction, winding up his course of familiarization with all functions of the powerful lifting machines. He had been assigned supervision of all deck equipment, and it would be his responsibility to see that all systems were "go," and report any malfunction well prior to loading and discharging operations.

"I feel like king of the ocean," he said, beaming, to the technician, with whom he had been training for the past week. It would be an enjoyable addition to his duties, he thought, and felt exhilarated, spinning the crane round and round, surveying three hundred and sixty degrees of empty, blue, shimmering horizon from his lofty perch. The early summer weather had held out, with sunny days and starry nights through the whole week.

The day being Sunday, a holiday spirit already prevailed on board, but the seamen deserved to be awarded the rest of the day for their leisure before arrival. A skeleton staff, consisting of the Captain, the Chief Mate and the Chief Engineer, manned the bridge and control room.

Captain Selgren, the ship's Master, produced a bottle of expensive

Cognac, poured a round of drinks for everyone, and toasted the crew for a job well done. The men and women raised their glasses and drank to the Captain's health with gusto. He presented the bottle to the group and took his leave to join the Mate on the bridge.

The brandy was soon consumed to the last drop. The ship-bound merry-makers drank toast after toast to their favoured heroes, patrons and champions.

"To Canada!"

"Skoal!"

"To all the Swedish hockey players in Canada!"

"Skoal!"

The men's enthusiasm was building up, but the brandy gave out before their inventory of salutations had. Then someone brought from his cabin a nearly full bottle of akvavit. He liked brandy, he said, but preferred the delicate aroma of his own country's best-loved schnapps. Another man, the deck-crane manufacturers' troubleshooter, an outsider in the pack, who had come on board in Los Angeles, brought out, as his contribution to the party, a bag of pistachios he had bought there. The salted nuts whetted appetites anew. A half-full bottle of whisky also appeared on the table, and everyone drank with renewed gusto, all vying to propose the most unexpected yet significant toasts.

"To our Ship and our Company!"

"Skoal!"

"To the hi-tech shipbuilders of Sweden!"

"Skoal!"

"To the cranes! To the magnificent deck cranes on our ship, all six of them, like marble statues of the god Thor, lined up as in procession for battle, sparkling in their white-painted armour of steel!" The proposer of the toast was young Second Officer Lars-Erik Johansson. He had been assigned responsibility for supervision of the cranes, and for the past week at sea had been eagerly working with the manufacturer's technician, learning all he could about the machines' functions and operation.

"Skoal! Skoal! Skoal!" The revelers responded warmly to Johansson's toast.

The festive fervour began to ebb. The drop of the curtain seemed to call for a more indulgent flavour to pamper the palate, and a more profound closing toast.

Ulla, the Radio Officer, one of the two women on the crew, a rather plain-looking but shapely blonde in her early forties, said the best after-dinner liqueur, to her taste, to top all others, was neither brandy nor akvavit. She tottered to her cabin, came back with a bottle of Grand Marnier, and poured everyone a glass for a final toast.

"To all the good folk back home!"

"To all the long-suffering, uncomplaining and forgiving wives and girl-friends whose lonesome menfolk are plying the distant oceans!"

"To Life!"

"To Health!"

"Skoal!"

The strong aroma of percolating coffee permeated the air, signaling a winding down of the merriment, inducing an aura of quiet contentment. Ingrid, a golden-haired young nursing student working her summer break at sea as cook's helper and 'Girl Friday,' put out cups with biscuits on the counter. Some of the men took their coffee and quietly drifted to their cabins. Others lingered in the lounge, smoking pensively. Supper, in due course, would be optional, in the form of an open smorgasbord. The men were not expected on duty until midnight, some until dawn.

Lars-Erik Johansson, alone, had not had his fill of the cranes. The day was still young, the sailing smooth, and the weather clear and warm. He changed quickly back into his coveralls and slipped into his clogs.

"We are going back on the crane, you and I, one more time," he said to the factory technician, slapping him on the back.

The man eyed him with disbelief, for he felt numbness creeping into his limbs. But he complied and also donned his coveralls.

"I applaud your enthusiasm about the cranes," he said, "and there's certainly much more we can learn as we go along. But it seems we have so far neglected one of the most important rules of crane operation: 'Never operate a crane, or even climb into one, after drinking any amount of alcohol.'"

Johansson relished the cool breeze caressing his face as he walked windward along the railing on the cargo deck. His cheeks tingled, and it was about the only sensation he felt. He was not conscious of his feet. It was as though he were being carried along on wings of a bird, gliding the full length of the vessel to the foremost crane, scaling the cold steel ladder inside the tall pedestal, exerting no effort at all. He even entertained a fleeting sensation that he had become endowed with the faculty of flight, and could hardly keep from bursting into hysterical laughter at the thought.

The physical exertion of the long walk in fresh air, and the caution demanded in scaling the pedestal, served to clear Johansson's head and sobered him up somewhat. Satisfied, at last, with his final learning session of crane operating procedure, he and his companion climbed down the ladder, step after careful step, and walked safely astern.

It was quiet at the ship's quarters, except for the muffled pulsation of the engines, and the odd deckhand on duty, who dropped in and out, now and then, for a snack or coffee. A buffet spread had been laid and an urn of coffee brewed in the lounge. Johansson sat down to relax with a cup of coffee. His head throbbed. He needed the rest. But he must try and stay awake at all costs. In a few hours the ship would rendezvous with the pilot's tugboat at the approaches of the narrow inlet to Gold River, and it would be his duty to see that the pilot came aboard safely.

He must have dozed off, Johansson realized, for he was jolted awake by a clamorous commotion in the hallway. Boisterous shouts of men and the clatter of footsteps in chase, punctuated by the gleeful screams of Ingrid, rang through the corridors and up and down stairs.

It wasn't an everyday occurrence. The men were in high spirits, Johansson rationalized, yet viewed the display with mixed emotions of desire and resignation. Besides, he further consoled himself, he was in no condition, nor would his call of duty allow him to join in the chase. Moreover, his observation of Ingrid during the weeks at sea had taught him that she was nobody's easy target. It was true; her lighthearted and jovial presence on board had helped ameliorate the loneliness of life at sea. But she had demonstrated a mature sense of responsibility and had given no cause for rivalries among the men. Johansson knew that the ruckus would soon subside and they would all be exhausted and sleeping in their own cabins. He took his coffee and stepped out onto the deck to let the cold breeze flow over his throbbing head.

He found, to his surprise, that it was already nightfall. The eastern horizon had become obliterated, blending sea and sky, and a faint purple glow on the western distance was fast disappearing in the wake of the setting sun. The weather had become overcast as the ship advanced northward, deepening the night to pitch-black darkness.

Johansson was seized in the grips of a frightening experience as he stepped out into the fresh air. He felt the ship had suddenly been thrown into a powerful spin, as though caught in the eddy of a gigantic whirlpool. He let go of his coffee and held tightly onto the railing, in a useless effort to stop the ship's gyration. But the tighter he held the more violently the ship seemed to pull him along. And then, joining the merry-go-round, as though in a dream, a carousel of brightly lit faces—familiar blondes and brunettes—circled, like a halo, above his head. And he thought he heard their names spoken as they floated past before his eyes.

When the whirling stopped and his head had gained its balance, Johansson found himself kneeling on the deck, his hands still holding tightly onto the railing, a tender whisper of a name on his lips: "Ingrid...Ingrid..."

He raised himself up slowly, and looked around. Thankfully, he was alone. It was the sudden exposure of his aching head to the cool breeze, or his effort to breathe deeper than his lungs could take, that had caused his giddiness, he reasoned. Perhaps he was also famished. A hot and cold shower in his cabin suite should take care of his head. And snacks or sandwiches, as well as tea and coffee were always available in the kitchen. He would feel fine and be well prepared to receive the pilot when he arrived in a few hours.

An intermittent beacon from a distant lighthouse signaled the approaches to the inlet at Nootka Sound. Light-buoys on shore-side guided the ship into a placid cove, and she reduced speed to dead slow in anticipation of the pilot's arrival. A faint speck of light that had been bobbing for some time, now hiding, now appearing on the undulating water far away, drew closer and was soon revealed to be the awaited tugboat. It flashed a strong but momentary beam of light toward the ship, and its horn sounded a sharp, falsetto greeting. The ship answered with a short but powerful boom that echoed in the stillness of the night, rebounding against a wall of cliffs, apparently close by, but invisible in the darkness.

In the flood of light from lamps above the gangway Johansson could see two men standing on the stern of the tug below. He had the gangway lowered ahead of time, and when the tug had come safely close, the men grabbed the railing post, hopped on to the landing and climbed the seemingly interminable stairs to the ship's deck, with their bags slung on their shoulders. They introduced themselves to Johansson: The Pilot, from the Canadian Pilotage Authority, and an officer from Canada Customs and Immigration.

"Maiden voyage?" asked the Customs Officer as Johansson led the men to the Captain's Office.

"Yes, Sir."

"Another entry for the Big Rock Mountain Ship Register, I presume?" the Pilot quipped with a smile. Then, sensing Johansson's bewilderment, "You'll find out when we get there," he added.

The ship entered the inlet at Nootka Sound well past midnight and crept cautiously at idling pace over the sleepy waters of the dark and narrow channel. Towering cliffs and mountains thick with forests, faintly visible in the ship's glow, rose in the darkness, like sheer black walls lining both sides of the waterway. Marker lights, warning of hazardous spots, or indicating the ship's course, appeared at various places along the route, though drifting fog occasionally obliterated all vision.

A putrid odour blew into the channel at one point. The ship rounded a corner to the left and, at long last, the mill loomed in the distance at the far end of the cove. Lit up in a deluge of light from surrounding cluster lamps, inundated in clouds of fumes and steam that billowed from its flues and smokestacks, it glittered in solitary brilliance in the encircling gloom.

By the time the ship was moored at the mill's wharf, a blush of the breaking day had begun to tinge the patch of sky, revealing the forested peaks that circled the little cove in a dark, gradually discernible silhouette. It was enough to reflect in the water below and lend a measure of visibility to features of the landscape and sources of sounds of activity on the water and on shore.

What intrigued Johansson, as he surveyed the periphery of the cove, was the peculiar formation of the hillside beyond the lights of the mill. Advancing dawn revealed the whole mountainside jutting out in what appeared like a gigantic pile of oversized boulders.

With improving visibility Johansson realized that the boulders were not heaped in a loose pile, as he had thought, but were rather fused together, as though, during some volcanic era, molten rock had bubbled up, then frozen in a mountain of lumpy mass, each lump a large hemisphere of clean, smooth granite.

There was something about the spectacle of the "boulders" besides their quaint collective configuration that riveted Johansson's gaze. As dawning day afforded increasingly better clarity of vision, it became apparent that almost every globular surface on the lumpy hillside had been touched by human hands. They seemed to be covered with what Johansson thought looked like graffiti, many artfully designed, in various colours and large sized lettering.

As the inscriptions became more legible with hastening daylight, and their significance began to sink in, Johansson's heart leapt. Each lump of granite bore the name of a ship, its nationality and date of sojourn at Gold River. They were beautifully airbrushed in various colours and characters of exotic languages of the world. And there were dates that went back decades! The whole face of "Big Rock Mountain" had thus become a virtual registry of ships, which the pilot had alluded to when he had come on board in the night. More than that, Johansson thought, it was a veritable open-air art gallery, each picture hung on an imposing granite protrusion on the mountainside.

Johansson felt excited. His ship would, indeed, be the next entry!

Squamish Highway

Harry and his wife, Andrea, were getting ready to go out for the evening when the telephone rang. Andrea picked up the receiver and a ripple of displeasure quivered on her brow.

"It's for you," she told her husband, cupping the mouthpiece with her palm. "It's a man with a foreign accent. Sounds like a call from a ship. Tell them you can't go, Harry," she pleaded, with a note of impatience in her voice. "Not in this weather...and not on a Sunday night! Can't they leave you alone on a weekend at least?" she added, stamping her foot as she handed the receiver to her husband.

"The Company brochures promise twenty-four-hour service, seven days a week," whispered Harry. "Let's see what they want."

The call was from the chief engineer of a freighter docked at Squamish Sawmill, about forty miles by road from their home in Vancouver. One of the ship's deck cranes had broken down. It was critically located to cover two holds at the fore end. The next crane in line was too far out of range. There was no substitute. If it weren't repaired by the following morning the ship could be declared 'off hire.'

Harry was familiar with the term. It was a situation ship-owners dreaded and chief engineers were anxious to avoid at all costs. It meant the vessel would be towed offshore and remain idle at anchor; her turn at the dock would be given to freighters next in line until repairs were completed, costing the owners a great deal of money. It could reflect, besides, on the negligence and incompetence of the chief engineer himself.

The Chief's voice sounded desperate. First thing in the morning was not good enough. The problem had to be attended to "now," have repairs completed overnight and the crane ready for operation in the morning.

Harry was usually willing to make allowances, but prevailing weather conditions could possibly hamper the process, he reasoned. Besides, if the ship had been at a more distant location, or if he had previously been dispatched to another vessel at a different port, it would have taken him much longer—perhaps a day, or more—to arrive on board. Moreover, this was an exceptionally cold, even ice-bound weekend, and family demands and plans as well had to be considered.

"I'll try and be there sometime not too long after midnight," Harry promised as he hung up.

"It's insane to drive to Squamish in the middle of the night in this freezing weather!" Andrea protested. "The highway is probably covered with ice, if it hasn't been closed. Are you trying to kill yourself? You must learn to say no sometimes. They'll respect you more for it."

Harry mused for a moment on the validity of Andrea's statement, smiling to himself. He could recall the many arguments his 'no' had generated and wondered if it had also gained him much respect.

"At least it's close to home, Honey," he said. "I should be back by the evening."

It was midnight when Harry packed his test kit, changed into his long johns and padded coveralls, put on his parka, his gloves and wool cap, and took off in his van.

The city roads, plowed previously and salted for the night, were lined with deep snowbanks burying many cars parked at the curbs. It didn't surprise Harry that the streets were quiet, virtually devoid of traffic on a Sunday night, especially on such a cold one.

When he crossed Lions Gate Bridge and entered the freeway, on the upper levels high above the city, his wife's apprehensive caution appeared to Harry to be justified. A heavy blanket of snow that had fallen a day or two earlier had evidently been touched by a brief, erratic spell of misty warm air. Its surface had barely begun moistening when, overnight, a freak arctic weather pattern had descended, holding the region hostage in its icy grip. The snow, now frozen into a thick crust of hard, unrelenting ice, sprawled all over the area, glistening like the gelatinous effusion of some phantasmagoric oozy creature from outer space or the ocean depths, clinging to every inch of rock, roof and shrub. Menacing giant icicles, like translucent tentacles of the creeping monster, hung in creeks and down cliffs on the roadside, casting eerie reflections and ghastly shadows as

Harry's lights swept past. They even hung from the overladen arms of ice-encrusted fir, pine and hemlock ghosts that covered the whole mountainside in crystalline mounds, and also congregated here and there on the roadside along the way.

The road had been sanded and generously salted, but the highway was mostly dark and wound along with sharp twists and turns at every mile. Harry had to concentrate hard to avoid an accident, skidding over the icy shoulder on the curves.

He had passed Horseshoe Bay when he became aware of the presence of another car in the distance ahead. His had seemed to be the only vehicle on the road at that hour. The faint glow of red taillights came into view and disappeared as he rounded corners. They appeared a little closer each time. When he caught up with the car he realized it had not been moving. It was parked at one of the numerous lookout points on Harry's left. The trunk of a tree could be seen in the beam of its headlights.

Harry shook his head and drove past. Lovers have curious appetites, he thought. Extremes of weather, apparently, were no deterrent.

The neon sign of a truck-stop restaurant at Britannia Beach, halfway to Squamish, was a welcome surprise. It said: "Open 24 Hours."

The matronly owner greeted Harry with a smile. "We get truckers, workers and skiers on their way to and from Squamish and Whistler," she said. "But not too many people are out on a night like this, save for the snowplows and sanding trucks, maybe."

Harry ordered eggs and ham to sustain him until the morning, and coffee to keep him awake. He also needed a break from the exhausting drive.

"Lovers!?" Harry almost said the word aloud, suddenly shaking off a sleepy sensation that had been creeping over him, awakened by a vivid flash, a replay on his mental screen of what he had just seen on the road. It was the steam rising from his coffee, as he gazed at it, holding the cup in his palms for warmth that reminded him of the car parked on the roadside. It had not impressed on his consciousness at the time when he drove past, but recalling the scene in his mental image, he felt almost certain that he had seen a blurry stir against the tree trunk lit up in the car's headlights. It must have been steam wafting from its radiator, he decided.

When he restarted his van and entered the highway again, instead of turning right, toward Squamish, Harry turned left, toward where he had seen the parked car.

What am I doing this for? Harry reproached himself, questioning the sanity of his uncalled-for undertaking, as he drove back on the icy road. It's really none of my business! Besides, I have work to attend to! He was reminded of an occasion when a friend had asked him what he enjoyed about his job, traveling to faraway ports, working at all hours of the day or night, leaving the comforts of home for days or weeks at a time. Was it not hard work, and dangerous, climbing up and down the tall cranes of cargo ships?

It was the challenge of detective work, he had replied. Troubleshooting broken-down machinery, finding the faults and effecting repairs gave him much satisfaction and made the ships' people very grateful.

But I don't have to do this! he kept chiding himself again and again as he maneuvered his van back up the treacherous highway. I'm no Sherlock Holmes, or a real detective! And yet, by some trait of his character, he was driven to investigate.

The lights of the parked car had waned somewhat when Harry reached it. But, weak as they were, if it weren't for them, he thought, he probably would not have seen the vehicle in the pitch-black darkness. Its presence, still at the same spot, as well as its fading headlights, seemed to confirm his suspicion of an accident. He made a careful U-turn on the narrow space of the icy ground and aimed his headlights at the rear of the car. He could see no one inside. He rolled down his window and called out.

"Hullo! Is anyone out there?"

There was no answer. It was quiet, but for the purring of his own vehicle. He turned off the engine. A muffled hush prevailed. He called again.

"Hullo!"

The silence breathed a spellbinding whisper, as of a mysterious waterfall hidden in a dark canyon far away.

Harry reached for his flashlight in the tool-kit and surveyed the surrounding area, sitting in his van.

No soul stirred—inside or outside the parked car. There seemed to be no one about.

As the beam from his flashlight swept back and forth over and around the car Harry began having second thoughts about the situation. He had at first assumed that the car's front end must be smashed against the trunk of the pine tree. He now could see that the tree was in fact several paces further ahead, down the drop of the hillside. Had he been wrong about seeing steam rising from the radiator? That was entirely possible, of course, he admitted to himself. It must have been a cursory impression on his subconscious, he concluded, based on a fleeting glance as he drove cautiously past, paying more attention to the road than to mindless lovers in a side show; an impression, however, that had brewed, in his imagination, into the possibility of a skidding accident.

Whether or not an accident was involved, there was still a mystery surrounding the case, Harry conjectured. The car may have broken down or run out of gas, in which case the driver may have been lucky enough to make contact and find alternate transportation. On the other hand, if there was a driver collapsed on the seat, he must be frozen to death by now. In either case, Harry felt duty bound to investigate, though a sense of some lurking danger nagged the very depths of his consciousness. Cautiously he stepped out of his van and, taking one careful step after another on the slippery ice, he approached the car on the passenger side.

The windows had become frosty. He couldn't tell whether there was anyone, dead or alive, inside. He felt uneasy about attempting to open the doors, or even just touching the car. He began chiding himself again for becoming enmeshed in something that was none of his business. He wished he had listened to his wife's intuitive cautions. This was more than he had bargained for.

He was beginning to be plagued with thoughts of regret when his flashlight revealed a strange accumulation of ice on the car's hood. He took a step forward and was startled to see signs that the windshield had been struck and perhaps broken through by a large chunk of what looked like one of those giant icicles his headlights had lit up hanging from ice-laden trees on the roadside. How far it had imbedded itself, or how badly the windshield was smashed,

Harry couldn't tell, but by all appearances, enough to do substantial damage. He had heard of rocks rolling from the steep mountainside smashing windshields, causing death on this highway; why not bulky blocks of ice falling off trees, he thought, though such extreme severity of weather must be a rare occurrence, if it had ever happened at all.

He stole over to the driver's side of the car, lighting his footsteps over the roughened surface of ice. The driver's door appeared ajar. Harry's steps froze on the spot. Could there be someone inside? If so, it must be more dead than alive. Why else would his calls have gone unanswered? Or...could this be a trap by a deranged assassin to lure and pounce on the curious innocent? He was about to call again when, peering through the slit of the unshut door, he could see a man's shoed foot.

Frozen to death! was Harry's spontaneous assessment. Nevertheless, he was overcome by a creepy sensation of being surrounded by a host of dispossessed souls hiding in the shadows of the dark. Instinctively he pulled back a step and quickly surveyed the immediate vicinity with his flashlight, his heart beating fast. He was seized by an uneasy suspicion that he was being watched.

He waited a moment to regain his composure and peered again through the door.

The general interior of the car looked unkempt and disheveled, as did the man's appearance, though he lay facedown, slumped over the gear control. His clothes seemed roughed up, as though he had been in a life-and-death struggle. Upon an impulse, Harry called "hullo"—rather to shake himself back to reality, hearing his own voice, and make sure he wasn't having a nightmare—but not expecting a reply. The man could only be dead.

Understandable, under the circumstances, thought Harry. He decided to rush to a telephone booth—perhaps at the truck-stop café—call the police, report his discovery of a fatal accident on the highway, and hurry off to his job. He felt uncomfortable facing the eerie situation any longer. An undefined sense of guilt had also begun to torment him.

He pulled back from the gruesome scene, swinging his light left and right for a final view of the car's interior. Suddenly he stopped short, gaping. Something plunged his mind into confusion. His gaze froze on one spot. He had noted dark blotches of blood on the man's clothing. That had been understandable. But when his light shone upon the windshield it came as a stupefying ominous blow. He was stunned and not a little shaken that in his probing of a presumed accident he had failed to observe a striking inconsistency that now glared at him with menacing clarity. The windshield was not smashed—as it had appeared to have been when he had viewed it from outside. Nor was it broken into shards to cause any piercing wounds to the driver—or passenger, if there had been one.

A cold, prickly sensation crept up Harry's spine, tingling the hair on the back of his neck, despite the heavy parka he wore. "Murder!" he gasped and could not help his mind becoming engulfed in a flood of regrets. What business was it of his to know what lay in the sidelines of his path? I must be crazy, he told himself, and his wife's words began ringing in his ears: "It's insane to go out on a night like this!" A woman's intuition, he thought. I should have listened to her.

The unexpected discovery upset his stomach and he turned away, fighting a strong urge to throw up. The dead man was now no longer a victim of an accident, caused in part by nature's contribution to the predicament, as Harry had believed, but a prey to human violence, foul play, man's brutality against man, and unnatural.

Impulse prompted Harry to flee. But, considering that the murder was of such recent execution, his mind began concocting obstacles of caution and fear. What if the perpetrators were lurking in the surrounding darkness? He had misgivings. He was paralyzed; his legs felt heavy as lead, mired in the thick, strangling aura of tangible evil that seemed to pervade the very air he breathed.

But flee he must. A sense of duty compelled him to report his discovery to the authorities without delay and let a professional detective solve the crime. He took a headlong step toward his van and slipped over the ice. In the erratic flailing of his flashlight, as he tried to steady himself, ice-encrusted trees glared back like a multitude of gigantic ghosts, their frozen limbs spread down in hostile posture; menacing shadows danced before Harry's eyes; dark figures whirled and vanished. Was it an invasion of evil spirits? Harry thought he saw a solid dark figure slip in through the open door of his van. He was sure he saw the van rocking. His imagination fell captive to fantastic stories of kidnappings by extraterrestrial aliens; or abductions by the Sasquatch, the legendary, hairy, human-like giant of the local forest, whom some people claimed to have seen.

A short pause, spent in focused self-reflection in the sleepy silence of the frozen night, helped Harry recapture his mental balance. Nightmarish situations such as this—he admonished himself—give rise to wild imaginings in weaker minds. He wasn't one of those simpletons. He was a man of sound and rational mind. He wasn't going to allow himself to be swayed by such preternatural, hypnotic influences. He took a deep breath of invigorating cold air and stomped to the door of his van. A quick glance inside revealed nothing but his tools and test equipment. He jumped into his seat and started the engine. After a few hectic seconds, with the tires spinning in forward and backward attempts, the van took off and was on its way.

He had driven perhaps a hundred yards when the cliffs at the approaching curve loomed ahead in the beam of his headlights. Overhung with heavy pillars of ice, they were reminiscent, Harry thought, of the columned gates of mythological castles in fairy tales. The comparison captured his imagination as he drove on, oblivious to the bend of the icy road when, as though through supernatural intervention in wish-fulfillment, the columns were suddenly flooded with a powerful, penetrating brightness, a heavenly brilliance that seemed to light up the whole mountainside, transforming the columns, in Harry's vision, into a sparkling crystal gateway to a story-book castle. And Harry, overwhelmed by the unearthly light, thought he saw a familiar figure, larger than life, standing at the gates, beckoning him to enter. The sound of a thousand trumpets blared accompanying the harbinger of light, as though heralding his arrival, and the beautiful figure stood at the gates beckoning, ushering him in, and Harry heard a voice bidding him to "enter the crystal gates of glory!" and a thousand bells chimed and tinkled as he crashed through, and in that brief moment of evanescent consciousness Harry wondered why the voice had sounded like his own, and found himself in the comforting arms of his wife, "Andrea!"

Harry lay sedated at Lions' Gate Hospital. Andrea sat beside his bed, her hand gently resting on his bandaged arm. Several men—one or two in uniform, another in coveralls—as well as a nurse were present in the room.

"I must thank all of you people for finding my husband in good time, flying him to hospital and caring for him to save his life," Andrea spoke. "I'm also very grateful to the RCMP for arranging for me to be with my husband. You men must each have a story about him. I'd like to hear you all."

"All we did is our everyday duty to the public, Ma'am. Routine." It was the helicopter pilot who spoke. "I believe the paramedics will agree. But if there's one man who really deserves your thanks it has to be the sanding truck driver who first notified everyone."

"I had sanded and salted the road, all the way to Squamish," the man in work clothes responded. "I was now running back to base to reload. I had just turned a blind corner, and I see this van, some distance away, speeding down as if he had lost control. At that speed, I could tell, he wouldn't be able to swing the curve safely. I was sure he would have skidded and crashed or rolled into the ice-bound cliffs. Or, if he did manage to stay on the road, he would have come plowing onto my snow-blade. I had to do something to make him aware of my presence on the road, and, maybe, to wake him up. I turned on my searchlight and blew the horn loud and long. But...I'm sorry Ma'am; it didn't help. He drove straight into the columns of ice on the cliffs. I'm sorry Ma'am."

"Please don't feel badly, Sir," Andrea said, softly. "My husband is a dreamer. He gets carried away sometimes. The time was late. He may even have fallen asleep on the wheel. It's hard to tell what happened. He should never have been on the road," she said, dabbing her eyes. "But he would surely have frozen to death if it weren't for your presence there to save him. So, thank you!"

A police detective, accompanied by a nurse, entered the room.

"This officer wants to ask the patient about a car parked on the roadside not far from where the patient crashed," said the nurse, introducing the officer to the attending nurse.

"We want to know if the patient had seen the dead man in the parked car," said the officer.

"What dead man? What would a dead man have anything to do with my husband?" Andrea asked, agitated.

"Nothing, really, Ma'am. Just that he happened to be a crew member of the ship your husband was en route to. There's no other connection or involvement. He carried a suicide note. The story will be in the news in the morning, so, I guess, maybe I can let you know. It seems he had been 'commissioned' to perform a dangerous, criminal assignment, but had changed his mind. 'I am not afraid to die,' said the note, 'but I want no part of the dirty job. It is wrong.' It's just routine investigation, Ma'am, that's all. But it can wait for a more suitable time. Nothing to be concerned about, really. Thank you."

Long Beach Holiday

The wide expanse of clean, smooth sand which stretched for miles at Long Beach, on the west coast of Vancouver Island, was an inviting sight on a hot summer morning and promised a welcome holiday. My wife and I could cast our cares on the mighty breakers that whipped the shore wave after pounding wave. And, with our cares, arguments, if not drowned, would at least be muffled for a short week in the deafening roar of the surf. Our daughter, Linda, eight years of age, would have no trouble keeping busy building sand castles or collecting shells. Our fifteen-year-old son, Richard, who had lived his impressionable years and reached his teens in the rebellious 'sixties, would have an opportunity to experience the closeness of family.

We had arrived early in the day, it seemed, for, though there were numerous cars, campers and tents put up along the edge of the sandy strip farthest from the water, the beach was, as yet, not crowded. At a suitable spot we parked our car and set about unpacking, I, the tent and related equipment for an immediate shady retreat from the blazing sun, and my wife, Alice, the food and accessories for the picnic. We were hungry as well as tired after the long drive from Vancouver.

"Where is that boy going? My God! Call him back, Jerry, call him back!"

My wife's frantic voice suddenly interrupted my leisurely absorption in the intricacies of setting up the tent and alerted me to the fact that the wild surf that had attracted us in the first place could instantly turn into a monster ready to devour the unwary.

Raising my head from the trunk of the car, I was just in time to see our son running into the water with the air mattress in his embrace. He had found it among the pile of paraphernalia in the car, inflated it and was hurrying now to enjoy its use as a float. By the time I reached the water he had already gained a fair distance and almost disappeared.

"Go after him! Call him back!" his mother urged.

Our panic acquired an even more distressing urgency when we noticed, just at that moment, a sign on a large board that warned of "Dangerous Undertow."

What did undertow mean?

There was no time to find out. Whatever it meant, it was obvious that the ocean could not be taken for granted.

I waded into the water and, with my hands cupped around my mouth, called after him. He didn't hear me. I could hardly hear myself in the thunder of the surf. He seemed to be heading toward a small island, about two hundred yards away, that appeared to be swarming with sea birds.

Keeping my feet on solid bottom became more and more difficult as I kept wading further in, bouncing upward to keep my head above the rolling waves. Suddenly the bottom was no longer there, and, just as suddenly the meaning of undertow came home to me in a flash. I had lost the ability to control my direction and kept drifting away—not offshore, fortunately, but not toward land either. No swimming expertise (which, I admit, I possessed in no great degree) seemed to help. The waves raced toward the shore, row after row, yet I was being driven sideways, caught in the fast-flowing current of a sub-surface river. There was no telling if at some point the current might change direction and carry me outward into the ocean. Why not call for help? "Help! Help!" Not so loud! Aren't you ashamed? A little girl playing in the shallows heard me and ran away, scared.

Several hundred yards from where I had entered the water my feet touched bottom again and I could wade back ashore.

We watched anxiously as our son floated, apparently unperturbed, paddling facedown, and headed straight toward the island. How he kept so accurately on course and made such steady progress against the rolling waters I could not understand. Although he seemed to blur into the background on the shady side of the island, still, we were able to discern his movements at that distance and saw, with a sigh of relief, when he landed on his rocky destination.

No lifeguards whom we could notify were to be seen on the beach and the few campers in the vicinity seemed unaware of our predicament.

We waited in suspense and prayed for Richard's safe return.

Our prayers may have risen to heaven in silence but were uttered vocally in the form of argument and were expressed in blame, guilt and remorse. We came to the decision that I should spend more time with my son, and I agreed to go fishing with him when, by the grace of God, he returned to us safe and sound.

He did come back.

When next we raised our heads, there he was, standing in the shallow edge of the water, washing himself and his float. The island, he said, was deeply covered with mushy bird droppings.

That afternoon I took out the rods and bait (which had been intended for use in some lake or river) and, with the blessing of my wife, took my son on a fishing expedition.

We looked left and we looked right and as far as our eyes could see in either direction the water was at war with the land. The sea kept battering the shore with unbridled fury.

Where or how does an ignorant greenhorn take his son fishing in an angry ocean?

But then, our purpose was to spend some time in each other's close company doing something enjoyable together.

And so we walked and walked, looking for a suitable spot.

Whether the idea had appealed to Richard, or perhaps in atonement for the anxiety he had caused us earlier, he came along without protest.

At a considerable distance northward, far from any campers, the sandy beach tapered off and came to an end beside a rocky protrusion: a small, low-lying peninsula that stretched into the water for about fifty yards. Hopping from rock to jagged rock we made our way to the head point. It stood safely above the wash of the waves yet low enough so that we could sit and cast our lines. One or two straggling cypress trees, thwarted and windswept, clung in seemingly soilless crevices. It was a small area but we settled comfortably and looked forward to several hours of leisurely fishing in the afternoon sun.

The hope and anticipation of a bite — a little signal of communication with the hidden world of the sea—that may never occur, can keep one captive for hours without sensing the passage of time. It is good exercise in patience and it was good practice for a fifteen-year-old adolescent as well as for his father.

Before we knew it the clouds in the watery western horizon began to acquire a variety of fiery colours. The sunset was not to be missed! We would savour the fleeting moment of beauty in silent meditation and then make our return to the campsite where my wife and daughter must be waiting to have dinner.

We collected our gear and turned to start our descent to the beach only to find, to our surprise, that we had been standing on a small island. The tide had come in and surrounded us, and the sea, wild as ever, still raged on.

What could we do? Dive into the maelstrom of the seething waters and try to swim ashore? The possibility of being battered over the rocks or carried away in the undertow, perhaps even drowning, would be too big a risk to take.

If we waited for the tide to go out again we would be certain to incur the reproof of Alice and Linda. That would be a risk of an emotional storm—hopefully a temporary one—but would at least ensure our physical survival.

It was cold and pitch-dark after the sun had gone down. I dug into my pockets and was lucky to find the crumpled remnant of a book of matches. We scrounged for twigs, bits of driftwood and dried branches from the trees, built a fire and waited.

We had established good rapport, my son and I. The atmosphere between us was relaxed. He took the situation in stride and this additional course in the virtue of patience served as a lesson in being prepared to accept calmly a predicament that we could not change.

Above the surge and wash of the waves that raged beneath us we could hear a repetitive splash as we sat huddled in the warmth of the fire. We turned around to find the water had risen close to our perch, and were more than a little startled at the sight of a man swimming in the dark swirl. He clambered up the rocky side of our little island, panting heavily, and we could see, in the light of our fire, that he clenched an open knife between his teeth. He was clothed in shirt and ragged jeans. His face showed a stubble of several days' growth. His eyes, a blurry greyish green, appeared out of focus: he faced us yet seemed to be looking beyond.

"What are you doing here, man?" he said, gazing at the fire with a hungry look. His teeth chattered and he shivered in his dripping clothes as he spoke.

Trying to keep my cool—though I could feel my heart racing in my chest—I told him of our embarrassing situation.

"I thought you were cooking on the fire," he said. "I'm hungry, man. I haven't eaten anything for three days." And he babbled on deliriously. Though I could make no sense of what he said, it sounded like a story of violent fights, killings and escapes.

"I gotta go," he said suddenly, put the knife back between his teeth, dove into the dark billow, and swam—away from shore, as though escaping capture.

My son and I stared at each other. Could we have done that? Swum ashore, that is? What were we doing here waiting for the tide to go out while two helpless women were probably wondering whether we were dead or alive? Were we cowards or what?

The tide turned and we headed back to the beach, groping our way over rocks and through puddles, in the blackness of the night. We had no watch to tell the time, but I figured it must be well past midnight. Though returning empty-handed and outrageously late, we stepped on dry sand ecstatic at our deliverance and walked with a lightness in our feet and a curious sense of contentment in our hearts. We had had a day of unusual experiences, survived an ordeal together and developed friendly, non-confrontational communication between father and son. (Though our contentment was tinged with a painful sense of guilt and penitence, in anticipation of the deserved chiding that awaited us.)

How We Raised a Robin Chick

Something stirred among the driven leaves at the curb, a few paces from my van, as I parked under the maple trees on our boulevard. I stopped to investigate before going inside, and found, as I had suspected, a recently hatched baby robin. Probably fallen out of its nest, I surmised, and its mother still unaware of its absence, or reconciled to its loss. If I ignored it and let it be, cats would be sure to find it, though it had an almost perfect camouflage, sitting still. I would not forgive myself in that event. I took the cheeping, wide-mouthed, hungry little ball of fluff in my palm, carried it into the house and presented it to my daughter, Linda, who was thirteen at the time.

I dug a can of squirmy worms in the backyard and fashioned a cozy little nest with rags in a small plastic bucket. My daughter assumed the duty of foster mother and started feeding the insatiable, ever-demanding mouth.

It didn't take long for the voracious orphan to identify Linda as its source of sustenance. Every time it saw her passing by, regardless of the time of day (or night) it would rise on its legs, stick up its head, with mouth wide open, and raise a racket in the house with heart-rending shrills of hunger, wings fluttering, bouncing up and down in desperate effort to reach above the rim of the bucket.

Placing the "nest" higher up on the refrigerator provided a temporary solution. But our winged little foster child was growing by leaps and bounds. Very soon its beak could reach the rim of the pail and its sharp eyes began to survey its surroundings. Its body grew in size and its wings in strength. It would no longer chirp and beg and wait to be fed.

One evening, having quietly espied Linda studying at the dining table with her back turned, our little robin decided it was time to embrace Nature's purpose for its wings and obey the command of its instinct. It hopped out of the bucket and, wildly flapping its wings, became safely, if somewhat awkwardly, airborne. Chirping, as though with the excitement of victory, it flew through the kitchen doorway and, with no hesitation, perched on top of Linda's head. The chirping now became an insistent, clamorous demand for immediate gratification of an insatiable, perpetual hunger.

This newly discovered ability became a frequent performance, noisier and noisier every time. Landing on Linda's head, the ravenous little robin, its wide-open mouth gaping to Heaven, would cry and quiver, chirp and twitter for more and more food. The only time of day when there was peace and quiet in the house was when the lights were out at night. We learned, for the mutual comfort of bird and man, to simulate its natural environment by placing a dark cloth over its "nest."

But our foster child had learned to fly and was no longer a helpless baby. It had to be let go. We worried whether it would be able to fend for itself, or become prey to an alley cat. I took the bird, with the bucket, outdoors, set it on the grass and started feeding it. My daughter remained inside. The bird, not seeing Linda, did not attempt to fly, but took the worms from my hand, chirping and twittering as usual.

Then, unexpectedly, a strange situation ensued. Apparently attracted by the commotion, an adult robin suddenly appeared on the scene. It swooped down into the yard, chattering excitedly, and made an obvious attempt to get close to the bucket and the chick — but for the presence of a meddling human in the relationship. The visitor hopped from grass to shrub, then back and forth several times, chattering in an agitated, restless manner, obviously trying to make contact with the chick. I decided to withdraw and observe the unfolding spectacle from the kitchen porch.

What followed was nothing short of a miracle. Upon my withdrawal from the scene the adult robin made a sudden exit from the yard, disappearing for a very short time. It promptly returned with a worm in its beak. The chick gulped it down without hesitation, as though in its natural nest. The process was repeated several times, the adult bird flying off on its mission, chirping happily, returning with yet another squirmy worm, feeding the chick with motherly attention. Then, as the adult bird flew away for the next feed, the young robin also took off after it.

We stood gaping at each other, my wife and daughter and I. Had our little foster bird found its natural mother? Were we ever going to see it again, or recognize it if we did? Had the adult bird identified her young from its chirpings? (I had heard or read somewhere—as well as witnessed of many a spring daybreak—that robins teach their young their individual code of communication by singing to them, over and over, in the cool and quiet hours of early dawn, a series of four or five notes, sung in soft and dreamy chirps. The chick responds in a hardly audible chip-chip-chirrup.)

Just as we turned to go inside, with mixed emotion, a robin swooped down and perched on the railing of the kitchen porch, chirping, quivering, and looking at us wistfully. Was it the chick? Did it expect to be fed? If my daughter had been closer would it have landed on her head?

It flew away.

The next day 'it' came back and perched again on the same spot, chattering. But its chatter this time was a calm and composed attention getter. If it was the mother bird, it may have come to say thank you for keeping her offspring alive. On the other hand, if it was the chick, all grown-up, it most likely came for a final farewell, perhaps to say thank you, and to tell us not to worry, it had discovered its roots and all was now well.

My Daughter's Wedding

I have albums and boxes of photos at home, accumulated over a period of time when, like many people, I used to take a lot of pictures. I was not and never became a serious amateur. And, even though in my younger days I had worked with a professional photographer for a year, I never became anything approaching a professional, either. Nevertheless, some of the pictures in my collection—I could even dare to say, many of those pictures—are really not bad at all. Representing different eras in our family's life, they come in three general groupings: the earlier ones in black-and-white; then, colour slides; and finally, colour prints.

A number of the pictures, on the other hand, are, really, very good. And that is no thanks to my skill as a photographer; but rather because I've had beautiful, inspiring models. The best of the pictures are, perhaps, among the colour slides, which were taken when our daughter, Linda, was a beautiful, sparkly-eyed, exuberant, photogenic, bubbly little blonde "Shirley Temple."

I must confess, of course, that by that time I had had some practice in taking pictures of beautiful girls. The best pictures in the black-and-white series, you see, are those of Linda's mother, who was a beauty in her own right. She still is—my beautiful wife, Alice.

In the Colour Slides series there is a picture of 3-year-old Linda playing on the beach next to an inflatable swan. It was a warm and balmy summer day in Vancouver. Her mother and I watched Linda as she seriously patted a pyramid of wet sand, oblivious to her surroundings, rapt in her creative endeavour.

I remember the occasion, because, though she had been deeply absorbed in her project of building a castle, Linda suddenly sprang to her feet, laughing, obviously pleased with her achievement, and, flapping her arms, as though in rapture, flying like a bird on the wing, dashed into the water, leaving behind her swan, which was supposed to be her safety floater. I jumped and ran after her. Just as I reached her she tripped and fell facedown into the water. I immediately picked her up—and she was still laughing ecstatically.

For some years after that incident, I wondered—though I never mentioned it to her mother—I wondered if there would be occasion in Linda's future when I would have to run to her rescue.

My concern proved to be unfounded and unwarranted. Linda grew into her teens, graduated from university, and reached adulthood, with a well-balanced personality. Her amiable character and caring spirit is evidenced by the great number of warm and intelligent friendships she cultivated, and the many words of praise and appreciation she was bestowed upon, as well as tribute paid by parents, associates and others involved in her work as a child therapist and counsellor. She was even made an honourary member of a Native First Nation, in gratitude. And throughout, she never lost her zest for life or sense of humour, and always filled our home with joy and laughter.

When Linda was fourteen, her mother and I took her overseas so she could meet her grandparents and other kinfolk. One admiring relative predicted that it wouldn't be long before we saw Linda married.

And so we waited...and waited...and wondered what she was waiting for.

And then, one day, on one of British Columbia's picturesque islands, at a centre where seekers after Truth, and people of kind heart congregate, Linda met a kindred spirit. His name was Michael. She then flew away, one day, straight to a place called Bend, in Oregon, to visit him. On her way back, she called to say she was coming home with Michael. They would be arriving late in the evening. "That's quite all right. I can pick you up from the airport any time of the night. Are you changing planes in Portland, or Seattle, perhaps?" "Oh, no. We are not flying." "Not flying? Taking the train, then?" "No. Not the train, either." "I see. Michael must be driving, then. Well; take your time. Drive safely." "Oh, no, Dad. We are on Michael's motorcycle." "What! Motorcycle!" Oh, my God! I thought. Now, there was my feared alarm call, at last! But how could I jump and rush to her rescue, now? And at this advanced age?

The jolly tone in Linda's voice, however, was reassuring.

They arrived. And, once again, my anxiety was proven unwarranted. She had been riding with an angel. No. Not the kind of "angel" we have learned to associate with motorbikes. This was a real angel; on two wheels instead of wings. And now we knew why Linda had been waiting all these years. They sure took a long time finding each other, though.

Michael, we greet you in words of our Armenian language—words which, somehow, I feel you will understand: Michael, menk kezee g'sirenk. We love you, Michael. We welcome you as our son, we embrace you and take you to our hearts.

And, finally, Ladies and Gentlemen, I wish to thank every one of you who have come from near and far, to honour us and celebrate Michael and Linda's wedding. May I ask you to join me, please, with a toast to their union.
TO MICHAEL AND LINDA! God bless you both!

Tales of Travel and Work

Sidetracked to Salvador

During my years as a technician of hydraulic deck cranes on cargo vessels, I often performed my duties at sea, while the freighter plied its course from one port to another. I operated as a freelance contractor, receiving my instructions from a Vancouver company which represented the European manufacturer of the cranes and also acted as agents for the East Coast representatives in New York. On one such occasion I completed a job en route to Panama, having boarded the ship at Houston, Texas.

In Colon, Panama's Atlantic seaport, the ship's agents asked me to call our Head Office in New York for a message. Heading north, on my way home, how would I like to stop by in El Salvador for a ship with crane trouble?

"Salvador? Isn't that where they're having some kind of revolution?"

"Oh, no! You're thinking of Nicaragua. Or, is it Guatemala? No, no! There's nothing going on in Salvador."

Armed with a letter of introduction, but without a visa, I arrived in early afternoon at San Salvador, Capital City of El Salvador, a small country on the Pacific coast of Central America.

My letter created quite a stir amid whispers and consultations. No one spoke English, and I spoke no Spanish. I was finally led to an adjoining empty room, offered a lone chair, and asked to wait and not go anywhere.

In late afternoon a young man strode into the room and introduced himself in fairly good English.

"My name is Miguel. I will be your driver. I will take you to your destination."

In the car Miguel produced a small book.

"I will be your driver and you will be my teacher," he said, handing me a thin manual of English conversation for beginners. "You will ask me the questions, and I will give the answers, so I practice my English."

Fair deal! No other ride of any distance had ever offered a more interesting prospect to fill the dull moments of the drive. Besides, I could probably pick up a few words of Spanish for myself in the bargain.

Sparse traffic on the highway afforded us a more leisurely drive and more comfortably to pursue our tutorial diversion, but images and impressions I carry in my memory lend a basic identity to my brief contact with El Salvador.

As we wheeled to enter our main route we came upon a crowd of women, bent over in the middle of the road, obstructing traffic, filling pots and pails from broken sacks of sugar which had apparently fallen off a truck.

A lone young man in blue jeans, sleeveless undershirt and cowboy hat, walked along the highway at a leisurely pace, as though he was in no hurry to get anywhere, casually swinging a bare machete in his hand. It was the tool of his trade, as I gathered.

Sugarcane fields were visible in the distance.

On our left, spread out over a wide and shallow, rock-strewn section of a river below the highway, a crowd of village women were washing laundry, beating stacks of soaking clothes with wooden paddles on squeaky-clean granite boulders.

A solitary canopy came into view in the distance. "Maybe we find something to eat there," Miguel said. "We are hungry, no?"

It was a welcome suggestion. I hadn't eaten anything since breakfast on the early morning flight from Panama.

The place wasn't much of a sidewalk café, but there were welcoming signs of the glowing embers of a wood-fire in a makeshift, raised stone grate, and a lump of cornmeal dough on an improvised counter. There was no table about, and the only furnishings on the dirt floor seemed to be two rustic, shaky chairs. A peasant woman slapped tortillas between her palms, "baked" them on the hot metal sheet that topped the fire, and served them spread with fresh-churned water buffalo butter. Miguel asked her whether she had any avocados. She produced a small bucketful and started cutting them open with a rusty machete, showing them to us for our approval, holding the threatening weapon right under our noses. Most of the avocados turned out to be bad, but two met our approval. We had our fill and were on our way.

In a valley, far below to our left, workers and machinery were busy, like ants, clearing shrubbery, combing and tilling the red soil in an area that formed a large basin between slopes. Miguel said it was a German company preparing the ground for a coffee plantation. Coffee was one of the Country's major exports, and German companies owned most plantations.

The sun set and darkness fell during the last leg of our drive, and the surrounding was no longer visible. And yet darkness offered one of the most spectacular sights I have ever been lucky enough to witness. Streaks of light started flashing all around us as the car sped along. Fireflies! Dozens of them at every pace!

At long last we arrived at our destination. The dockyard gates were manned by an armed military guard, which, I thought, was somewhat unusual. My driver was allowed entry and drove me to the ship. Our brief friendship had come to an end. We shook hands and parted, with gratitude on both sides.

The ship was discharging fertilizer, specifically for coffee plantations.

In the morning a message from our office in Vancouver advised me to call my wife. She had been informed of the digression in my itinerary, had apparently heard that a government minister of El Salvador had been assassinated a day or two earlier, and that a crisis situation prevailed in the Country. I assured her that I had seen or heard nothing to that effect, and that there was nothing to worry about.

I finished the job on board and returned safely home, still unaware of any crisis.

But we were soon to hear, read and see glimpses on television of continuing assassinations, political murders, suppression of protests, torture of the innocent poor, and how El Salvador dominated the news for many years as it sank deeper and deeper in the grip of violent, bloody revolution.

An Affair at an Arctic Hotel

"The job and working conditions may not be anything to get excited about, but I'm giving you a rare chance, an opportunity of a lifetime only very few people are lucky enough to have: A free trip to the Beaufort Sea, up north, in the Arctic Circle. Whadya say?"

My boss didn't have to try hard to persuade me. Although my travel assignments had not always yielded leisurely sightseeing diversions, still, just having been there often seemed privilege enough; and, indeed, I might never be presented with this undreamed-of Arctic opportunity ever again. The time of year was mid-August, the season of the midnight sun for a further few weeks. The sea was not ice-bound and would not be for some time yet. Offshore oil and gas exploration in the region was in full progress, and I was assured the job in question would not be in isolation over a godforsaken, desolate expanse of frigid water.

Some months earlier we had designed and installed the hydraulic system in a crane barge. It had been towed away and was now at its destination at a man-made island in the Beaufort Sea, northeast of Alaska. The control arrangement we had incorporated had proven unsuited for the Arctic climate, and I was being sent to modify the system.

The early morning flight from Vancouver covered some exhilarating scenery of boundless forest and rugged mountains over British Columbia and Yukon Territory, making one stop at Whitehorse. It afforded, as well, a brief view of the bleak, marshy tundra of the Northwest Territories before landing at Inuvik airport, on the McKenzie delta, at noontime, with a full load of passengers.

An agent of the companies operating in the area, a young man by the name of Bruce, met me and drove me down to the water's edge. A small seaplane soon arrived at the wooden dock and flew me a fair distance to a floating transfer station. Anchored in the middle of the ocean, with no land or human activity in sight, the structure looked like an impressive lodging house and apparently served arriving and departing employees, engineers and visitors connected with the activity abuzz in the area. The plane dropped me off at the dock with my bag and flew away. I looked about for a doorway and walked into what I assumed would be a lobby, only to discover that, impressive as it was, this lodging house wasn't anything close to a hotel. The "lobby"—such as it was—was a large hall, cool and clean, with polished floor, and empty. There was no reception desk anywhere, and not even a single soul to be seen. I felt suddenly abandoned and alone. I must be the only transient "patron" at that moment, I thought—it was so lonely.

I called "Hullo!" and waited. Two men finally appeared, with apologies, and said they hadn't been expecting anyone at that hour, but had been quite busy during the day. They offered me coffee—which, I discovered, had been brewing at a self-serve counter—and introduced me to the manager in the office. I was asked to wait for the helicopter, which was away on an errand. I had noticed the empty landing pad at one end of the roof and, though weary and bored, I now waited with some anticipation. It would be my very first helicopter ride.

Whether waiting patiently or fidgeting with boredom, the hours were slipping away. And unless you watched the clock, and had it marked for am or pm, you couldn't tell, by the light of day, morning from evening, or east from west, for that matter: the sun was forever undulating all around a circular horizon.

The Manager, who must have been aware of the working hours on the "islands," called me into the office and said it would be wise to take a boat ride rather than wait for the helicopter that was being delayed indefinitely. He would man the boat himself and deliver me personally to the post of my appointment.

There goes my fantasy of a helicopter ride, I thought, somewhat let down. But then, I consoled myself, a boat ride on a bleak ocean, where the sunrise doesn't truly light up, or the sunset truly darken, may have its own, perhaps hidden, panoramic rewards!

The Manager, who also, apparently, bore the title of Captain, brought the boat out to the dock for our trip. It turned out to be enough of a novelty to compensate for my disappointment over the helicopter. The craft was a bare, open hull of a boat, with a pilot's seat near the fore end, and a bench-like seat at the rear. What made it unusual was the propeller that drove it. Not the conventional marine propeller, immersed in the water, but an aerial propeller, like an oversize fan, mounted on the stern, encaged in heavy wire mesh, blowing backward, driving the vessel forward.

The weather was calm and clear, almost warm; the sea placid, with not a ripple of a wave. Our boat glided on the surface without agitating the water, as other boats do. Other than the novelty of the boat, however, the ride, as I remember it, was dull, with the Captain at the controls at the fore end, me isolated at the rear. The colour of the ocean was dull, as was that of the sky. I did see the top ends of two or three drill rigs in the far distance, but nothing else to engage my interest.

My enthusiasm over the Arctic experience, however, did not dull, regardless. I do gratefully admit that the good ship as well as the good captain delivered me to the island of my destination, safe and sound, in less than an hour. A neatly packed and leveled platform of sand, fine gravel and cement, the size of a football field or two, contained in a surrounding wall of boulders and concrete, the island rose perhaps twelve feet above the surface of the water. All human activity, through what remained of the working day, was centred on the main dock area where my barge was stationed. Equipment of all kinds was being unloaded and busily carried and stored in sheds or hangars.

There was not much excitement after work. A few of the men kicked or threw a ball back and forth. Then, a soothing silence descended, caressing this dot of a solitary islet in the vast and empty sea, and it was quiet in the camp. Bedtime crept wearily, and a sense of loneliness and isolation, like a dark and gloomy cloud, now seemed to hang over the group of men—each man an island to himself. Blinds were drawn for darkness.

Amateurish sounds of a piano tinkled from a corner of the dormitory.

"Your daughter?" asked a voice from a different corner.

"Yes."

"It's good."

"Thanks."

By the end of the following working day I had completed my job, showered, packed and made ready for my return home in the morning. I was to be picked up and flown to Inuvik by helicopter. While we waited—with the site manager and a few men to help with the craft's landing—the Arctic weather, which had been calm and almost balmy, suddenly put on a freak display of its wintry possibilities. A cold gust of wind, driving a maelstrom of dry snow, originating from no apparent source, blew in bursts of wildly shifting directions, propelling the swirling flakes into a confused dance, now spiraling upward, now fluttering every which way, hesitating in mid-air, then darting away into thin air, never settling. Just then the helicopter arrived overhead. It was a large passenger transport and appeared quite full. Apparently battling the wind, it made several attempts at landing. But at every precarious attempt, before it could touch ground, it seemed to be caught in a rattling side-to-side motion. It took off quickly into safer heights to avoid crashing. Regaining control, it came back again and again. Finally it abandoned the plan and flew away. (I have since learned that what the helicopter had been experiencing was what is called wind shear: an erratic pattern of shifting wind dreaded by all pilots at takeoff and landing.) I flew back to Inuvik by seaplane. My hoped-for helicopter ride was not to be.

Bruce met me at the dock and checked me into a hotel. Although the sun would not set, and though, now brighter now dimmer, it was daylight all day, yet, by the clock it would be said to have been nightfall when I arrived back on land. Considering that I was scheduled to fly home to Vancouver by noon the next day, I thought I'd use to advantage the short time that I had on this rare opportunity in the Arctic and explore, if not the town in detail, at least my immediate surroundings. Traveling alone can be a lonely affair if you don't take an interest in the novelty of your new environment. Locking yourself up in your hotel room, especially when it's daylight outside—even with a good book or television—calls for a great deal of saintly meditation in order not to succumb to depression. I stepped outside. And though I had noticed that houses in the Arctic are built on stilts, I also soon learned that the permafrost melts in the summer, and if you do not walk on raised wooden sidewalks or paved roads you are liable to step into soft and deep mud. A pack of massive husky dogs didn't seem to mind the mud. Probably fed up of a summer without snow, frustrated with idleness, they were having an apparently friendly, yet "full of sound and fury" dogfight, barking and yelping, biting and scuffling, howling and growling... to themselves; not bothering with passers-by.

Behind my hotel were a number of grey-haired natives of the frozen north, lined up, crouched or squatting along the raised wooden sidewalk, waiting, it seemed, in patient anticipation. They sat in a row, silent and motionless, like ancient relics carved of stone, their eyes fixed vacantly on a door above which a Neon sign proclaimed it to be the town's liquor store.

Across the square was The Hudson's Bay Company's "Trading Post." Not a large department store, it carried regional necessities in general merchandise, but also items of visitors' interest. A full-grown polar bear skin, complete with stuffed head, eyes and teeth gleaming, covered a large area of the display floor.

Neon lights beckoned from an elevated area a short distance away. Even more beckoning was the sound of music that came from inside a complex of low-rise buildings. My hotel, I learned, was not the only one in town. Here was a larger one, with a spacious hall for a pub, full of young people drinking beer and eating french-fries. A band of guitars and drums rattled away on stage. This truly reflected the spirit of the boomtown that was Inuvik. I sat down and ordered a beer. Although I am not a regular drinker, I do have a fair tolerance for the stuff when occasion demands it. I had hardly taken my first sip when I thought I recognized Bruce strumming a guitar and singing into a microphone on stage! Bruce! The agent who had checked me into the smaller, quiet and boring hotel! He noticed me and came to my table during the break. He said many of the men and women "moonlight," or work on more than one job, in order to make as much money as they can on high wages in a short time, because they can't tolerate the weather, the boredom and loneliness for too long. He apologized for what he had done, but said he knew I would appreciate it because this was a noisy hotel full of rougher men; and since I had been working hard, he thought I needed a good sleep before flying back home. And, of course, he was right.

I don't think I drank to excess. But I was not and am not now accustomed to the beer parlour atmosphere, and with the tedious beat of the music and the monotonous buzzing of the crowd I felt numbness in my head and thought it best to go to bed. I waved to Bruce and set out toward my quiet, neat little hotel. As I came closer I was already longing to put my head on my pillow and drop off to sleep when, lo and behold, music more welcome to my ears echoed from the lobby! A charming blonde, dressed in sparkling white attire, with sequins and tassels and cowboy hat, sang country-western, accompanying herself on the piano. The place was not crowded or noisy, and all seemed to appreciate her singing, which was good and was only excelled by her beauty. She seemed to have a wide repertoire and sang the patrons' favourites, encouraging them to put down their requests in writing. And they passed them on to her on paper napkins, folding them together with dollar bills...or fives... or tens; and she obliged them with increasing eagerness; and the barman kept serving cocktails or beer, but mostly hard liquor. But there comes a time when one must make an exit and still be able to maintain one's dignity. And that is how I arrived at my room and lay down...dreaming.

I had not been able to fall into deep sleep when, at three o'clock in the morning, there was a determined knock on my door. I sat up with a start, suddenly drenched in perspiration, my heart pounding, my imagination flashing images of the beautiful country singer at my door. I was plunged into a panic. A confusion of thoughts and emotions immediately engulfed me. Surely I hadn't put my room number on the napkin? It had only been a passing whim! Had I really acted on it? I couldn't have! I had never done anything of the sort in all my life. Surely I hadn't been so drunk as to be unaware of what I had done? I wouldn't even know how I should behave with a beautiful woman in my hotel room! I didn't even have anything I could offer her. I should have been better prepared, perhaps with a bottle of champagne...or chocolates? Resigning to the possibility that I might have done a foolish thing at a moment of thoughtless excitement and wishful abandon, I was torn between conflicting emotions of apprehension and desire. My heart racing with anticipation, my head throbbing with an oncoming hangover and spinning in a labyrinth of possible repercussions and a muddle of regrets, I crept over and, holding my breath, cracked open the door.

Had I been dreaming I would have felt captive to the power of a sorceress. I was not dreaming, and the figure that stood before me in the dimly lit hotel corridor was quite real. And she was not only willing but also determined to come into my room. I felt my heartbeat accelerate. The confusion in my head vanished and ushered caution. Apprehension took hold of my consciousness, for, the apparition, though real, was also quite unreal. What faced me, as though emerging from ten-thousand-year-old mists of time, was an ancient crone. Small in stature, her long, braided hair the colour of her ice-encrusted northern homeland; her weather-withered face covered, every inch and in all directions, in a network of fine furrows; her eyes devoid of expression; her mind set on a single object that seemed to drive her whole existence. It was the only word she uttered, as she tried to push the door open and barge into my room. But her effort offered no greater resistance than a bird's plucked down-feather.

"Weesh-kee!" rang her plaintive cry again and again, as I closed and locked my door.

Stranded in Panama

My work as a freelance service technician on ships' cranes took me to various countries and many ports in the Western Hemisphere. When called upon, I would catch the first available flight; land at the airport closest to the job; be met by the shipping agency's representative; hire a taxi or rent a car, and head to where a freighter was having trouble loading or unloading its cargo.

Although, in the back of my mind I always had the notion that I would someday write stories based on experiences and observations gathered on these travels, yet I never took notes nor kept a journal. Certain events and encounters, on the other hand — especially if accompanied by powerful emotion — seem to be stored in a mental 'file of quick recall.' One place that provided such memorable involvement was the Republic of Panama.

It was perhaps my third or fourth trip to that country, where, according to instructions I had been given, I would be boarding a ship in Colon, which is the city at the Atlantic, or Caribbean end of the Canal. The major airport where my plane landed, however, is closer to the Capital City of Panama, at the Pacific end — about fifty miles from Colon.

In view of the possibility that the job might last longer than anticipated, and perhaps also prompted by the great distance from my home base of Vancouver, I had overstuffed my bag and made the mistake of checking it in, rather than carrying it on board, as I usually did on shorter flights. Upon landing in Panama, all passengers picked up their luggage and proceeded to Customs. I alone remained at the platform waiting for mine. The porter with the tractor came back with an empty trailer. There are no more bags, I surmised, he said, in Spanish, with a shrug and a curious grin.

I found an official in uniform and showed him my baggage check. He sent the porter back to investigate. The man returned empty-handed once again, but with a bigger grin, as well as a shrug.

The shipping agent who had been assigned to meet me, and had apparently been waiting outside and wondering, was allowed into the passenger area. He introduced himself and wanted to know what was delaying me. He had checked the passenger list and knew I had arrived on that flight. When he learned of my predicament he immediately reported to higher authority. The porter was sent back again. He soon returned, head hung sheepishly, carrying a solitary piece of luggage on his trailer: mine.

My bag now safely in my possession, intact and unpilfered, I rode with the agent to the Panama Railway Station. I was to take the train and would be met by the representative at the Colon terminal.

On a previous occasion I had covered the distance by taxi, and enjoyed the rare experience of a glimpse of the tropical jungle it afforded. The sun, at places, hardly penetrated the canopy of the forest, the gloom below lending a sense of foreboding to the journey. Our car was the only vehicle throughout on the narrow, dreamy highway, which seemed to be in a struggle to keep clear of the overlapping undergrowth that assailed it on both sides. A blue butterfly, large as a fair-sized pocketbook, almost luminous against the dark leafy ceiling, floated lazily across the tall arcade of the hushed, dusky gallery. A strange, green, giant lizard crossed the road, in an unhurried, waddling pace, oblivious of the approaching car, wagging its tail a warning to alien trespassers on its territory.

I had hoped the train ride would offer similar sights, but, although it was a welcome variety as a mode of transport, it proved uneventful.

The Colon terminal, where the rails came to an abrupt end, appeared to be a bare shed rather than a manned station—a shelter, perhaps, from the rain (for, I have observed, when it rains in Panama, it pours like waterfalls; and when it stops raining, rooftops and streets steam and sizzle dry instantly.) The train, which, apparently, was more of a shuttle of convenience between the two cities, contained few cars, and not many commuters. They detrained and dispersed quickly. The few motor vehicles that had been waiting for their passengers vanished, along with the train that returned to base, without warning, before I became aware, with a shudder, that the agent who was to meet me had not come, and that I had been forgotten and abandoned in the thick of an impenetrable jungle, utterly alone.

The station seemed to be buried in deep bush. No sign of a city or any human habitation was visible anywhere. The narrow road that had led the cars away from the station receded into a dark tunnel of trees and shrubbery. From the slight elevation where I stood, all I could see was a lush, dark green carpet spreading throughout the land below. And the day was waning. So was a vague hope I had held that the train might make another trip, and I gradually became convinced that that must have been the one and only run of each day.

I still held a belief, however, that the agent's representative might still show up any time. Surely he hadn't forgotten about me! Surely he must be on his way to pick me up! Just let me wait a little longer to give him a chance. But...if he had forgotten...then I shouldn't wait any longer. Then...what do I do? Where would I go?

If only I could call a taxi! They'd know where to take me. Surely there must be a hotel...wherever the City is hiding! I tried the station door and found it locked. The windows were permanently framed panels that couldn't be opened. I peered through the hazy glass but could see no telephones or facilities of any kind.

I began to question my own personality. The reason I stood waiting and at a loss, I decided, was not because I believed the agent would, sooner or later, come to pick me up. Rather, I honestly admitted to myself, I was mentally paralyzed, and didn't know what to do. If I were the aggressive, "go-getter" type—as I had heard it said—I would pick up my bag, this minute, and march confidently up that road, and eventually walk into...civilisation?

My mind began dwelling on recent and past events. The morning's incident at the airport, where the porter thought to get away with stealing my bag, assumed a level of lesser offence, when, in an involuntary surrender to paranoia, I recalled my very first trip to Panama, perhaps a year or two earlier. I had completed a job on a ship, and had a whole day free before my flight home. I asked my driver—who, for a fee, gave me a guided tour of the city—if he would recommend a "duty-free" store where I could purchase a camera. He was a tall and impressively handsome African descendant, who worked on contract for the shipping agents. He spoke good English and called himself Mister King. "I know just the place," he said. "Others may cheat you; especially, if you don't speak Spanish."

Armed, thus, with a brand-new camera, I strutted down the main boulevard past my hotel, and thought to spend the afternoon shooting pictures, right and left. I noticed a sign across a busy street pointing to a stairway leading up to, what I imagined to be, a recreation park. It proved a disappointment. It was merely a spread-out concrete plaza—possibly a parade ground—with few benches and fewer plants. It was empty, except for a cluster of young men (clean-dressed, white men—probably students, judging by their uniforms: dark trousers and white shirts), all in their teens, huddled together at a distance from the edge. They all turned, in unison, to face me, as soon as I appeared on the scene, and began walking toward me with amused smiles, as though I were an object of strange curiosity. "You American?" asked their apparent leader, hardly twenty, towering, in height over the rest.

"No. Canadian."

"Ah! Canadian good! This camera good! This camera for me, yes?" They ganged up on me and surrounded me like a swarm of ants, grabbing and pulling at the strap of my camera, pushing me back and forth among them, testing my resolve and my strength.

I managed, with difficulty, to move closer to the edge of the terrace. When they thought they were becoming visible from the street they eased up gradually and backed away. Breaking loose, I hurried down the stairs to the sidewalk, ruffled and agitated, but uninjured, and with my camera and my wallet intact. A black policeman waved from across the street, and caught up with me. "I was coming to warn you," he said, in good English, "to stay, always, on the main road. Don't stray into side streets. It can be dangerous." I understood, then, why pretty heads had been popping out through windows and curiously smiling, in a street further up the road. They must have been laughing at this idiot tourist, walking alone in the streets of Panama, showing off his camera. (I found out later that I could have bought the same camera for less, back home, in Vancouver).

꽁 꽁 꽁

As I mused on these past experiences, I wondered which jungle would prove more dangerous for a stranded stranger: the concrete one, well-lit but peopled with unfriendly humans; or the dark forest inhabited by the wild unknown?

The sun was now on its way down, and I no longer had any doubt that I had been forgotten and that no agent would be coming to meet me. What would I do if it got any darker? I wasn't going to spend the night in the jungle, alone! I felt marooned!

My anxiety was exacerbated by a pressing call of Nature that had been demanding relief for some time. I made a frantic search around the station. I could find no outhouse. I looked for a telephone booth. There wasn't one anywhere. Don't despair! I kept telling myself. Something's got to happen! This is an adventure you're having. Think of it as a privilege. You're going to come through, you'll see! Have faith! Miracles do happen, you know! Have faith in God! Say a prayer! You used to, remember, when you were a child? I feel like a helpless child, God!

Just then, to my surprise and astonishment, I noticed a figure standing motionless a short distance down the incline. I could have been dreaming! It looked like a picture from the pages of National Geographic Magazine: a remnant of the ancient natives of the Americas; dressed in colourful, knitted apparel, from headgear to footwear, a perfect camouflage in the brush, emerging, as though from five hundred years of hiding in the depths of the jungle.

In spite of an eerie sense of having traveled back in time, apprehensive and cautious in face of this alien, otherworldly visitation, and uncertain whether I myself had been seen, I was, nevertheless, emboldened by desperation to communicate. "Do you speak English?" I called, in a loud voice, to make sure I was heard, not knowing what response to expect. The figure (which, judging from its garb—it wore knitted pants—I assumed was male) did not reply nor made any gesture of acknowledgement, but continued standing on the same spot, somewhat hesitantly, I thought, for he appeared to be rocking, in a hardly discernible, left-to-right, twisting motion. I noticed, again to my surprise, that he was standing beside what looked like a free-standing closet—the station's "outhouse," or common toilet, I presumed, elated at the discovery.

A moment later a second figure, obviously a woman, just as uniformly outfitted as the first, emerged from the closet, her knitted, tubiform skirt reaching down to her ankles, almost hiding her footwear.

I repeated my question, but, though desperate for information, did not press for an answer. How do you communicate with aliens from a different world, or bridge a time-gap of five hundred years? Ignoring my enquiry, as well as my very presence—perhaps regarding me, an unwelcome intruder in their domain, with contempt—the two small figures disappeared into the thicket, on whatever mission had prompted their nocturnal outing, heads hung shyly, walking side by side in tiny steps.

The emergence of the young native couple, like apparitions, from their forest hideout, convinced me that dusk signaled the time of day when the jungle reverted, if only temporarily, until dawn, back to its original owners, and that it was time for me to make myself scarce.

Before making a desperate bolt into the menacing unknown, however, I felt a driving urge to look into and take advantage of a discovery I had just made. I walked down to the closet I had just seen used. I opened the door, and it took the restraining awe, the dread of the solitude and deafening silence of the jungle, to chide and prevent me from screaming with disgust at the top of my voice. Come hell or high water, I would not, could not step into the accumulated, sickening mess on the floor inside, where I could see no receptacle of any sort! Better risk all hideous, imagined hazards or threats of the unknown and obey Nature the way all creatures of the wild do!

I grabbed my bag and ran. But my desperation had not yet crossed the boundaries of caution into insanity. The dark end that the road ran into stopped me. I began exploring my surroundings again. A tall wire fence ran along the station and the railway tracks, far into the distance. Though the farther reaches were obscured by the ever-invading vegetation, the closer end stood free of any entanglements and was fitted with a padlocked gate facing a clearing beside the station. While I had unconsciously accepted its presence, taking it for an enclosure of the station, its true significance, I found out, had escaped me. Walking up to it now I realized that it was not meant to enclose the station at all, but rather to protect the vast grounds I could see on the other side, which seemed to include houses that looked like army barracks, and fields that could have been parade grounds. My observation was confirmed when, further straining my eyes, I could make out a flagpole. It looked no taller than two or three matchsticks placed end to end; and though the banner hung limply in the stillness, and I could discern no colour in the dusk and the distance, I became convinced, judging by the neatness of the grounds, that it must be the Stars and Stripes. And it suddenly dawned on me, in a flash of elation and boundless excitement, that this was the Canal Zone! United States Territory! I had been standing next door to civilization all along!

Thank you, God! I whispered. My salvation was close at hand! I now had to find someone who would hear my plea, here, on earth.

The field beyond the wire fence looked empty. It was the time of day when all outside activity had, apparently, ceased. Or, perhaps there had been no activity, the day being Sunday. I watched to see any movement in the farther distance, by the houses in the vicinity of the fence. Someone had to come out and lower the flag for the night, I surmised. But objects were not well defined and colours seemed to blend in the waning light. I waited and gazed without blinking. There was no movement, and not a soul was in sight. It would soon be dark. How would I spend the night? I thought of breaking the station window and taking refuge inside—facing the consequences in the morning. Or, perhaps I could climb the fence and cling all night, for my life. Impossible feats can be performed under duress of the unknown, I reassured myself. All kinds of hideous thoughts, fed by pictures from television and enhanced by the moment's roused imagination, crept into my head: The forest would soon be shrieking with the screams of creatures of the night; panthers with glowing eyes would be prowling in the shadows; snakes and scorpions would creep at my feet; insects and tarantulas would crawl up my back and neck; and bats, like swarms of devils, would set upon my head!

Be quiet, and shun these evil thoughts from your head! I chided myself. Thank God for the more hopeful situation you are in at this moment. Something might happen yet!

Thank You, God! You must be watching over me. Thank you! But... couldn't You...at least...also...please...send someone...an angel...to the gates? Don't wait till I am dead, to open the Gates of Heaven before me!

What could I hope for, under the circumstances, but a miracle? I focused my eyes near and far as hard as I could and it felt as though they began playing tricks on my mind. Was it my imagination? Something the size of an ant seemed to stir by the flagpole! It was hardly noticeable, blending with the surrounding background in the approaching twilight. A man in khaki! Just a solitary figure in a boundless field! He must be out to lower the flag, I thought. But he seemed to be casually loitering instead. Whatever he was out for didn't matter. I had to capture his attention before he disappeared. He was the godsend angel of my salvation. I must not let him go! "Hulloa!" I called, as loudly as I could, not sure whether I could be heard over the distance. I thought if I could hit the fence post with a rock or metal bar it would reverberate to his end of the fence. But I could find neither. My voice would be my only medium of communication. I had read, in an autobiography of a Nineteenth Century opera singer — later confirmed in a public speaking course — how to project your voice with the application of abdominal breathing, using the diaphragm, by-passing the throat. "Hulloa!" I called again — this was my life-or-death situation to put the knowledge into practice — "Hulloa," waving my arms wildly. He heard me over the distance! I could see him stop and look around to see where the voice came from. "Hulloa!" I called, waving frantically. "Can you help me, please?" He noticed me and started moving toward me. His steps seemed cautious and hesitant, at first. The situation must have been as strange for him as it was nightmarish for me.

He gained more confidence as he came closer and saw that I meant no harm. I told him of my plight and asked if he would order a taxi for me, and whether there was a hotel in Colon. "I thought you had come out to lower the flag for the night," I said.

"We never lower the flag," he said.

"You must be an angel," I said.

"I don't know about that," he said, as he unlocked the gate. "I am the only man in camp, manning the office. I got bored and came out for a breath of fresh air. You come in," he said, "and wait here. I'll go call a cab for you."

"You are an angel," I said, "and I thank you very much."

"You're a very lucky man," he said, as he walked back to the barracks.

It was already nightfall when the taxi of my deliverance drove up to the gates of The Washington, a palatial hotel, built to celebrate the completion of the Canal, early in the Twentieth Century. I ordered a glass of wine with my meal and drank to the health of my American angel.

I had been very lucky indeed!

Bizarre Philippine Encounters

As a troubleshooting technician on freighters of many nationalities, I once was called to supervise the repair of one of the hydraulic pedestal cranes on a Philippine carrier.

Moored at a remote dock somewhere in southern California, the aging vessel was loading scrap steel for shipment to China. The choice of the isolated site was, very likely, governed by environmental considerations. A reddish-brown haze of rusty dust hung above the bustling scrap-yard that covered acres of land along the water's edge. The hovering dust-cloud served as a beacon, coming to view upon veering off the turnpike, as I drove to the job site for several miles each morning. I don't remember the name of the town or the hotel where I lodged for the duration of my stay, but no sign of a significant settlement was visible in the immediate vicinity of the dock area, and the general surroundings, as I remember, were an undulating, desert landscape.

Much of my first day of engagement was taken up by travel, as usual, but there was enough workday remaining to carry out tests on the crane in question—the most forward in a series of four cranes—and determine the faulty component. It was found to be a malfunctioning hoisting pump, a major unit of the crane's power plant with the most frequent use and bearing the heaviest load. A replacement pump was, fortunately, available in the ship's spares.

When I arrived on board the second day, the ship's Electrician, whose duties included the proper maintenance of the cranes, had already begun the dismantling process. He had completely drained the hydraulic fluid reservoir, removed the side cover plate, wiped the floor of the steel tank dry, and squeezed himself inside. He lay on his back, tool in hand, in the constricted space beneath a labyrinth of rigid pipes that connected the cluster of pumps to their respective functional systems. The California sun had already begun to warm up, but the job was on the shady side of the crane, and the electrician appeared comfortable, sprawled on the cold steel floor. He worked with calm absorption at an unhurried pace, oblivious to the jarring racket of crashing steel where the feverish loading operation was raging a hold or two aft. Where muscular exertion is demanded but movement is restricted, concentrated effort is called for, applied with patience and perseverance. He seemed unmindful also of my presence as I knelt at his level in readiness to receive any parts he had removed.

An ominous sound, emanating initially in a low-pitched groan, crept unexpectedly, alarmingly, from the snarl of the crane's machinery. Gathering force and magnified within the gaping shell of the crane, it quickly rose, like the scream of a beast in a slaughterhouse, into a deafening, high-pitched growling whine. The mighty electric motor, whose purpose it was to drive the pumps during operation, had burst into action, unbidden, out of place.

"Who the hell is up there?" I exclaimed, jolted into what I impulsively perceived as a crisis situation. Jumping to my feet without a second thought, I scrambled up toward the control cockpit. Someone must have pressed the start button, I swore, alarmed, though I had assumed the electrician to have been the only man in the crane.

There was no one at the controls. It didn't surprise me. I had felt, deep down, a nagging sense of omission upon first hearing the motor start with a groan. I now lost no time in reaching for the main switch. Pulling hard at the stiff lever I cut off all power to the crane. It ought to have been done as a first step before starting the job. Spontaneous induction is an uncommon occurrence. To prevent the possibility, repairmen are advised to disconnect all current entering the work at hand.

I returned to the job level, somewhat ruffled, yet relieved. No accident had resulted, and none, thankfully, would have been likely to. There were no exposed rotating gears or shafts in the oil tank of this model of crane. The electrician lay unperturbed, quiet, still absorbed in his work.

"I knew it was going to happen," he muttered, almost to himself, after a long, inattentive silence, as though, by his aloofness, chiding me for my needless agitation.

His comment immediately evoked, in my mind, images that I had recently seen on television, of Philippine "healers" performing non-invasive "surgery," "removing," with somewhat bloodied fingertips, offending particles of fleshy substance, leaving the "patient's" skin slightly bruised but intact. Are these people endowed with the gift of harnessing the powers of the mind? I thought for a fleeting moment. Are they "psychic"?

I had already dismissed the incident from my mind when I arrived on board the next morning, but was soon to witness a more outlandish episode of what may be called extrasensory misperception. Our repair work was coming to a conclusion. A number of the ship's deckhands and fitters were brought over to clean up and prepare the crane for test. As I stood by, casually watching the men go about their job gathering tools and pumping oil back into the tank, I became aware, in a flash of creepy revelation, that I myself had become an object of searching surveillance. One of the deckhands, it seemed to me, was making an unmistakable effort to watch me, with obvious intent, eying me with a scrutinizing squint at every turn. Had he, perhaps, seen me before on another Philippine vessel? I wouldn't remember. But I nodded to him in acknowledgement of the likelihood. Did he return my nod? I wasn't sure. He didn't shift his eyes from me, and there was no smile in his expression; rather, a reflection of dark and sinister thought in his persistent squinty stare.

Offensive though his ominous gaze was, it aroused my curiosity to know its implication. I must encourage him to approach me and express himself. But no effort seemed to be required on my part. His need to communicate was apparently more urgent. When, at the conclusion of the job, we all came down on deck, and the rest of the men had walked ahead, he lingered behind. Hesitantly, almost fearfully, he moved closer to me with every step, his gaze more focused and searching. He seemed driven to have it out with me. I nodded to him again, and said hullo, though I was beginning to sense hostility as well as fear, or perhaps deep anxiety in his eyes. His lips trembled nervously.

When he finally managed to give utterance to his distress and began to get it off his chest, his very first words came as a bombshell.

"You have come to punish me, haven't you?" he stammered,

breaking into a sweat, with a tremour in his voice.

His behaviour had prepared me for a jolt, somewhat, but I hadn't anticipated the shock and the drift of his assumption. Where had it originated? What experience in his past had given rise to it? We were total strangers to each other. I had never met him before on any ship. He was obviously mistaking me for someone he had met only casually — which, I assumed, explained his long and agonized scrutiny of a likeness he had perceived in my appearance — and who might, for some misdeed committed, be carrying a grudge against him. I tried to convince him that I was not who he thought I was. But try as I might, I could as well had been pleading with the steel hull of the ship. He was not looking for confirmation. His mind was made up. He even became impatient with my inability to understand his convoluted reasoning.

"I know you are not the same person," he protested, "but you look very much like him, and you have come, on his behalf, to wreak vengeance on me. You have come to avenge him. Three years ago in Iran..." he continued, his mien and tone conveying a hint that he was recounting an occurrence I should remember.

"I am not Iranian," I stressed, "and I have never been in Iran. What were you doing there?"

"I was working. Many Filipinos are employed as labourers in the oil fields of Iran. We were having an argument; it turned into a tussle, and during our struggle he fell and hit his head on a rock. It wasn't my fault. I did not kill him. I want you to know, it was an accident. You understand? I want you to understand. It was an accident."

What I understood was that I faced a wreck of a tortured soul, whose unbearable concealment of a possibly incriminating secret and overwhelming consequent sense of guilt had driven him to the cliff-edge of insanity. I could also deduce that, having become privy to his secret, I was now marked to be silenced. I was therefore glad I had booked to stay at a hotel rather than on board ship, as I had often done on my assignments. But I wasn't leaving before giving him a piece of my mind.

"Listen, my friend," I said. "I understand very well what you are telling me. But I want you to understand something. When I came to repair your ship's equipment, I did not know you; for all intents and purposes, as far as I am concerned, you might as well have not existed at all. I have now completed my job; I'm tired and am on my way to the hotel to wash up, have a peaceful sleep, and forget that I had ever met you. I advise you to do the same. In the morning I still won't know your name nor who you are, or what you have done. I am not God's Avenging Angel. But let me give you some advice, if you are willing to listen. You are young. You can't live the rest of your long life looking for and seeing a vengeance seeker in every other stranger you meet. Be brave enough to face your past and find a way to make peace with yourself and with your God. Go have a peaceful sleep tonight, and forget that you ever met me."

California Fireworks

I arrived at a late hour one summer evening on a troubleshooting appointment on board a freighter at Long Beach, California. The vessel was in the process of docking and I met the Chief Engineer on deck wrapping up the operation.

Although it had always been my preference to arrange for accommodation before presenting myself for the engagement, no inn had come to my attention as I drove to the site in my rented car. I therefore asked the Chief whether he knew of a hotel nearby. He said that wouldn't be necessary. The "owner's suite" was vacant and available on board.

It had been my unexpected privilege to be assigned the "owner's suite" on other ships once or twice before and I now, instinctively, looked forward to the comfort and luxury of fixtures and fittings that I remembered.

We discussed briefly the problems they had been experiencing with their equipment, so that I could anticipate them in the morning, my expertise covering mainly hydraulic deck cranes and winches on deep-sea vessels.

As we were leaving the deck a faint flicker of fireworks in the distant darkening horizon captured my attention. I wondered what the occasion was and where based. The Chief hadn't noticed and had no knowledge of any celebration.

The "owner's suite" promised a disappointment when I was led to it up only a short flight of stairs above the cargo deck; whereas I had envisioned it on the same level as the Captain's suite. But my varied experience had taught me to be adaptable. The Chief fetched the key and further warned me that the room hadn't been used for some time.

I opened the door, looked for the light switch and turned it on. The light was strong enough to reveal a single bed, fully made, with a pillow and blanket. There were, as well, two plain chairs close to the bed, all in a very austere setting. For all its weakness, however, the light could not hide the fuzzy dust that lay at a thickness of perhaps three quarters of an inch, and covered, wall to wall, the whole surface of the concrete floor. I stood, as though paralyzed, gazing at the fuzzy ocean of the floor, wondering how to navigate through without upsetting the tranquility that had lain undisturbed for—who knew how long. The solution, such as it was, I found in a massive bundle of newspaper I had bought at the airport, and which I kept in a shopping bag, along with other items. I opened the paper and laid down a full sheet for each step that I took, until I reached the bed and chairs without visibly raising any dust. I used the same method of stepping-paper to reach the bathroom, which was well equipped with tub and shower as well as soap and towel, and, of course hot water, with the usual warnings against scalding.

The single bulb electric light did not appear to be conducive to reading for relaxation—though the bulb had been placed fairly low on the wall at the head of the bed—nevertheless, I thought it would be wiser not to give in to frustration but rather surrender to sleep.

I was debating whether to put on my pyjamas, considering the cold atmosphere of the room, when an unexpected knock on the door prodded me to a fast decision. I quickly donned my pyjamas and, carefully treading back the sheets of newspaper on the floor, walked over and opened the door, expecting the Chief Engineer, with whatever additional message he might have for the job. I had a bewildering surprise to find, facing me at the door, not the Chief Engineer, but a well-groomed and very beautiful, young Afro-American woman.

My immediate assumption was that she had knocked on the wrong door.

"I think you're looking for the Captain, Ma'am," I said. "On an upper floor."

"No," she said. "I want you!"

"What? Ma'am," I said, "I don't belong with the ship. I'm a visitor, a technician. I'll be working to-morrow and leave when I finish the job. I need to sleep now. You want the Captain, or some officer of the ship, whatever your business is. You don't want me."

"I want you," she said.

"I'm afraid you don't understand, Ma'am," I said. "You don't want me."

"I want you," she repeated.

"Why?" I said.

"Um'm," she hesitated. "Um'm." She moved further in and sat on the vacant chair. "You want to have a good time?"

"What!" I was taken by surprise and couldn't figure her out. In every aspect of her appearance she looked too well-groomed, even dignified, cultured and educated to be a common prostitute, or, so called, "escort." She must be hiding something, I thought. "You don't look like nor do you sound like a common hooker," I said.

"Um'm. Yes," she said.

"Yes, what?"

"I am."

"No, you aren't!" I exclaimed. I was angry at the blatancy of her preposterous, low-down claim. It sounded hollow and was uncharacteristic and totally incompatible with the image she portrayed.

I wondered how she would react if I called her bluff.

"Listen," I said. "I don't engage in entanglements with hookers. I don't believe you are a hooker. But to prove your claim I'm willing to offer you whatever you charge for your services. Will you tell me how much?"

She gave me a long and blank stare, fumbling for a figure.

"Mm'm, mm'm. Twenty dollars?"

"Well, that proves to me you're no hooker." I said. "But there's one catch I should have told you. I have no U.S. dollars. Will you take Canadian money?"

"Um'm...Uh...Um'm...I must ask my manager."

With that excuse she left the room and I knew she wasn't coming back.

In the morning, before any word about the job at hand, the Chief Engineer had an urgent question: "Last night," he said, "we were warned by the harbour security to watch for suspicious visitors. Do you know why they gave us such a warning?"

"O-o-oh," I sighed, suddenly remembering. That's what the fireworks were about! It was the opening night of the Summer Olympics in Los Angeles!"

"Oh, that must have been it," the Chief said, relieved.

I never mentioned to the Chief my encounter with the amateurish "hooker," secretly laughed at the thought that she was indeed even more amateurish as a Security sleuth.

Fast Taxi to Caracas Airport

I had completed a troubleshooting assignment on a ship's cranes at a small seaport in Venezuela, and on my return trip home to Vancouver had to stay overnight in Caracas, the capital city. The small plane dropped me off at the airport and I took a taxi to what I was given to understand was a first class hotel—"the best hotel in town." My flight home was scheduled to start on its first leg at 8 a.m. the next morning.

I can't say that I was tired, but certainly in need of better sleep than I had on board, and more hungry than tired. I took a quick shower and went down to the lobby to inquire about a restaurant. I was directed to the hotel's dining room: a sprawling hall on the ground floor, or "basement" of the hotel, with a surprisingly low ceiling for its expanse or intended use. I could tell I had arrived somewhat late in the day, for "meal-time" seemed to be well under way and almost every table was taken—which, I assumed, should reflect the popularity of the place, based presumably on the quality of the cuisine. What simultaneously captured my attention was a curling column of fire that burst forth above a table occasionally, subsided momentarily, only to flare upward again, its reach just short of the ceiling. Manipulating the flame was a man dressed in black suit, white shirt and black bowtie and moustache. Then I noticed the fluffy blanket of smoke that floated overhead and clung thickly to every inch of the ceiling.

A waiter arrived with a menu.

"I'd like steak," was my hunger-driven, impulsive yet calculated behest, taking into account that Venezuela was probably among the top beef producing countries of South America, along with Argentina and Brazil.

"Aahh!" beamed the waiter. "Today everybody want steak! Tell Chef," he said, pointing to the 'flame master,' "how you like your steak, when he coming to your table."

So, that's what was happening! The man was barbecuing the

diners' steaks at every table, generating the clouds of smoke. And it was now no longer hugging the ceiling. Combined with cigarette smoke rising from every table, the thickened mass of fumes already weighed down now to the level of the patrons, masking their heads in a shroud of grey haze.

When at last the 'flame master' Chef arrived at my table with his portable gas paraphernalia, the smoke had taken up the full capacity of the dining hall—chock-full, from ceiling to floor. The haze had thickened, drastically diminishing visibility; the asphyxiating fumes permeated every single breath of air inhaled; and my head had started pounding (reminiscent of a case of carbon monoxide poisoning that had nearly killed me once). The restaurant with all its accoutrements, as well as the whole dining crowd had acquired a dark and sinister aspect of a nightmarish scene from hell, and the Chef, with his whirling column of fire, had become the Devil himself.

"Ss...Sess...Senor! Your sst...steak?"

His words came out muddled; his eyes could not focus or stay fully open; his bowtie was cocked to one side, his hair disheveled, his face pale and sweaty. I wasn't surprised at his befuddled state. What with tending to his fire for so long, breathing greasy fumes, and the glasses of wine offered to him by patrons at the tables, it was a wonder he wasn't heat-struck, and ready to drop dead.

"I've changed my mind," I said. "I have a headache."

I paid for a glass of wine and a roll or two that I had consumed while waiting, and walked out into fresh air. It was no use looking for a coffee house or restaurant in a neighbourhood where obviously there weren't any. I took a short stroll to ease the throbbing of my head, and headed toward my room, stopping at the Desk to ask for an aspirin. I was told there was aspirin in my room refrigerator.

The first thing I noticed when I opened the refrigerator door was a big, live, brown cockroach inside. It wasn't in the main area of edibles, thankfully. It had somehow been trapped in a small chamber on the inner side of the refrigerator door, where there was a typewritten list of all items placed at the patrons' disposal. I watched it for a long time and was convinced it couldn't leave its prison and roam about over the chocolates. There was no telling how it had found its way in or how long it had been there, but its little chamber was apparently not cold enough to kill it, and not big enough to allow for much movement. Its foremost legs moved one step left, then one step right, and that was all the movement it could muster; except for its feelers, which were in constant motion, flat against the clear plastic cover.

But the cockroach was not my primary concern, I told myself, though I thought it had helped to relieve my headache, somewhat. I looked about and found my aspirin. I also allowed myself to be tempted to a bar of chocolate, a bag of chips and a can of Seven-Up, since I was still hungry. I set my little alarm clock for six o'clock, and went to bed.

I couldn't tell if I had slept at all, or how long, but on waking up at the alarm I called the Desk and said I'd need a taxi for the airport at six-thirty. That would afford me enough time for a leisurely coffee and perhaps even a bite to eat at the airport café, whose existence I hadn't ascertained. I made the mistake of telling the clerk my departure time. He assured me the taxi would be ready in good time, "no problem."

Time kept going by, until I felt it becoming a "problem." My anxiety rising, I called the Desk again and again, and each time I was assured the taxi had been ordered and would be arriving at any moment, not to worry, the driver was a very good driver and he would get me there on time.

I hadn't quite recovered from the ordeal of the night before. The lingering residue of a headache, lack of adequate sleep, and a persistent hunger still gnawing at my stomach served only to increase my anxiety. It was getting so close to departure time that I was certain I would miss my flight. I grabbed my bag and hurried down to the lobby in hopes of speeding things up, when the taxi pulled up at the same time.

I threw my bag onto the back seat and jumped into the passengers' front seat.

"Buenas dias," the driver greeted me with an unruffled, innocent yet playful smile and took off with a jolt. He was a boyish young man, with a perfectly round head, thick but closely cropped hair and impish eyes. I showed him my watch and indicated with gestures that my plane was leaving in twenty-five minutes. He nodded, again with that reassuring smile, and stepped on the gas.

The streets of Caracas, built in a valley on undulating terrain, rise and drop with the hills. Hence the path leading to the highway for the airport on lower ground, as my driver took it, seemed to follow a series of sharp drops and sudden turns.

Without reducing speed at an intersection, blind to what he might be faced with, he turned headlong into a narrow street to the right.

My heart pounding and suffocating me in my throat, I turned, gaping and speechless, to face him. He glanced with the corner of his eye, and again treated me to that shy, unperturbed, confident smile of his.

He was not going to slow down. He was determined to take me to the airport on time! Whether it was the time of day that worked in his favour, or he knew the short-cuts with no traffic to face him, he kept going at the same breakneck speed, all downhill, until, lo and behold, he came to another intersection and did exactly the same kind of reckless swerve to the right, and again gave me a glance, and the same shy, unperturbed smile.

And now I began wondering whether I would ever make it to my flight.

I had sensed a rapid movement of his hands as he maneuvered the wheel and negotiated the turns, and yet there seemed to be no tenseness in his performance, and his smile reflected only a serene confidence. Would I ever know his secret?

Let him take me to the airport safely and on time, and I don't care how he does it, I was thinking, no longer concerned about my headache, or how hungry or sleepless I was. And, surely there can't be another corner to turn!

I was wrong. He made another and the last sudden turn, safely, yet again! And this time I discovered his secret! I caught him in the last stroke of crossing himself! He had been relying on Divine Providence to see him safely through!

He smiled and, as I could construe his words, "It works every time!" he mumbled.

Additional Writings

Khatchatur Abovian (1808-1848)

Khatchatur Abovian is held in worshipful reverence as the torchbearer and founder of modern Armenian literature. He was a brilliant young man who, nevertheless, came, tragically, to symbolize a missed opportunity in the process of that revival and cultural enlightenment, and whose work, belatedly brought into public attention, proclaimed him, in the end, to have been the protagonist of the movement, and heralded the change that was set in motion.

Abovian began his schooling at age 9 in Etchmiadzin Monastery in Armenia and, later, at Church sponsored schools in Georgia. At around age 20 he was back at the monastery of Etchmiadzin, the See of the Armenian Church, employed as secretary to the Catholicos (the Head of the Church), as well as teaching and further preparing for the priesthood, for which he had initially been intended. By his return to Etchmiadzin, eastern Armenia had been wrested from oppressive Persian rule and was annexed by Russia, rousing hopes of cultural emancipation.

If Abovian had remained in the service of the Church he might have attained a prominent rank in that Establishment and perhaps even been remembered for a measure of intellectual achievement. But literature, and, hence, the nation's cultural direction would have continued to remain for a further indefinite period within narrow, traditional confines, a self-indulgent preoccupation, the domain of and serving a coterie of scholars who alone were versed in the classical medium. (Perhaps they are not to be disdained. They had endowed the creation of their alphabet with the mystery of a divine miracle, canonized the "Holy Translators" and idolized the language that had so magnificently Armenianized the "Asdvadzashoonch"—"Breath of God," the Armenian name given to the Bible—a rendering that foreign scholars have called "the queen of translations.") And, further, the language the masses of the population spoke and understood in early nineteenth century, had suffered, as had the land and its people, through centuries of upheavals, invasions and tyranny, and had become a hodge-podge of regional "dialects" full of Arabisms, Pharseeisms and, especially Turkisms. No unified version had come to the fore and none was considered to have any redeeming literary quality. Were the common people, then, to be ignored, while the purity of the language was being preserved within the confines of the Church establishment and its monasteries? Concern had begun to grow. But overt concern for cultural perpetuation was tantamount to nationalism and nationalism under intolerant foreign occupation was punishable by death and exile. Where, then, was the thrust for change to come from?

In 1829 a professor from a German university in the Baltic country of Estonia came to Armenia for the purpose of climbing Mount Ararat. In his search for a guide and interpreter he was introduced to Abovian who, besides the languages he had learned naturally as he grew up, had acquired or brushed up on a few, including German, at school. It was a fortuitous encounter. Professor Friedrich Parrot was so impressed by the character and intelligence of the young man that at the end of the expedition he offered to take the twenty-one-year-old Khatchatur Abovian to Europe with him for an all-expenses paid tuition in his university in Estonia. Abovian was excited at the prospect. The Catholicos disapproved, but Abovian prevailed. He envisioned an array of rural schools and generations of young students in his homeland imbued with progressive thought. His weeks of sojourn with Professor Parrot, as well as his previous schooling in Georgia, had convinced him that a European concept of education was indispensable to dispel the cultural darkness that had set in throughout centuries of barbaric domination of Armenia, and reintroduce the enlightenment that had inspired the Translators of the Fifth Century's Golden Age.

After more than six years of study and exposure to the great thinkers of Europe, such as Rousseau, Schiller, as well as Pushkin, and a thorough introduction to modern pedagogical methods, Abovian returned home to Armenia in 1836, with enthusiastic plans to spread the light of knowledge among his people. He soon found that his return had not been anticipated. He applied to the Catholicos to have a school established to train teachers for rural schools. The churchman's reply was curt and dismissive. "You seem well able to mold the minds of innocents," he said, unable to hide his prejudice, "but to train them is not your job." Abovian secured a position as a superintendent at a state sponsored Russian school in Georgia for his livelihood, now that the Caucasus had become part of Russia, and stayed at it for thirteen years, sharing, to his minimal satisfaction, even a limited measure of his treasured education for the benefit of the children. He applied several times for a position in the Etchmiadzin School, but was rejected every time.

Abovian requested the Church to release him from the vows of the priesthood and married a girl he had met in the German community of Tbilisi. He finally found a similar job of superintendent at another state school closer to home, and moved with his family to Armenia. On the day he was to start work he came out of the house before the appointed time and went for an early morning walk. He was never seen or heard of again, and his end has been a mystery to this day.

The Secret Mission of Tissaron Stonaris

He had been abandoned as an infant at the door of the village church. Rumours circulated concerning his birth. No one claimed parentage or ancestry, but gossip pointed to a wealthy widower, a recluse, who held the church in contempt and whose property abutted the vast holdings of the ancient monastery perched on a bluff high above the village. It was said about the widower that his wicked ways accounted for the flight from the village of many a young woman and her family who could not abide the disgrace of an illegitimate pregnancy.

As for the infant's mother, wagging tongues referred to the coincidence that on the day of the child's discovery at the church door there had been a fire at a lowly hovel in the outskirts of the hamlet where the charred body of a young woman had been found.

The child was fed, clothed and kept alive, but displayed no significant intelligence or capacity for learning to merit the Church's patronage. He remained in the margin of the community's charity and was commonly referred to as "the boy" or "the orphan."

In time, as he grew in strength and stature, he was taken into the full guardianship of the Church. He was placed in the care of the monastery, not as a novice, but as a servant and ward of the Church. He was treated as a simpleton and was assigned chores that required little intelligence: running errands to the village; taking care of the monastery's only donkey, grooming, feeding and watering it; fetching loads of water from the spring in the valley; keeping the saddlery in good order, and generally managing the stable, where he also slept. Often he would be assigned chores in the kitchen and, on weekends, when visitors and pilgrims were most numerous and there was a higher demand to provide free meals for them, he would also be called upon to chop wood and help in the cooking and preparation of a large cauldron of legumes, such as beans, chickpeas or lentils, over wood fire, out in the open.

On one such occasion an English professor, a scholar of Byzantine art and amateur anthropologist, who happened to be lodging at the monastery, doing research, conferred upon the "boy" the unusual and impressive-sounding designation of Tissaron Stonaris, a name he himself had made up, claiming that it encoded a certain quirk of personality he had observed in the young man's behaviour as he watched him at work.

In due course, having received, in the opinion of the Abbot, adequate instruction in religion and Church rites, the boy—by now a young man—was elevated to the responsible upkeep of the icon gallery. At first he worked under the supervision of the senior steward; then, as he gained the trust of his superiors, he was allowed full access to the chapel and entrusted, as well, with keys to other chambers and storage sheds.

At the end of each day, after the last of the pilgrims had departed, he would set about cleaning and tidying the gallery. He swept and mopped and scrubbed the marble floor 'til it shone and sparkled, "befitting the Holy Place." Awed by the array of lifelike Byzantine icons that lined the walls of the chapel, he kissed each one of the portraits with reverence and crossed himself as he went round. Their frames of gold had to be dusted, cleaned of all finger marks and lipstick, and gently buffed to a soft gleam. He replaced expiring candles of the altar, lighting new ones with the old stubs. New candles and tapers were tall and had more prominent flames. How he delighted at the sight of the fiery tongues as they waved and danced atop the many candles, tapers and oil lamps! Multiplied in reflection into an enormous galaxy of starlets, they twinkled in the polished frames of the icons as well as in the shiny gold, silver and crystal trimmings of the altar! Ah, the mystic flames of the flickering candles; the seductive, enduring scent of soul-caressing incense, and the lingering whiff of old beeswax whose fumes, for centuries, had penetrated and darkened the ancient beams and woodwork!

Stonaris learned the names of all the Saints represented by the icons, and believed with all his heart in the miraculous powers ascribed to each. Above many of the icons hung clay or wax replicas depicting body parts, placed by ailing pilgrims hopeful for a cure, or grateful for a cure granted. The icons had, little by little, unobtrusively acquired, in Stonaris's consciousness, such an aura of reality that he began to regard them as his night-time companions. So much so, that the atmosphere in the chapel seemed often conducive to the manifestation of the Saints in their living, physical presence. If he watched them for any sustained length of time, in the quiet and solitude of the late night, Stonaris felt, with a chill in his spine, that the Saints would come alive, shake themselves free from the restrictive frames, step down onto the floor and..."Kyrie eleison, Kyrie eleison..." Stonaris crossed himself, shuddering at the thought. These Saints had a way of asserting themselves. He must be careful not to dwell on each one for too long. Some of them had kindly expressions. He felt friendly toward them. He took particular solace gazing for long periods, in silence, at the icon of Saint Mary, and imagined himself, as Baby Jesus, nestling in the warmth of her cuddling arms. He felt strangely comforted but could not abide the spellbinding gloom for too long. Sometimes, when he was alone in the chapel, he would be overcome by an eerie sensation of being mobbed by the crowd of staring saints. Some of the icons had such fearsome scowls that he was afraid to look directly into their angry eyes, as though they could see the minutest sin in the very depths of his heart.

"If you have a pure heart you have nothing to fear," the Abbot had told him. "What sin are you harbouring in your heart, my child?"

Stonaris confessed that he was haunted by one ungodly thought he found impossible to shake off: to kill the widower. Often, when he went to the village on an errand, or to the spring to fetch water, he took a short-cut that ran across the widower's property, past the back of his ramshackle bungalow. The widower, when he happened to be at home, would come out with a shotgun and chase him away, swearing and cursing him, and uttering the foulest words of abuse against the boy's mother.

"Don't let that evil man upset you, my child," said the Abbot, "but avoid him if you can. He will burn in Hell, if he does not change his ways!"

Burn in Hell! The Abbot's pronouncement soon became an obsession in Stonaris's head. From time to time, now, he would catch himself hatching plans, and found it scary to contemplate their fulfillment. He had noticed, on his outings, that the widower kept a steel drum of gasoline on the shady side of his house, for use in his motorcycle, the only motorized vehicle in the village. It would not be difficult to set fire to the explosive fluid with a flaming taper!

But in what light would the deed of revenge be seen by the abbot and the Saints who had now all become his friends?

Some pilgrims hoped they'd win status in Heaven through the intercession of the Saints, and showered them with gifts of money or provisions of food and clothing for the monastery. Stonaris had neither; neither did his ambitions extend beyond the grave. But it was important to secure the certainty of the Saints' favour for the accomplishment of his goal. He had of late acquired skills that he could offer them freely, pouring out his heart in the process: he would dance for them! He had learned that, when he could find no words to contain the outpouring of his emotions, he could only express it in dance.

He already had the answers to most of the questions the plot demanded. The Abbot had now given him a general idea about How?

The question that now remained to be answered was When? The deed could never be done on a Sunday, of course. There was no argument about that. Sunday was Kyriaki, the Lord's Day, and the Monastery was buzzing with pilgrims, tourists and visitors. The contemplated 'Act of God,' to be delivered by God's steward, Tissaron Stonaris, must be served on a weekday.

He made observations to determine when the man would be at home. He thought carefully and chose a Wednesday to set the flaming taper to the gasoline.

There was no moon on the night he embarked on his mission. He produced from under his bed the few items he had assembled in preparation: a long taper of yellow wax; a box of matches; a barrel-cap wrench; and, as his divine protector and champion, a portable-sized icon of Saint George the Dragon Slayer which he had found in the cellar among gifts that pilgrims had brought.

He stole out in the quiet and total darkness of the late night, in the small hours of the Wednesday. His feet seemed to know every detail of the path.

Soon he was at his destination. His eyes had adjusted to the darkness and he could see the widower's motorcycle among a row of unkempt shrubbery. The drum of gasoline stood nearby. Stealthily Stonaris approached it, tested the tightness of the cap before risking a noisy struggle with the wrench. He was lucky. It was only hand-tight. He removed the cap, tipped the barrel—which appeared to be about half full—and, exerting his well-developed muscles, gently and noiselessly laid it on its side. The gasoline started gurgling out. But Stonaris was confident the widower wouldn't wake up. More than asleep, he thought, the man must be in a state of alcoholic torpor. He crossed himself, picked up his icon of Saint George, kissed it and held it to his breast to calm the palpitation of his heart. He then took out the matches, lit the taper and had hardly extended it toward the barrel when there was a sudden WHUMP! and mighty tongues of fire sprang up the side and front of the cottage, reaching up to the thatched roof, devouring the structure in roaring flames. Stonaris barely escaped being engulfed in the conflagration himself. He watched the spectacle from a distance, jumping up and down in gleeful madness, crossing himself and kissing the icon again and again.

"My Saint has revealed to me this day the secret encoded in the name that was give me," he cried, holding Saint George high above his head. "I am Tissaron Stonaris. I consign you to the flames of eternal Hell! By Saint George!"

The Foreboding

A stunned silence gripped the Police Station. Officers stared at each other in gaping bewilderment. Detective O'Malley sat at his desk, seemingly in deep concentration. But he could not gather his thoughts. His mind was a total blank, and he groped in a nameless vacuum. His stomach felt twisted in knots and...something nagged at his memory. He thought there must be some significant connection between what they had just witnessed happening on television and the pesky notion that nibbled and gnawed on his faculties of recall, but which he couldn't recapture or identify. He was also bothered by the blurry figure of a cat that seemed to haunt his thoughts, but he could not tie it in nor could he dismiss it.

He rose from his desk and walked over to the shelf of unsolved, all but forgotten—though not officially closed—cases. Sure enough, there was a folder there under "Cat," and it even contained a plastic envelope of evidence! The cursory investigation had been carried out and the evidence collected some three years earlier. A note attached to the file referred to another file under "Drug Op Blast." O'Malley began to remember. The explosion, at a rundown apartment in a seedy part of town, had occurred within a week or two following the cat incident. No perpetrators or victims had been discovered; both cases had gradually run into a dead end and eventually abandoned. The detective had been intrigued. The incidents had taken place in areas far removed from each other, the cat incident occurring at a well-maintained, respectable part of town. What seemed to tie the one to the other was a Jack of Hearts, found at the "Cat" scene, which unmistakably belonged to but was missing from a deck of cards taken as evidence from the "Drug Op" site.

O'Malley took both files and returned to his desk. He wasn't quite sure about the connection of the two cases with the tragedy which was, just then, unfolding before their eyes on television, but he was determined to delve into them, and even re-activate them if necessary, for he felt confident his notion would be justified with discoveries revealed under a new light.

On a summery day, three years earlier, the Station had received a call from a man, reporting the maltreatment and torture of a cat by a group of suspicious-looking young transients of foreign appearance, in an otherwise peaceful, well-groomed, middleclass neighborhood. The caller, Simpson by name, a retired widower who claimed to be an artist, said he had been watching the youths—two men, one perhaps older than the other, and a young girl—from his third-floor apartment across the street. He said he had lived there a long time and knew the neighborhood well. The three strangers had been sitting on Mrs. Rosedale's manicured front lawn, by the sidewalk, in the shade of the neighbor's hedge. They were ostensibly playing some kind of a card game. The girl, meantime, nibbled on a chocolate, while the younger man listened attentively to the older fellow who seemed to be engaged in an agitated discussion. At one point he grabbed the girl's wrist and wrenched off her bracelet, sending chocolate and bracelet flying from her hand.

Two chance occurrences coinciding with his brutal treatment of the girl, drove the man to further lose all sense of civilized behavior, and compelled the group to beat a hasty retreat. A cat, emerging from beneath the hedge, unseen by the group, approached the leader from behind and began rubbing its tail against his side. The sudden appearance and unexpected physical contact of the animal so startled the already-agitated man that he jumped to his feet panic-stricken, and in an uncontrolled and irrational rage, kicked the cat, flinging it against the wall of Mrs. Rosedale's house. His companions, sensing the peril their leader's action had plunged them into in an unfamiliar neighborhood, quickly gathered up their cards and were making ready to flee when a car glided slowly past them and pulled up by the curb next-door. The cat kicker nervously turned to view the movement of the car and at once became aware that his insane exploits had been witnessed by two children, a boy and a girl, who had apparently been playing on a jungle gym in the adjoining yard, and had now come out to the sidewalk to meet their father who was home from work. Sweating nervously, the shaken youth signaled his friends to start running.

Officer O'Malley had been meticulous in taking down details of Old Simpson's account, but had thought the incident didn't merit the Station's immediate response. He had let the report lie in the "Pending" tray for several days, but when the story of the injured cat had reached the ASPCA, as well as a prestigious animal clinic, he had decided it behooved the reputation of his precinct to overtake and act ahead of the rumors. He had personally driven to Mrs. Rosedale's house and, by sheer luck, had found the bracelet, the piece of chocolate and a Jack of Hearts still lying beneath the hedge, just as Simpson had described. Mrs. Rosedale wasn't in, but the neighbors said she was virtually blind and had probably not seen anyone. However, the children had heard the agonized cry of the cat but had only glimpsed the strangers as they ran away.

O'Malley had felt pleased with himself for the work he had done. He had placed the bracelet, the piece of chocolate and the Jack of Hearts in a plastic envelope as evidence, filed it with the report, and, for all practical purposes, considered the matter closed. He had not intended to take any more of the Station's valuable time further pursuing what he deemed to be clearly a misdemeanor... until a week or two later.

The explosion at the slummy tenement had revived interest in the "Cat" incident via the Jack of Hearts connection. The occupants had vanished into thin air and initial inquiries had yielded no culprits. It had been an amateurish job and rated as minor, considering the negligible extent of damage it had caused; which had given O'Malley all the more reason to consider both "juvenile" cases as one and the same, elevating the "Cat" incident, nevertheless, to a felony from the lesser category of misdemeanor, and treating the characters as suspects.

O'Malley had rung Old Simpson, his only contact who had seen the offenders. Simpson's answering machine had said he was away with a seniors' group of artists on a long painting expedition on the Oregon coast.

The case had, once again, been suspended, and the files, once again, pigeonholed.

All those incidents and follow-ups had taken place three years earlier. O'Malley now sat gazing at the files and fumbling with the few pieces of evidence he had collected, and wondered what had prompted him to dig up the case or even connect it with the shocking holocaust which was being telecast on the news at that very moment, holding every member of the precinct staff in gasping, angry and even tearful suspense. He thought of calling Simpson again—albeit after so long an interruption—in the questionable hope that he might shed further light on the matter. What more was there to know? Simpson had already given a thorough description of what he had seen. What did those young strangers look like? Simpson was an artist. Perhaps he could sketch their portraits. It wouldn't be reliable, though. He might not remember. What had they been talking about? Had anyone heard them? Mrs. Rosedale may not have seen them. She was blind. Was she perhaps also deaf? What language did they speak?

O'Malley mused while he waited for Simpson to answer the phone. Then, as though seeing it for the first time, his gaze fell upon the bracelet. He was struck by the beauty of its design and artisanship. His answer shone at him in several lines of decorative writing superbly etched on the inner surface of the jewel. O'Malley reckoned it to be a poetic or religious quotation and was knowledgeable enough to recognize the script as Arabic.

"NO!...NO!...NO!"
"OH, MY GOD!"
"OH, GOD! OH, GOD!"

Exclamations exploded in the Precinct like a peal of thunder as the world watched the Twin Towers of the World Trade Center in New York crumble in a dusty and fiery inferno, as though a raging volcano had opened its gaping crater, spewing dust and smoke, burning and consuming thousands of trapped and bewildered men and women.

"How could this be allowed to happen?"
"Who the hell is keeping watch over this country?"

"Hallo!" It was Old Simpson's voice answering O'Malley's call. O'Malley hung up. "It's no use!" he said to himself. "Too late! Too late!"

Woe Is Me-ow! (Big Red, the Alley Cat Meets Milady, the Aristo-Kit)

"Meo-o-o-w-wow-wow! Meow-meow-meow! Hullo! Hullo! What do we have here? The most beautiful, young, aristocratic house cat of the neighbourhood, Milady, far away from the safety of your mansion, and...hiding? You're hiding!...in the dark shadows of a scraggly shrub by the wayside! I nearly didn't see you!"

"Phpht!"

"Oh, please, don't get me wrong. I mean no offence, really. I pass by here every day, roaming the neighbourhood. I often see you sitting in the window of your luxurious house, surveying the outside world through the glass. Or, sometimes, cradled in the arms of the twin daughters of your Mistress, playing in the front yard. I've never seen you outside your boundaries, blocks away from your house, and on such a cold day, with lumps of snow still hanging on branches. But what worries me most is that you're alone, and you're obviously hiding from something! Are you in some kind of trouble? Running away from home?"

"Scat! Phpht!"

"I don't mean to pry into your private affairs; but if you're in any predicament, I feel duty-bound to come to the aid of my kind and kin."

"Go away! Leave me alone!"

"Something in your manner tells me you're not happy. I can see panic in your eyes, though you're turning away and won't face me when I speak. You're perched on a rotting stump, above ground, hiding among the tangled branches of this unkempt laurel, in a corner of a neglected yard, a fair distance from your home. You've really done a great job of hiding, I'll grant you that! Passers-by would never notice you, especially with the colour and patterns of your beautiful fur coat. Is it dark green, or blue, or violet? You're so beautiful, yet blending with the dark shadows of the foliage. Me? I could never miss you, of course. With my sharp eyesight, and keenly developed powers of observation nothing much escapes my eyes. Right now, I can see through your thoughts and feelings. You're running away from a situation, but you don't know where to go or where to turn. You wanna tell me what's troubling you? You can trust me. I understand your problems."

"No, you don't! You're a no-good alley cat. I'm not supposed to speak with you, anyway. Leave me alone!"

"Yeah. I know. That's what people call me. 'Watch out for Big Red, the Alley Cat, and keep your house-cats indoors!'"

"You're not even red. You're orange! It's a funny colour for a cat. I've never seen another orange cat."

"Yupp! I'm the only one this side of Darby's Pub. You're young, and you've been housebound. You haven't seen much. Me? I've been around and seen a lot. I've been through hard knocks, experienced and learned a lot. Every day I meet cats of all colours and quirks. I have many friends among them. I even have friends among dogs!"

"I hate dogs!"

"They are an arrogant bunch of rascals, aren't they? It's a game I play with them. I challenge them to a race, and when they start chasing, I'm up a tree, and..."

"Stop talking to me! You're making me nervous! Go away, please!"

"I'm sorry! I was just trying to tell you that I've had my share of problems. And I understand yours. You'll feel better when you tell me about them. But first, let me tell you about mine.

"I belonged, for a long time, in a family not far from this neighbourhood. I had a fairly comfortable life. But the family had come to a crossroads. The children had grown up, and the old folks moved to a different town. I heard them discussing whether they would take me along. 'What do we do with Big Red?' they said. 'Let's leave him in the kennels. Somebody will be sure to adopt him.' I had seen cats that had come from the kennels. I didn't wait for the day. I slipped out and embarked upon this independent life of a tramp. I've had no regrets. Most people are kind. They'll put out food and water for me. I am grateful. In return, I chase away the mice in the neighbourhood."

"Do you catch mice and eat them?"

"Oh, no! I haven't developed a taste for them. But they do get killed sometimes, in the chase. Have you ever caught a mouse?"

"Me? In the house? No! I wouldn't even know how! My folks used to say, 'Don't ever let Milady out! She might get lost and starve to death. She can't even catch a mouse!'"

"You shouldn't be expected to. It's no sport for a feline of good breeding. I wouldn't even try. But chasing squirrels, now, is a different thing. That's a real sport. Under different circumstances, if you were willing, I could take you to the front yard of a house, a few blocks from here, where you can watch squirrels doing acrobatics and clown acts under a pair of mighty trees at the entrance. I usually sneak over, hide under the hedge and watch them, sometimes for hours. They are very entertaining. I feel like joining them in their play. But as soon as they see me, they scramble up the branches of the trees...with me at their tails. We play hide-and-seek in the cavernous trees. They always win. I could take you there, but I have a feeling your mistresses will soon realize that you are missing and start looking for you."

"I'm not going back!"

"Why not? What do you mean? I don't understand!"

"They...they...they don't want me ba-a-ack...yowl, yowl, yowl."

"Of course they want you back! Who wouldn't want a beautiful kitten like you?"

"They...they don't love me any more...yowl, yowl."

"It can't be true! I wouldn't know what may have triggered this, but, whatever happened, it must have left you under a mistaken impression. I'm sure they love you and want you back. In fact, they may be out looking for you just now. You wanna tell me what happened?"

"It was Christmastide. They went to buy me presents. They came home with two boxes, wrapped in shiny paper. 'Look, Milady, we brought you two little friends you can play with and not be lonely,' they said. 'Here's Duke, and this is Prince.' At first I thought they were cats like me, and for a moment I felt very happy. When they opened the boxes, two ugly monsters sprang out, screaming and screeching with deafening yelps, running amok all over the floor. The first thing they discovered was me. They came barking into my ears: 'Yip-yip-yip!' 'Yap-yap-yap!' I was terrified. I ran away and hid in a closet. 'Oh, she'll get used to them,' they said. Next day—yesterday—the twin girls took their monsters out for a walk, leaving me at home, alone. I felt my world coming apart. I used to be their pet, their constant companion, and now—I didn't know where I belonged. So, early this morning, I sneaked out, and...here I am. I am not going back!"

"Mila-a-a-d-y-y-y!"
"Did you hear that?"
"I—I didn't hear anything! I—I'm not going back!"
"Mila-a-a-d-y-y-y! Where are you, Milady?"
"I told you they'd come looking for you. I better sneak away while you come out and meet them."
"I...I can't. Can...can I?"
"Sure, you can! I'm glad it turned out all right. It's been nice meeting you and talking with you. Keep looking out for me through your window. I'll wave to you as I pass by. Good-bye, now, good-bye!"
"Mila-a-d-y-y!"
"Meo-ow!"
"Oh, there you are, sweetheart! We're out with your little friends, looking for you. We have them on leashes, see? Don't be afraid, sweetheart. They're only chihuahuas, no bigger than you. They love you, and they want to wish you a Merry Christmas!"
"Yip-yip-yip!"
"Yap-yap-yap!"
"Come-on, sweetheart. Let's go home now! You have lots of toys around the Christmas Tree; you can play with your little friends."
"Yip-yip-yip."
"Yap-yap-yap."

"Meow. Purr. Purr. Purr."

Jerry has been an active member of the Brock House Writers Circle in Vancouver, B.C., for over 25 years.

About the Author

Jerry Shekerdemian was born the youngest son of survivors of the 1915 Armenian Genocide. He lived on the culturally rich and diverse Mediterranean island of Cyprus when it was still a British Colony. He grew up speaking 4 languages: Armenian, Greek, Turkish and English, as well as a little French. From a young age Jerry was interested in history, the arts and literature. Having been forced to leave his formal education prematurely, Shakespeare became his teacher, his friend, his inspiration and his salvation. He dreamt of being a photographer and a reporter but the realities of helping to support his family and then provide for a family of his own led him to develop his technical skills and train as an Aircraft Engineer. Forced from his beloved Cyprus by troubles brewing there in the late 1950's he moved with his young family to Beirut, Lebanon, and then to London, England and finally immigrated to Canada in 1959. Once Jerry was able to retire from a successful career as a hydraulic technician on large ships, during which he traveled extensively, he returned to his original love: writing. Jerry is also a painter in oil, acrylic and watercolor. He was an active member of the Armenian Community of Vancouver, B.C. where he often gave speeches, in English and Armenian, on important cultural holidays and served as host of the Armenian Cultural Association's radio program on Vancouver's community radio station. His family likes to call him a "True Renaissance Man." His 10-year-old grandson, Eli, credits his grandfather for his love of painting, drawing and writing. This is Jerry's first book, published on his 90th birthday.

Made in the USA
Monee, IL
05 June 2020